AN URBAN BOOK OF SHADOWS FOR THE 21ST CENTURY

Here is your magical guide to daily living! From brushing your teeth to driving to work, from doing chores to socializing with friends, you can learn to live a magical reality. *The Urban Pagan* could be considered the first Book of Shadows for the modern city magician. Not only will you learn how to live magically, but also how to *think* magically. In this book, you will discover the following—plus much, much more . . .

- The power of positive speech, word power for magic, inclusive language skills, creative communication
- How to create a magical living atmosphere even in the city with sound, light, and mood magic
- How to positively employ the magic of technology
- New symbols for a New Age—updated interpretations of symbolism for application in sympathetic magic, dream interpretation, and visualization
- How to make and find magical tools which fit your higher senses and your pocketbook
- How to help heal Gaia through magical ecology
- Urban herbalism—the use of storage space, indoor and window cultivation techniques, herbs for health, and useful recipes
- The urban wheel of the year
- Modern magical issues and exercises

ABOUT THE AUTHOR

Patricia Telesco is an ordained minister with the Universal Life Church and a professional member of the Wiccan-Pagan Press Alliance. Her hobbies include Celtic illumination, playing harp and dulcimer, historical costuming, writing and singing folk music, sufi dancing, historical herbalism studies, carving wood and soapstone, poetry, and the Society for Creative Anachronism (a historical recreation group). Many of these activities have extended themselves into her small mail order business called Hourglass Creations. Her articles and poems have appeared in journals such as *Circle, The Unicorn, Moonstone* (England), *Demeter's Emerald, Silver Chalice,* and *Llewellyn's New Worlds of Mind and Spirit* (formerly *New Times*), and she is also the author of *A Victorian Grimoire.* She welcomes the opportunity to do workshops and lectures. Patricia lives in Buffalo, New York, with her husband, young son, dog, and six cats.

TO WRITE TO THE AUTHOR

If you wish to contact the author or would like more information about this book, please write to the author in care of Llewellyn Worldwide, and we will forward your request. Both the author and publisher appreciate hearing from you and learning of your enjoyment of this book and how it has helped you. Llewellyn Worldwide cannot guarantee that every letter written to the author can be answered, but all will be forwarded. Please write to:

Patricia Telesco
c/o Llewellyn Worldwide
P.O. Box 64383-785, St. Paul, MN 55164-0383, U.S.A.

Please enclosed a self-addressed, stamped envelope or $1.00 to cover costs.
If outside the U.S.A., enclose international postal reply coupon.

FREE CATALOG FROM LLEWELLYN

For more than 90 years Llewellyn has brought its readers knowledge in the fields of metaphysics and human potential. Learn about the newest books in spiritual guidance, natural healing, astrology, occult philosophy and more. Enjoy book reviews, new age articles, a calendar of events, plus current advertised products and services. To get your free copy of *Llewellyn's New Worlds of Mind and Spirit*, send your name and address to:

Llewellyn's New Worlds of Mind and Spirit
P.O. Box 64383-785, St. Paul, MN 55164-0383, U.S.A.

LLEWELLYN'S PRACTICAL MAGIC
SERIES

The Urban Pagan

Magical Living in a 9-to-5 World

Patricia Telesco

1994
Llewellyn Publications
St. Paul, Minnesota 55164-0383, U.S.A.

FIRST EDITION
Second Printing, 1994

Cover art: Merle S. Insinga
Illustrations: Silver RavenWolf, Winston Allen
Book design and layout: Jessica Thoreson

Library of Congress Cataloging-in-Publication Data:
Telesco, Patricia, 1960—
     The urban pagan : magical living in a 9 to 5 world / Patricia
  Telesco
        p.   cm. -- (Llewellyn's practical magick series)
     Includes bibliographical references and index.
     ISBN 0-87542-785-5
  I. Title. II. Series.
  BF1571.T45   1993
  133.4'3 — dc20   93–15787
                                              CIP

Printed on recycled paper using soy ink

Llewellyn Publications
A Division of Llewellyn Worldwide, Ltd.
P.O. Box 64383, St. Paul, MN 55164-0383, U.S.A.

ABOUT LLEWELLYN'S PRACTICAL MAGIC SERIES

To some people, the idea that "Magic" is *practical* comes as a surprise.

It shouldn't. The entire basis for Magic is to exercise influence over one's environment. While Magic is also, and properly so, concerned with spiritual growth and psychological transformation, even the spiritual life must rest firmly on material foundations.

The material world and the psychic are intertwined, and it is this very fact that establishes the Magical Link: that the psychic can as easily influence the material as vice versa.

Magic can, and should, be used in one's daily life for better living! Each of us has been given Mind and Body, and surely we are under Spiritual obligation to make full usage of these wonderful gifts. Mind and Body work together, and Magic is simply the extension of this interaction into dimensions beyond the limits normally conceived. That's why we commonly talk of the "supernormal" in connection with the domain of magic.

The Body is alive, and all Life is an expression of the Divine. There is God-power in the Body and in the Earth, just as there is in Mind and Spirit. With Love and Will, we use Mind to link these aspects of Divinity together to bring about change.

With Magic we increase the flow of Divinity in our lives and in the world around us. We add to the beauty of it all—for to work Magic we must work in harmony with the laws of Nature and the Psyche. *Magic is the flowering of the Human Potential.*

Practical Magic is concerned with the Craft of Living well and in harmony with Nature, and with the Magic of the Earth, in the things of the Earth, in the seasons and cycles and in the things we make with hand and Mind.

Other Books by the Author
A Victorian Grimoire
Llewellyn's 1994 Magickal Almanac

Forthcoming
Victorian Oracle
Folkways
The Kitchen Witch's Cookbook
A Witch's Brew: The Art of Making Magical Beverages

ACKNOWLEDGMENTS

In writing, it is often difficult to pinpoint sources of inspiration because that amazing spark seems to come in waves from every corner of your life; your past, your present, those around you and even the media. With this in mind this book is shared lovingly with thanks to:

All the wonderful people at Llewellyn who have not only become friends, but who through their tenacious kindness and support have imparted to me the greatest gift imaginable; a heaping spoonful of self confidence. Especially to Nancy, a great companion, steppin' partner and advisor, even across the miles.

Dan Winter, who does not know how often his home and gentle kindness affected my life deeply when I first started to explore my spirituality.

To Dave, a welcome addition to our extended family, for bringing joy, adventure, and love into Jody's life.

To Mitchie, for helping me learn to say, "not the mama" to everyone except my son.

To MaryKay for the constant kindness, thoughtful care and immense support she has given to the Kroldart clan over the years.

My English teachers, specifically Dr. Frank, who encouraged me to write even though I couldn't spell ~~corektly~~ correctly.

Dawn, who has been a living reminder of the joy of discovery, and proof that an "old dog" can, indeed, learn new tricks and even improve on them!

The memory of Paul Karlis whose passing taught me that faith without thought and wisdom is foolish . . . and that religion should not be carved in stone, but act as a guideline with our hearts at the helm.

And finally to TamLyn, my fluffy four-footed, ever-constant companion for that special love and warmth only a familiar can give.

DEDICATED TO

Those that speak the truth in love
Those that know our world will be healed with Wisdom, not War
Those that gain respect by consistent word and deed
And finally my family
Those of blood, marriage and spirit
You enrich my life

CONTENTS

Introduction

*The old order changeth, yielding place to new and God fulfills himself in many
ways lest one good custom should corrupt the world.*

— A. Tennyson, *On Poets and Critics*

ven today, with all the wonderful teachers who speak out on magical issues, frequently the image portrayed for magic is terribly arcane. This is most obvious come Hallows (commonly known as Halloween), when the traditional ugly old hags on broomsticks continue to make appearances in all forms of the media. While this is not necessarily a direct, intentional assault on the modern magician, it is an important reminder that the views about magic, and Witches specifically, still need a lot of hard work and good public relations to change.

The question remains in my mind, however, of how these images affect the way even Wiccans and Pagans think about magic. I believe there is still a part of our minds and hearts which, out of habit, falls into the stereotype trap. It is good to ask ourselves from time to time if we wear our robes and jewelry, perform our rites, or even communicate in certain manners because it is the "way" others expect, or because it comes from our heart.

Magical traditions have grown and matured tremendously over the last twenty-five years, but this development is not without certain hazards. There is the temptation to become complacent, to allow the magical life to be restricted to our circles, instead of really incorporating those ideals in every part of our life. Even for those who do try to accomplish this, there are the problems of a modern world to grapple with.

While family and other older traditions serve to give important foundations for the modern magician to build on, that old spell from Aunt Martha calling for the fresh spleen of an animal or feathers from a bird on the endangered species list is simply no longer acceptable in the new environment of ecological awareness we live in. In some instances, the languages of spells, rituals, etc., is so antiquated that only the serious student, who has the time to research countless volumes of information, understands the intent fully.

When the opportunity for ritual arises, we are faced with busy city streets and a vast shortage of private natural space to worship in. The symbols that have been passed down to us are sometimes outmoded, technology surrounds, and there still exists the fear and misunderstanding that come with the infamous "M" and "W" words (magic and Witchcraft). This leaves many people, even the experienced magicians, scratching their heads, and trying desperately to sort out how to take practical magic into the twenty-first century.

Most things that have been labeled as magic in the past (and today) are actually sciences of the mind. Originally the meanings ascribed to the word "magic" were to "be able" or "have power." In other words, magic was historically based on the idea of adeptness, skill, and control. Real magic, therefore, comes from both a command of the self and an attunement to the world to see how new realities can be made from the marvelous patterns of the universe.

On a less lofty sounding level, magic is word and deed in accord. It is the thought and dream put into action; the moving of our minds and spirits to higher levels which release us from conventional perceptions. It is the twinkle in the eye of the God/dess.

To keep up with the ever-changing world around us, creativity must (and has thankfully begun to) find its way into our circles and our homes. Our magical traditions need to grow and blossom with us, with our Earth, without necessarily discarding the richness our history offers. Taking this one step further, living an urban magical lifestyle is then also the desire to move towards completeness; a unity of old and new, spirit and mundane.

Wholeness is not only a vision of self, it is also being able to see all souls as intricate, functional parts of the workings of the universe. It is being able to look beyond the surface and see the beauty people can create when they set aside differences to work together towards a common goal. Wholeness requires us to find peace with ourselves and our world and then take that harmony into our relationship with others. Instead of the struggle with truth, it is the acceptance of change; instead of fear, it offers us quiet knowing.

This text, as a collective Urban Book of Shadows, is meant to help with just such a quest. Through these pages, plus a little ingenuity, the modern user of magic can begin to incorporate earth-aware philosophies of days gone by with modern realities. We can look seriously at our role in the world today to find a harmony of desire and belief, sociology and science. With these tools in hand, we can then prepare for our tomorrows by developing original powerful rites that are part of the "ritual" of day to day existence.

We can not allow our magic to become stale and mechanical. I have always believed that to work magic well, you must live it; become it. Not unlike digging deep for that very fresh well of water, this special power is within us as part of our heritage; our birthright, if you will. Therefore, it is really a part of everything that touches our lives. All that remains is to allow our daily routines to become an expression of this principle.

So through this text and your own creative abilities, let's venture forward together, building a present and a future filled with positive, transformational magic.

The motivation for working magic is unlike superstition —
it is not fear, it is the desire to understand!
— Marion Weinstein

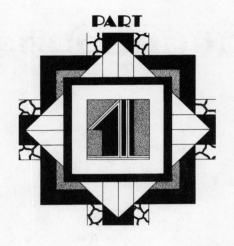

PART

SPIRITUAL SOJOURN

Exploring Inner Space

Mine is the moonlight
and stars stretched
like a fan
dancing the tree tops
flying with birds . . .

Mine is the morning
and sunsets on oceans
mine is the music which must ever
be heard.

— Marian

Meditations and Musings

The Mind Over Mundanity

The proper study of mankind is man.
    —A. Pope, *Essay on Criticism*

The examination of the human thought process is also an examination of culture, language, and the amazing human capacity for growth and change. In retrospect, there is some question in my mind as to how much we have shaped both mental and oral dialogue patterns and how much they have shaped us. From childhood onward we are definitively told the sky is blue, the sea is green, what is good and what is bad. Our minds, hungry to learn and understand, accept this information as truth. If left to our own, without society's trained responses, one wonders what words would develop to mold the way we think about the world, and the way we express those thoughts.

Since members of humanity are by no means isolated from each other, this question is only food for thought, but well worth chewing on. As I listen to conversations (including my own), I realize how much we banter about words with casual indifference, half the time not perceiving how much effect their vibration[1] can have on our lives and the world around us. Even within our own minds, we hold entire silent discourses for decision-making whose outcomes can be evolutionary.

So when we consider meditation and contemplation as a means for magical change, we must begin with our own deliberation process; the constructs of our language and personal vision. We can not remain aloof, continuing to wear rose-colored glasses and saying that no problems exist in our lifestyles. No one is perfect or we wouldn't be here. On the other hand, it may be equally harmful to constantly focus our reflections on the negative things until all hope has expired.

Learning to use thought-forms to reshape our magical lives will require us to first retrain our minds and mouths to find a fresh balance. There is a saying that goes, "Be sure your brain is in gear before shifting your tongue to high." It is a good one to remember. From the initial concept pondered to the eventual verbal/written construct of that idea, language can, and does, have powerful consequences. Before we can use this energy for magic, however, we need to begin freeing ourselves from the false images and negative terminology taught us by society to discover the God-Self[2] within.

If for a moment you can step back and envision the Divine being as a multi-faceted crystal, which at the dawn of time shattered leaving bits of itself within each human soul, you can begin to look for that fragment of the God/dess[3] deep in your heart. It is from this shining core, the best of what can be, that new sparks of creativity and belief are kindled. As we teach our minds to think in this manner, reflecting positive magical ideals and eventually "universal" terms,[4] it revolutionizes our way of living. These spiritually centered discernments start like a seed, which when properly cared for, grows outward to bloom in every portion of our reality, sharing its inestimable perfume of new-found freedom and peace.

From this outlook the individual is still of great import, but is also part of a much larger picture, granting tremendous perspective with which to work. This insight — combined with scientific knowledge, other metaphysical techniques, and good old-fashioned backbone — can give us the basic tools necessary to not only reform ourselves and our magic, but also the world . . . gently, sensitively, and powerfully.

The goal for this text is to help us build a vision for tomorrow which is life-affirming, then apply all our knowledge, magic, and talent towards realizing that vision. During this process it is important to set realistic goals and affirm those goals in word and deed. In this manner, our thoughts and actions move in one accord, sending out positive, creative energy on all levels, and building a more harmonious and functional foundation for any magical lifestyle.

At first, some of these activities will seem to have nothing to do with magic. While reading, try to remember the saying familiar to many magical people, "Love is the law; love under will," and these activities will begin to have a more obvious meaning for the urban magical life. Will is a function of the mind, while love is an emotional response. There is a difference between hoping for change and resolving to transform your life. Even then determination, if it is not centrally guided by love of self and others, can go astray — carrying your magical energy with it!

The idea behind the exercises in this chapter is to help rebuild self-confidence and a positive image. Without this foundation, any type of magic is difficult at best, since much of its effectiveness is based on your own trust of your abilities. Once this confidence is established, it allows you to work on other concerns with renewed conviction that you have the power to change your life!

I suggest, before you start these or any other activities detailed in these pages, purchasing a good-sized notebook to write your reactions, successes, failures, and other observations in for each activity. This spiritual diary serves a number of useful functions. First, after you are done writing you can return to it any time to read, and probably learn something new from your own insights. Second, writing things down helps aid the retention process so that as you find rituals, visualizations, etc., which work well for you, they can begin to be committed to memory. Third, these pages become a written record of your personal magical growth. Once or twice a year you can re-read them and watch yourself evolve into a beautiful, spiritual creation. The exciting thing about this aspect is that you can actually see with your own eyes what a vital role you have played in your own development. Finally, this book becomes the foundation for a Book of Shadows[5] which you can share with friends and loved ones as you deem appropriate.

In reading and working with these applications, please remember that your heart alone must be at the helm of guidance for your magical life. Teachers can act as guides, and share from their personal backgrounds to help you find your way, but ultimately what you incorporate into daily experience must sing the music of your soul. Listen closely to that small voice within, and begin to trust in it. The God/dess can manifest wonderfully in you and through you because you are a Divine creation with a special purpose. That same great Power combined with your own intuitive sense can help you discern and apply what is the truth for your life.

SELF-IMAGE

Negative self-images are perhaps the most difficult barriers for anyone to overcome. For some reason the human species tends to be its own worst critic. This is actually good up to a point, but when it begins to tear at the very fibers of your being, it is time to reevaluate where these images are coming from. Someone once said that the Earth, as the Mother of humanity, perfectly reflects the spiritual state of her children. With this in mind, it stands to reason that we can not hope to heal the world when we have not really learned to heal ourselves on all levels of being (body, mind, and soul).

Sometimes we know at least part of the cause for a poor self-image, such as bad childhood memories, taunting from peers, negative statements from family or friends, past failures, or cultural ideals for appearances. If you are aware of the people, circumstances, etc., which form the roots of self-doubt, then you already have half the obstacle breached. Now all that remains is to begin digging down to pull them completely out of your subconscious and conscious mind.

If on the other hand you are dubious as to why you have these nagging uncertainties, the process is a little more difficult. In the medical profession it is nearly impossible to treat symptoms effectively without knowing the source. So your first step towards wholeness is examining your life to find the origins of apprehension. This may be a rather painful process because it brings to light everything from disturbing memories to the way you really perceive yourself on a daily basis.

I will not tell you that these exercises are a quick fix in either case. Rebuilding the self is sometimes a life-long process. The more you are willing to release negative feelings and leave the past where it belongs, the more effective these types of practices become. Like anything else in life, the intense desire to help yourself is your most powerful tool. Learn to be your own best friend.

EXERCISE 1: SELF-HELP LISTS

This exercise is reflective in nature. It should be done on a day when you do not have to rush, feel fairly rested, and are emotionally centered for introspective work. Begin by finding a quiet place where you feel comfortable and can think without interruption, such as your home, a park, a church, or even a museum, and be sure to bring your notebook with you. Once there, sit down and take a few deep, cleansing breaths, allowing yourself to relax.

On one sheet of paper make a list of everything you can think of which you dislike about yourself. On another piece of paper list all your personal doubts, and on a third, list all of what you feel are your positive points. Make sure to encompass your feelings regarding all portions of your life, including spiritual. When you are finished, put the paper aside and try to forget about it for a few minutes, again breathing deeply. Take a moment to enjoy your surroundings.

For an instant now, I want you to pretend that your lists are really about someone else, someone that you care about. Try and read them from this perspective. With this outlook, many of the things which you thought were terrible suddenly don't seem so bad compared to all the good. Once you can see even the worst things about yourself and still say with confidence, "I am worthwhile, I am important, I am beautiful, I am Divine," you have taken the most important step forward.

Now look at the list again, and mark on it the things that you do have the power to change, such as bad habits. Eliminating negative tendencies will often help to eliminate certain self doubts. For example, if you feel you don't exercise enough, and change your life pattern to make time to include this on a daily basis, you may quickly discover the way you view your physical self is more optimistic because you are doing something constructive and achieving a goal. So put a target date next to the things you want to work on in yourself.

Try not to be overly idealistic about how quickly you can do this or you will become discouraged. Instead, try to set reasonable goals that take into consideration your other responsibilities and circumstances.

This type of list can be useful for other things besides self-image. Another application might be for decision-making, where you have "yes" and "no" or "should" and "should not" for sheets. Or you can just have one piece of paper which lists your personal objectives. This last list can be used in ritual as a magical focus for increased energy in achieving your goals (see Chapter Ten).

Foundational to this whole approach is the fact that sometimes we have difficulty sorting out the many thoughts going through our minds. By writing them down, organizing, examining, and finally reconciling them, we are helping ourselves to swim through the waters of confusion instead of just treading water and getting nowhere.

EXERCISE 2: BUILDING THE GOD/DESS WITHIN

For this exercise you will need a mirror; a full-length one being best. Take the mirror to a private part of your home where it is quiet. I suggest trying this during a waxing moon[6] with some soft music playing in the background; maybe a few red candles[7] burning, and perhaps other items around you which make you feel safe and comfortable. I also encourage you to be sure you will have at least one to two hours of privacy by turning off your phone and locking the doors.

You will need to have a picture of your personal favorite God/dess image with you for this work. This can be mythic or fictional, from posters, cards, calendars, or other art, but whatever medium you choose make certain it is pleasing to the eye and spirit. In other words, you should not only enjoy looking at it, but have some type of positive emotional response while you view the piece.

Next, stand fully clothed in front of the mirror. Look at yourself with your most critical eye. See wrinkles, blemishes; the bits of fat here and there. Once you have reviewed all the physically negative aspects, do just the reverse. Now notice all the positive things; how your eyes reflect the light in the room and the joy within your heart; the strength of the oak tree in your back to keep you standing . . . the incredible tools your hands are as they slowly remove your clothing.

As you take off each garment, consider for a moment what it represents. High heels may be a representation of society which is overly concerned about physical appearance instead of comfort, dark pants might be the business side of you which sometimes keeps you from the intuitive, a tie embodies the bonds of materialism, etc. When the clothing is being removed, begin to also remove the symbols from your life that are not positive and self-affirming. As the attire drops to the floor, leave it there along with any negative attitudes.

Continue in this manner until you have stripped away all the outward, non-productive images of self, and are left with naked radiance. This portion of the exercise is difficult for some people because many of us don't enjoy looking at our own bodies. This may be due to self-consciousness, a feeling that we are not "beautiful" or "handsome" enough, or the puritanical mindset which says nakedness is evil, but whatever holds you back, now is the time to try to overcome it.

Begin by realizing that your body is holy; it bears your soul through the lessons of life. View yourself for one moment from a more scientific angle to see what a marvelous "machine" you have been given. Look at how it bends and moves; the flow and curve of the muscles; the strength of the skeleton. These things are all part of you. Discard everything the media portrays as the perfect physical appearance, and focus instead on what you see before you — this cloth of flesh and blood which sustains your existence and allows you to grow!

Now, for one moment change your perspective to the picture of the God/dess you brought with you. Concentrate on it until you can see the image clearly, even with your eyes closed. Sit down on the floor in front of the mirror and look into your own eyes. Breath slowly and evenly. In the center of your eye, visualize a small flame burning and focus your attention on that flame. It is the center of your being, vital and full of energy.

In the center of the fire, now see the God/dess image you concentrated on before. As you fill the flames with that image, consider all the positive associations which go with that picture, such as strength, natural beauty, peace, and wisdom. Let these associations and the mental image of this Divinity grow until it is no longer just part of the fire or just in the center of your eye, but filling out every portion of your body, like a crayon shading inside the black lines of a coloring book.

When you feel as if the likeness has filled you to almost overflowing, open your eyes and look into the face of the God/dess! The energy of the Divine is within you waiting for expression. Look on to the body of the God/dess and know that the Divine being doesn't create junk. Look on your whole being and know it is magical! You are beautiful as you are. You are what you were born to be. Accept new self-love and find freedom.

When you are finished, relax, and slowly bring your breathing and perceptions back to normal. Dress in something comfortable and write down your observations and feelings, especially how they are different from when you began, in your diary. You can repeat this exercise any time you feel those old negative energies creeping in to disrupt your self assurance, or any time you want to reconnect with the God/dess within. I also feel this is an excellent practice for people who feel they lack sensuality, to help them accept their bodies and enjoy them.

This visualization can be applied, with some minor alteration, for rituals where you wish to "Draw Down the Moon." [8] In this case, instead of discarding negative images with the clothing you might take off "worldly" things to help release your mind for magical work, and focus on your intuition.

EXERCISE 3: FREE-FLOW WRITING

For this you will need a fair amount of paper, a pen, a green candle (to encourage creativity and growth), and again, perhaps some music to help you relax. To begin, decide on one particular issue regarding yourself, your life, spiritual or mundane circumstances to focus your attention on, and especially how you would like this concern to change.

Next, light your candle, stating your intentions. For example, you may dislike the fact that you loose your anger too easily. In this scenario, you ignite the candle saying something like, "I light this fire to remind me to be tolerant and to help spread the radiance of peace in my life."

Allow the candle to burn freely while you begin to write. Try not to think too much about the words, sentence structure, etc. Instead, focus all your energy on the specifics of the matter at hand. For this illustration it would be why you get angry, what makes you angry, how you know when you're going to "blow up," and reflections on what you think might help keep the internal volcano under control. For the individual who is trying to cope with extreme emotional swings, learning that they can have command over their feelings is a means to take back the reins of their life and discover far more control in their magical energy.

When you feel you have finished writing, put the pen down and rest for a few moments. Close your eyes and notice how much of your foreboding has poured out of you onto the pieces of paper. Writing in this manner is very liberating. It acts like a pressure release valve. After about ten minutes of peace and quiet, return to your notes and read them. By simply writing whatever comes to mind, you will often open a doorway to your own instinctive nature. In most cases you will find something very revealing about yourself or that situation which before now went unnoticed.

For those people who find that writing is not a really productive medium for them, I suggest trying alternative methods, such as speaking out loud or painting. Once you find an approach that helps you to rise above your circumstances and get things in perspective, use it consistently for just that. Remember, no one else has ever to see or hear your personal free-flow work, so you don't have to worry about how other people might react to it. This is something you do just for you!

I often recommend this exercise for artists who are experiencing creative blocks. Sometimes we focus so much attention on one thing that it keeps us from attaining our goals. By releasing our expectations we also release a good deal of tension and can often find new approaches to any problem in the process.

EXERCISE 4: BANDAGE VISUALIZATION

This visualization is specifically for those times when you feel as if life and the universe have been beating up on you. These are the moments when there is seemingly no energy left within to care about anything. You may feel discouraged, rather worthless, and as if hope has left you.

First, draw yourself a warm bath with some lavender and camomile in the water for peacefulness. Light a stick of incense, place a burning candle on the back of the tub, and set yourself in to soak. As you lie in the water, allow yourself to reach that half-sleepy stage, with the water slowly massaging away your tensions and worries.

When you feel calmer and more centered, close your eyes and visualize yourself standing some place where you have always felt secure and full of energy. It may be an area that you retreat to for contemplation, it might be the image of your parents' house, or any other place which gives you the sense of warmth and welcome.

Next, allow the picture forming in your mind's eye to include someone you trust totally and feel very close to. This person should be carrying a human-size bandage with them (or some other item you personally associate with healing, comfort, etc.). When you have this depiction firmly in your mind, see your companion moving towards you and placing the bandage around you like a huge hug. Sense the warmth and comfort it provides, like a salve for emotional wounds. Allow your companion to hold you inside this healing cocoon until you feel your depression lifting and a little personal energy return. This may take a little time, and you might have to repeat the visualization to get past this period, so try to be patient. Healing is a gentle art, sometimes trying our patience with its slow, subtle movements. When it comes, however, it will be worth the effort and wait (more exercises for healing may be found in Chapter Ten).

One word of caution for this exercise: I do not recommend attempting it when you are extremely weary. Falling asleep in the bathtub is not a healthy pastime.

OUTMODED HABITS AND VIEWS

When we are children, we speak and think as children. When we "grow up," suddenly a whole different adult world presents itself to us and we discover that many of our childhood perceptions no longer fit this reality. Even through adulthood we continue to find that life surprises us, and we need to change to meet those revelations with positive, creative power. Sometimes these modifications compel us to rethink the way we view things, or the habits we have acquired over the years.

EXERCISE 1: A FLOWERING SPELL

There is a wonderful application for an old folk spell when you are trying to either break a habit, change your outlook, or make the best of a bad situation. Take the seed of any flowering plant whose scent in full bloom is pleasant to you. Name the seed according to your need. Visualize your need filling that seed with life — you may even want to see a little sprout forming in your mind's eye — then plant it in rich soil to grow. If your climate is a little uncertain, grow your plant indoors.

Begin to make honest efforts to bring about the change desired. Magic requires that we match energy for energy and effort with intent for truly remarkable results. As the plant grows, tend to it with loving care, allowing it to remind you of your goal. Come the first signs of sprouting, you should begin to notice a difference in yourself. By the time the flower blooms your desire should be answered, although it is not always in the way you might expect.

Sometimes we must simply accept and work through things for whatever reason. If this is the case, by the time the plant bears a flower you will have built the inner strength needed to do just that.

EXERCISE 2: PERSPECTIVE

Sometimes before we can begin to work constructively towards change in our lives, we first have to acquire a better perspective of the "whys" and "hows" pertaining to specific situations. I know that I personally find it difficult to desire real transformation when I don't have the faintest notion of what brought about the problem(s) in the first place. In some ways, it is kind of like closing the barn door after the horse is already loose! During those times, I use this bit of productive daydreaming to help.

Begin as you might for any type of meditation,[9] using slow, rhythmic breathing to help bring yourself into a calm, centered frame of mind. When you are really at ease, focus your thoughts on the circumstances you wish to understand better, in as much detail as you can recall, replaying everything slowly in your reflections. This time, though, you are not an active participant in the situation, but an unbiased observer. Think of it like a movie theater (if it helps, make popcorn!). Now watch the people involved; their feelings, their perspectives. Even try to put yourself quite literally for a moment in their shoes and see what they see. You may be surprised at what you discover.

Say, for instance, you are trying to learn how to organize your time better. In this visualization you would simply replay your entire day mentally to see what types of situations distract you the most from accomplishing your goals. For this, and most problems in life, acknowledgement and understanding win half the battle for you. Along these lines, after this exercise you could then begin to watch for the identified diversions and hopefully avoid them until you finish what you set out to do.

This type of visualization is also very productive for decision-making. When you have an important choice to make, play out the scenario in your imagination in several ways, taking care to look a little forward in time, too, so you can discover what impact your judgment is likely to have. This is not always a perfect method of previewing the future, but it may grant enough emotional distance to make a choice and be at peace with that answer.

EXERCISE 3: TIME TRAVEL VISUALIZATION AND SYMBOLISM

The idea behind this activity is the belief that magic can work both forwards and backwards in time.[10] If we begin working with magical symbols as children, more than likely they will have powerful impacts on our adult life. However, since many of us grew up in Christian-based homes, we didn't have this advantage. In this case, I believe instead that we can use time travel visualization and symbolism to build some of the attributes in our lives that we need.

For instance, my greatest downfall is the fact that I don't like confrontation and will often keep my peace rather than come forward and stand up for myself. In recent years I have learned how emotionally damaging this can be. Sometimes the repression of honest feelings even manifests physically by aches and pains, exhaustion, or sickness. This is one way that our bodies can give us a mental (and much needed) kick in the butt and tell us, "Hey! Wake up!"

To help myself work on being stronger and more self-assured, I began using this magically-based visualization. Before you begin, though, I recommend setting up a protected sacred space[11] for yourself in which to work. Generally speaking, this is an excellent habit to get in to whenever you are embarking on metaphysical workings. Not unlike locking your doors when you go on vacation, establishing lines of protection before magic helps keep the energy where it belongs, and keeps any negative influences where they belong; outside.

Get comfortable in a chair or on a sofa where you know you can sit undisturbed by phones, pets, children, etc. After preparing your sacred space, begin to see yourself as you are right now in your mind. Once that image is secure, slowly begin rolling back the years of your life. If it helps, review pictures of yourself at younger ages prior to this exercise so they are fresh in your memory. When you get back to the age of reason (usually about seven years old), stop. This is your starting point.

See yourself as an adult walking up to this youthful image, and sitting down. From here the visualization can take two forms. You may either act as your own teacher, sharing with the child the things you feel are most important verbally, or you may give the child a symbolic gift of the attribute you wish to incorporate into your life. I personally used the rune of strength as my emblem for change, not only giving it to the child, but also tracing it on her third eye. I repeated this procedure in the visualization about three times, each time with a older version of me, the last instance being slightly in the future.

By repeating the process, you are reaffirming to your own subconscious that you have the power to transform your weaknesses into strengths, your sorrows into joys, and your struggles into productive learning experiences. When you are done, slowly allow your sensations to return to normal and write down your impressions of the experience. Repeat the procedure as often as necessary to help you reach your goal.

AWAKENING THE CHILD WITHIN

There is a growing understanding in the spiritual community of the power of perfect trust and love. It is one thing to know the words, and another to experience the breadth, depth, and height magic can reach when motivated by these two things. After years of having negative experiences in relationships, being trodden on along the business ladder, and the other realities of our hurried world, however, it is often difficult to remember what trust really is, let alone to want to give it freely. We come to magical lifestyles in the hopes of making a better world, yet the "old person" fights hard to maintain ground. So how do we begin to rediscover that trust and love? Through the child within.

Even if you are not a parent, the first step is pretty easy. Go to a park and watch the kids. Talk to them if you can. Watch how their eyes light up when you take interest in their games. See how willing they are to believe the best in you. Observe the pure joy in their playing, and the simplicity of things which bring that delight. Try for a while to watch the world through their eyes and carry that perspective in your heart.

Next, I suggest recreating some of the most enjoyed activities of your own youth. Go out and play hopscotch, run through an open field, pick daisies, or catch guppies in a country stream. Sing silly songs that make no sense whatsoever, speak in your childhood voice, dance with the wind, color a few pages in a book, and refresh the child within you.

At first this type of activity may seem rather silly, but I can honestly tell you that it is not only fun, but has a healing quality. Since I have had a child of my own, I love going to get toys not only for him, but for me! Adults need to frolic too; it relieves stress, brings pleasure, and gets us back in touch with the simple things which are really important to happy, healthy living.

Once you release this youthful part of yourself, love and trust will begin to flow in your life again. This doesn't mean taking everything at face value or losing the wisdom you have gained from life experiences, but instead it allows you to combine the two into a harmonious balance, powerful for magic and for personal transformation.

Exercises for Developing Awareness

In changing the way we think and view the world around us, the issue of awareness becomes very important; awareness of self, personal energy, attention to detail and the lessons being presented through your living experience, appreciation for nature and Her many gifts, just to name a few. In magic, we depend on our intuitive senses to guide us through many rituals, spells, and personal rites. So, developing these senses from the physical level up is a tremendous aid to the effectiveness of their application for magical living.

In cultivating our awareness of ourselves and our world, we also help to put our priorities into a fresh perspective which is not solitary. The ability to recognize how much our actions can affect the lives of those around us is going to be very important for the future of humanity as a whole. The more we can become attentive and attuned to the Earth and all its inhabitants, the more our lifestyles and magic can reflect global objectives.

EXERCISE 1: CRYSTAL FACETS

This exercise is simple and may be done with almost any object, but crystals tend to work exceptionally well. Take the stone and set it in front of you on a table at a comfortable eye level. Now take a casual look at it, first for things such as color and aesthetic value, then to see where it is on the table and in relationship to other objects in the room, including yourself.

Next move the crystal slightly in any direction. Build on your original observations, but notice how the light may strike it differently now, or how it appears to be a different color due to the proximity of another object. Make a few notes about your observations.

The third step is to examine each facet of the stone as it relates to the other sides and to the room. See the shape, hue, and texture. Make a few more notes and compare them to earlier parts of the exercise. Do you now have a clear mental picture of the stone when your eyes are closed? Do you find you appreciate it more, or perhaps have some intuitive feeling for its matrix?[12] Frequently the answer is a resounding yes. That is why this exercise is especially useful for writers or artists experiencing a temporary blockage.

At first you may feel a little absurd sitting and playing with a rock, but in the process of working with it you are actually retraining your mind to be more alert and observant of your surroundings. You are forcing your reasoning to hone in on all aspects of one item instead of the myriad of input it normally tries to gather. This particular ability is employed in many Eastern traditions to help increase focus. This skill also acts as an important building block for almost all visualization and meditation techniques.

EXERCISE 2: ENVIRONMENTAL AWARENESS

There are many ways to wake up your senses and learn to use them consistently. One of the most simple is to go out into different types of surroundings and concentrate not on what is actually there, but how these environments make you feel. What do you smell? What kind of texture lingers on the air? Is the ground beneath you hard, or alive with life? What songs are whispered on the winds? Each area or climate will have a music and feeling all its own. Discover them!

EXERCISE 3: SENSUAL FOCUSING

For this you will need a friend to help you, or to work with a group. Get a small chime or bell to be given to the "leader" of the activity. This person should be sensitive to group energy, have a good speaking voice, and be able to be creative with the phrases, if need be.

The leader begins by sounding the chime to give your mind a physical focus to signal magical effects and aid in centering. They then say one phrase, allowing everyone in the group to visualize or assimilate it in their own manner. It is good beforehand to have the entire group do some simple relaxation breathing to prepare. Again, the bell should be rung before each phrase is spoken, then appropriate time given so the group can experience the imagery. Here are some examples:

See forever in your closed eyes

Visualize breath as light which fills your being

Consider the sounds of silence

Listen to the music of your soul

Hear the song of time as it whispers of past lives

Sense the drumming of your heartbeat

Feel the air as it touches your skin

Become one with the movements of the earth beneath you

Discern the texture of your own aura[13]

Taste the salt of the sea in the wind

Savor the flavor of white, cleansing light

Taste the fresh water in your well of creativity

Inhale the strength of the earth to your body

Smell the perfume of peace as it settles on your spirit

Breathe the colors of the rainbow

EXERCISE 4: INVOCATION FOR THE SENSES

The definition of "invoking" is to summon, beseech or arouse. After creating appropriate magical space to work in, you can use the invocation as a means to draw attention to each of your senses and bring them into focus.

As you speak the invocation, it is sometimes helpful to light an appropriately colored candle for each element/sense (yellow for air, brown or green for earth, red and orange for fire, blue or purple for water). I also suggest having a little fresh soil, some spring water, a fan, and the lit candles to help bring the fullness of feeling to each sense.

You will notice for the fifth part of the invocation I have included the "self," where all the elements and senses may come together to produce that wonderful essence of magic!

Air: Imagine sitting towards a spring wind, drinking in the warm, fresh scents with only the chants from breathing bows to touch your ears.

Fire: Imagine sitting beside a roaring hearth, drinking in the crimson sparks with only the melody of friendly flames to fill the night.

Water: Imagine sitting near a moon-lit sea, drinking in each salty drop with only the echo of washing waves to hold you safe.

Earth: Imagine sitting amidst a rich, green forest, drinking in the colors of life with only the song of an enchanted Earth to anchor your soul.

Self: Imagine sitting atop a starry universe, drinking in the energy of ages with only the silent weave of space and time to make you free.

So fly . . .

There are tapes available on the market now with the sounds of various natural settings on them. If you are feeling really creative you may want to record appropriate sounds on cassette for each section of the invocation to be played in the background to intensify the impact.

OVERCOMING FEAR OR BLOCKAGE

Fear can be one of the most inhibiting emotions we experience in our lives, to the point where it strangles and stagnates any attempts towards individual expression or spiritual exploration. In discussing this one day, a friend of mine made the marvelous observation that fear turned inside out was actually courage! At first we laughed about this, but the more I considered her words the more I knew there was an important truth in them. We can use this illustration for a visualization of our fears.

EXERCISE 1: TURNING FEAR

Thanks to a story shared by my best friend, generally I envision fear as a black cloudy figure, not really quite formed but always lingering near by. When I name that figure (fear of flying, fear of heights, fear of vulnerability, etc.), I then grab it by the top of its "head" and shake it like I do my socks to turn them right side out. Sure enough, the inside of that cloud is bright and shining with confidence! This visualization alone may not be enough to cure you of long-time phobias, but it may give you the chance to look at them differently with a sense of humor which is always a good friend to have along.

EXERCISE 2: BREAKING THE BRICK WALL

This visualization has been created specifically for those moments when you feel you are getting nowhere and that doors are firmly shut to progress. Begin as you normally do to prepare yourself for meditation.

In your mind's eye, develop the image of a huge brick wall. See yourself standing next to this barrier with a magic marker or bucket of paint, and begin to write all your feelings and problems on the wall itself. Be as specific as possible.

Next, reach down to the ground and pick up an axe or hammer and begin breaking down that wall a little at a time until it is completely cleared away. It may take some practice and repetition of the exercise to accomplish this, and even after you do I suggest repeating the visualization at least three times to magnify the impact this has for your life. By duplicating the activity you are helping yourself on the conscious and subconscious levels to truly believe this wall can, indeed, be brought down and kept down. The energy of belief is very powerful. Once it is established you will usually find that the barrier slowly dissipates, or that you come up with alternative answers to your situation.

As an interesting point, I have heard of individuals who have successfully employed this type of technique to help improve their mental attitudes during serious illnesses. In this case they proceed to name the wall after the physical problem, and then tear it down. Medical science has long known that the patients' outlook on their situation can have a drastic influence on how well they respond to treatment, the most notable example of this being the use of placebos in place of pain killers. Here the patient believes the pain should go away, so it does. This is a potent example of the tremendous authority our mind has over our physical well-being. I do caution, however, that any type of metaphysical approach to healing should not take the place of professional care, but act as a tool to help facilitate the process of returning to wholeness.

Exercises for Channeling Anger

Being only human, there are times when everyone becomes angry. Finding constructive ways to deal with anger is not easy for anyone. Our animal instincts often call to us to react, to fight, while in spirit we know that anger can be terribly destructive if not handled carefully.

One of the best ways to initially deal with animosity is through physical exertion. Run, swim, dance, yell at a tree, or whatever it takes to release the pent-up emotions so that you can be in control again. Another means is by pouring your anger into an artistic medium, such as painting and music.

The third method I have recently come up with for a friend is unique. Go out and buy yourself some inexpensive breakables such as bowls or glasses. The next time you are furious, take one of them somewhere safe and visualize all your negative feelings filling it like black sludge. If your anger is directed at an individual, you may want to envision their face in the glass. Build the image in your mind until you feel the full force of your anger moving down your arm, then release it (throwing the glass at a wall or other hard object). Your anger now is literally broken! The pieces of the glass, once collected, might then be put to some type of constructive use, such as making them part of a "Witch bottle"[14] over which you can plant a tree or flowering plant to represent your desire for a positive, peaceful outcome to the situation.

While on the surface this activity may seem rather violent, I would much rather see a little broken glass than a broken body. Some people need a physical release for their emotions, and this type of exercise gives them a means to visually and bodily disengage the fury from themselves. More often than not, this will get rid of enough anxiety to allow that individual to think more rationally about the situation instead of having a heated argument or participating in some other, more destructive activity.

THE POWER OF YOUR NAME

We know that the written, spoken, chanted, or sung word can affect the human psyche tremendously. This evidences itself most dramatically in the individual name. If you don't believe this is the case, see what happens when you continually mispronounce someone's name. The emotional response can be astounding. On the surface this may appear only a function of the ego desiring to be recognized, but on deeper levels it is more than this. Our name is a symbol for everything we have become. When people speak it, that individual image fills their mind along with associated memories. Over time this becomes a powerful identification which, depending on thought and action, can be constructive or destructive.

If you don't like your name, you need to ask yourself why. What associations does it create in your mind to illicit a negative reaction? You may discover that you dislike your name because you also don't like yourself, or have a poor self-image. On the other hand, there could be far deeper reasons for these feelings, not the least of which may have to do with a past life memory.[15] There may have been another life when this name was central to something painful happening to you. Whatever the scenario, however, you need to resolve the feelings you have towards your name as a step towards self-love.

EXERCISE 1: RESEARCH FOR POSITIVE ASSOCIATIONS

It is sometimes interesting to look at our given names from the detached perspective history can offer. What does your name mean? What other people in history have had your name? What celebrities presently have your name? Believe it or not, this type of information can often be found in baby books.

Once you have this information in hand, weed out any negative connections and focus your attention on only those things which are positive. Make a list of these and use them as a declaration. For example, my name *Patricia* means "noble" or "peacemaker," so when I do name affirmations I might stand before the mirror and say, "I am Patricia, and nobility is in that name!" or "I am Patricia, one who can make and find peace." You will probably feel a little awkward at first, but don't be afraid to let your voice rise with energy. Feel the strength and power in the title you have used all your life filling your being. Listen to the words you speak, knowing they represent the best of you. Sing your name, dance your name, whisper your name to the winds and let them carry it like a blessing back to you.

This type of exercise is something you can do every day while you are brushing your hair, shaving, or whatever. It doesn't take a lot of time, but eventually you will notice your way of thinking about your name changing to reflect the growing awareness of its meaning in a more positive light.

If you happen to work with a group, this activity can be changed slightly. In this case you can stand in the center of the group while the people around you softly chant your name. As they feel inspired, each in turn will say what they think of when your name is spoken, and this statement will be reflected by the group.

To illustrate, if your name is Mary, then the entire group quietly and rhythmically chants "Mary, Mary, Mary." As they do, each member takes a turn sharing something positive such as "Mary is generous." The last word in the statement is then carried by the rest of the group in the chant which now will slowly change from the name to the attribute of "generous." This process continues until everyone has spoken and the energy of the circle naturally calms. Afterwards, warm hugs may be exchanged as a physical expression of the group's support.

EXERCISE 2: A NAMING RITUAL

Sometimes, especially in magical realms, we feel the need to take a new name to mark the ending of one cycle and the beginning of another. In the everyday world this is seen at marriages. In the realms of the spiritual this is most often experienced during someone's initiation[16] into a particular magical tradition. Each person's reason for taking a specific name is a private matter; however, the new name should reflect the best of what they hope to become by studying on this new Path.

While the ritual shared here is a personal one, I feel it can be used privately or with a group simply by making some adjustments which reflect the individual and their tradition more intimately. I began by decorating my sacred space just outside the circle with images that represented the "old person." For me, since I was coming from a fundamentalist faith into magic, these icons consisted of a cross along with other religious items from that belief system. On the other side of the circle, at the altar, I placed my new magical tools and a robe.

As I cast the circle,[17] I left the final quarter open, where the old life was, for last. I then turned my back to those tokens and closed the magic space to walk towards the altar, thus symbolically shutting that door behind me. At the altar I donned all my magical regalia, lit the candles, and stood in silent thought for a few minutes. I then spoke out loud the things on my heart, declaring to the four winds the new name I had chosen for magical work and my desire to cultivate mystical knowledge and wisdom. It was a wonderful experience which left me with a sense of liberation I had not known before. For the first time in my life I was able to be called by a name which I chose for myself, and that reflected my beliefs.

Even though we continue to use our given names on a daily basis, the employment of a magical name is very powerful for ritual. When we enter a circle, we are called by this name to remind ourselves that this is another type of reality. Here, this alternate designation helps to focus our minds on intuitive thought patterns where time and space no longer exist in the traditional sense, and our spirits are free to use their gifts, bringing transformation within and without.

AFFIRMATION FOR THE WHOLE PSYCHE

The preceding activities are meant to help narrow our focus and constructively deal with singular mental processes and thought forms. Along with these, it is good to also work with yourself in a more rounded manner. For this, we return to what is often called a *mantra;* a ritualistic hymn or prayer of self affirmation. In many Eastern traditions, the "om" or "I am" is used.

To begin your mantra you can use the "om," but I suggest a slightly different approach. Think for a moment about all the personal and spiritual qualities you would like to bring into your life. Narrow this list down to three items which you will use over the duration of three months, during which time you plan to also actively cultivate those characteristics.

Get comfortable and begin slow breathing as you have in the other exercises here, only this time as you exhale, speak the affirmation of what you are going to acquire. Phrases such as "I am peaceful," "My body is holy," or "I am consistent" are good illustrations. Each phrase should be repeated three times. First, visualize bringing that characteristic into yourself as you inhale; then as you exhale, release the energy with your words to create the change.

This activity should be performed daily over the three-month period; just as you would exercise your body, you are now exercising your will. Note your progress in your journal. Don't be discouraged if the changes are not 100% effected at the end of three months. Some things, especially life-long habits, take a little longer to eliminate or alter. The important thing is that you center your mental energy on your goals consistently, mirroring those aspirations with actions. You will feel better about yourself, have more energy to give to your projects, and should quickly discover your attitudes becoming more positive, life-affirming, and full of joy.

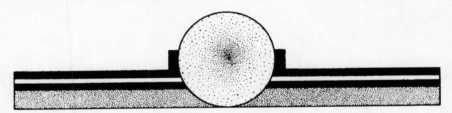

NOTES FOR CHAPTER 1

1. *Vibration*, commonly defined, is a type of energy wave. Words in spoken form carry energy with them. The power of the sound created with language can affect the way we react to it. For example, if someone is angry we will sense that emotion in their words.

2. *God-Self* is a New Age term created to represent the basic belief that all intelligent beings are in essence Divine. This belief is founded on the idea that in the process of creation a small portion of the energy of "god" was given to each soul to help them grow and develop until they can return to the Eternal Source in perfect harmony.

3. *God/dess* is a way of writing about the Divine being so that both the male and female aspects are represented. Many cultures throughout history have worshiped a female visage of God, while Western traditions have remained predominantly male-oriented. This term allows for more balance.

4. Carl Jung, in his studies of human mental processes, spoke of a "collective unconscious" where there are certain universal symbols and ideas inherent to all human beings. The idea of universal terminology is based on this, with a broader perspective that takes into account the individual's effect not only on this world, but all of creation.

5. A *Book of Shadows* is a magical book of spells, rituals, notes, herbals, and other pertinent information for use by either an individual or a group of Witches. This basically acts as a magical diary.

6. The time of the waxing moon is often used as a symbol of growth and change for magical workings. Here the image of the moon growing to fullness in the sky acts as a focus to bring abundance or completeness to mystical endeavors.

7. The color red is often used to symbolize love. We know that the human mind responds on an emotional level to color. Long exposure to bright colors often brings energetic responses from children, while darkness makes many people depressed. This basic intuitive reaction is the reason that color symbolism is employed for magical work.

8. *Drawing Down the Moon* is a phrase used by Witches to describe the act of taking on the role of God or Goddess for a ritual. Here, the priest/ess draws in the essence of the Divine for the duration of the working, not unlike the transformation which Christians believe takes place during communion.

9. *Meditation* is an age-old practice among many religions. In the simplest form it is quiet contemplation and relaxation. In more advanced forms it can lead to the awakening of communion with the hidden self, trance states, and visionary experiences. Most meditation techniques employ a combination of breathing tech-

niques, visualization, sound, and other sensory input to achieve a heightened state of awareness.

10. It is believed that magic works "out of space, out of time;" in other words, just beyond the normal range of awareness or through what some call the *Astral plane* where spirits abide.

11. *Sacred space* is any area which has been blessed or consecrated for ritual work (both Christian and magical). Here, some type of prayers or other actions are used to cleanse the space and prepare it for spiritual endeavors.

12. The *matrix* of any object is basically a foundational blueprint to its form and function. For example, the quartz crystal has a basic matrix that allows it to be the perfect conduit for electrical energy. Likewise, other objects can have a make-up that predisposes them for certain magical functions which are determined by the individual employing them. Similar to regular tools, the way they are employed is often a matter of personal preference.

13. An *aura* is the natural field of energy created by any living thing. Most noticeable through body heat, being aware of one's aura can often help with relaxation techniques, personal communication skills, etc.

14. A *Witch bottle* is commonly made out of an old coffee can or other jar which can be sealed. Inside, pieces of mirrors and other sharp objects along with salt or vinegar are placed and sealed after having been blessed for protection. The salt and vinegar represent cleansing, the mirror reflects back negative energy to the sender, and the pieces of glass act to trap any malicious intent directed towards the individual. The bottle is usually planted near the door of a home or in another area where it won't be disturbed.

15. *Reincarnation* is the belief that the soul, the thing which makes each human being a unique individual, is by its very nature immortal. This soul, until it reaches a state of perfect understanding, will return to live on this plane again in physical form as a tool for learning.

16. *Initiation* is rather like baptism in Christian traditions. An initiation is a ritual to mark the acceptance of a specific magical path, and recognition of this path by others who practice.

17. *Casting a Circle* is the term used to describe the creating of sacred space for magic. Often done by calling on the powers of the fundamental elements (Earth, Air, Fire, and Water) as protectors.

When passion comes to pierce the fray
I'm moved to write; let letters play
across the page, and to my heart
the dawning of some inner art . . .

When light, they come like soaring birds
I think again upon my words
then free this song in hopes it's heard

Great Spirit,
teach me to sing and sleep
when to sow, and when to reap
teach me again, the simple ways,
Great Spirit, teach me to pray.

— Marian

Chapter

Creative Communication

Learning to Trust Again

Dare to be true.
— G. Herbert

The young person feels uncomfortable standing firm against injustice for fear their peers won't understand; the working parent feels bad when they can't give 100% to their family. The housewife struggles with sharing her needs with her husband; the husband strives to be more open with his wife. The single woman contends with her sense of independence versus what society portrays; the single man grapples to balance sensitivity with strength. The elderly wonder about their lives and what they have meant.

No matter which kind of person you are, there is a common thread that binds us together — change. The inner struggle that occurs with change is perhaps the most difficult thing we face today. In the last few decades, a person's role in society and the legalities relating to it have shifted drastically, leaving many people lost in the shuffle. Many women are still unaware that there are "women's issues" outside the home and family. Many men are unaware that there is a growing "men's movement" that offers them new understanding of self. Because of this, it has become increasingly important that spiritually-centered people work together and share their strength with one another. In order to accomplish this, four factors must exist: effective lines of communication, transformation of our perspectives, tolerance (including forgiveness of past mistakes), and a sense of trust.

Any time two or more "enlightened" souls get together it represents a wonderful opportunity for expression and learning. All too often, though, our fear of being hurt builds walls which leave us with nothing more than superficiality. This is a situation which we can and should change. We need to reclaim our spiritual family so that balance between the sexes, between different spiritual Paths, and within ourselves can begin to be reestablished.

Our media bombards us with negative images, which leave us looking elsewhere for an alternate vision of ourselves and our world that is positive and refreshing. Our physically oriented society fosters jealousy, centering attention on the outer person rather than inner realities. It would like us to sectionalize ourselves into "this group" and "that faction" instead of uniting with a foundation of understanding, respect, and kinship. The heavy emphasis on appearance also encourages us to hide our true feelings and stick with the "status quo" so no one is made to feel uncomfortable with public displays of emotion. Society calls this being proper and considerate. I call it bondage for both men and women.

While there is a time and place for most things in life, there should always be a little room to support someone when they need it, whether or not it is in the public eye. Need does not always recognize propriety in its timing, much to the disconcertion of Emily Post.

Magical people must learn, and make way for all people, to step out of this complacent, comfortable, and even stagnant role. We are taught to be strong, self-sufficient, and to "handle it," when the truth of the matter is that we need each other. We need to retrain our minds to believe not only in ourselves, but each other.

The spiritually awakening atmosphere we live in calls to us to toss aside preconditioned feelings and begin exploring our true emotions with one another. There is no shame or weakness in saying, "I need, I hurt, I make mistakes." Yes, this means letting down some walls, but the alternative is remaining as super-people on isolated islands simply because we've been "burned" before. In other words, the choice is between safe aloneness or taking a risk and reaching out. I think the rewards of the latter are well worth stretching for.

So it is that an adventure begins in trusting. Then what? First we need to accept each others' viewpoints as valid, if only from their perspective. Love cannot grow where there is no respect. Then we need to recognize possibilities as they occur.

Whether you are talking over coffee with a friend, writing a ritual, singing at a rally, or sharing at Circle, take advantage of the great opportunity this represents. Don't be afraid to be real. Begin to trust the inner voice and get inspired. Shout, sing, hug, dance, or whatever feels right at that moment. In most cases people will not turn away, but probably join you!

There is an amazing amount of relief that occurs when people connected in groups discover their own humanity. Suddenly there is no longer the need for pretense or appearances, but instead just honest sharing. I find the more I open myself to people, the less shy I feel about asking questions, crying, or even requesting a hug. This was one of the most difficult barriers for me to overcome, but once I began I was surprised at the reactions from those around me. I found that as we reaffirm each other, new strongholds develop based on the perfect love and trust we speak so much about.

Like other matters in your urban magical life, it is easy to become distracted by everyday activities or caught up in the work ladder, and casually overlook a cry for help disguised as an "annoying" interruption. I experience this most predominantly with my son. If I am busy writing, cleaning, or just trying to get our home in some sort of reasonable order, I will sometimes catch myself "tuning" him out, like a television or radio. Usually the result is that Karl will purposely do something bad just to get my attention. This illustration is no different with other people, especially those who are life or magical partners. How often do we tune them out?

In Chapter One we were exploring our own inner expressions to bring peace with the self. Good communication skills help us to build and keep the peace with each other. The exercises in this chapter are meant to give some foundations for acquiring and maintaining those skills, including what is perhaps the most important one of listening with heart and mind.

USING INCLUSIVE LANGUAGE

The women's liberation movement has served to teach us much about ourselves and what has been a predominantly masculine-written history. From this angle we have read about war and peace, politics and pleasure; the entire myriad of human existence portrayed dominantly by one point of view.

As a balance to this, many women's diaries are proving a valuable resource to show the other side of the story. For example, when I was in Scotland I heard a tale from a Highland woman about a small scuttle between two clans. It was late in the winter and the men had grown restless, so they went out looking for trouble. The women of the two clans, in the meantime, got together and discussed how tired they were of their husbands' brutish ways. They decided to withhold their "favors" from the men until they came to their senses. Needless to say, this particular battle didn't last long, but I am willing to bet the men involved would have given you a totally different tale!

Either way, the past is behind us. What we need to do now is build positive language patterns for the future. The new phraseology we incorporate into our speech our children will learn and carry forward to many generations. The first step in this process is examining your own common dialogues. How frequently do you use sexist or other biased terms (mankind versus humanity, wise woman versus wise person, etc.) without even thinking about it? Sometimes to really notice this you will need to tape your conversations for a couple of days, then listen to the recordings.

Next, for one entire week make a note — on a little piece of paper or in a spiral notebook which can be easily carried — of each time you are aware of using this type of phrasing. At the end of the week review the list and next to each word, write an unbiased alternative. Continue to carry the list with you for another week, only now when you catch yourself beginning to use a biased word, change it. Make a conscious connection to the alternative term you have chosen, and put it to use regularly, not just orally but in written form as well (the writing serves to reinforce your memory).

If you continue doing this for a month you should begin to notice measurable changes in the way you talk to and about people. You may also find that your thinking changes to reflect your new awareness. For example, instead of considering someone in terms of being a male or female, you are now considering the whole person, who may have both male and female attributes[1] within them.

THE POWER OF POSITIVE SPEECH

In the last seven years the one great lesson my husband has taught me is that God/dess doesn't make junk. When I speak of myself in negative, demeaning terms, it is in some ways a slap in the face to those that love me. When we put ourselves down it is like saying that these people are stupid for caring about us, that for some reason we do not deserve love. Nothing could be less true.

We don't always realize just how much of our self-doubt and fear comes to light in our language patterns. For example, a positive person will say, "Today I am going to be kind to others," while a less secure individual might put it, "I'll try not to be so grumpy today." In the first illustration the person affirms themselves and their intentions by the "I am," whereas the second individual is uncertain of their ability to succeed as indicated by the word "try."

This simple cross section of common, everyday sentences serves to show exactly how much we can transform our lives by improving the way we express ourselves. The initial process is very mundane in nature; that of relearning and watching our words. However, the effects this type of reconstruction can have when blended with personal creativity are very magical.

Say you feel led to start performing past life readings[2] for people, yet fear of failure or a lack of security with your gift hold you back. In this instance you might want to help change your perspective by adding affirmative phrases into your meditation process, while you are walking around the house, or whenever you have the chance to speak out loud to yourself. Good examples are, "I have a gift, which I will share in love and trust!" or "I will look to the past to bring understanding today," or "The God/dess is within me; I will find new strength."

EXERCISE 1: LISTENING TO YOURSELF

If you are not aware of what you are saying about yourself and your perceptions of the world, more than likely you are also unaware of what others are trying to communicate to you. For this activity, all you really need are two good ears and the willingness to be more attentive to your conversations. As you talk, ask yourself these kinds of questions:

○ *Are my words positive and life-affirming?* If not, begin to make some changes in the way you present your ideas. Instead of accentuating the negative, such as "I had a really horrible day," and brooding over that, emphasize things like, "It was a rough day, but I learned something from it."

○ *Am I putting myself down frequently?* If so, stop right here and return to the exercises in Chapter One on rebuilding your self image and then ask yourself why you do this. You are a worthwhile, important, magical individual who is here for a reason, but you have to believe this before anyone else will.

○ *Do I share my opinions in a beneficial manner?* Sometimes in the effort to "prove" our point, we can be very harsh and really hurt someone's feelings. No matter how strongly you feel on an issue, words need to be tempered with wisdom, knowledge, and love if they are to be effective. Expressing your convictions is healthy, but they can be even more powerful if channeled in a constructive manner so that something positive results — understanding.

○ *Am I quick to accept other people's decisions about my own welfare?* Ah, this person is the perpetual volunteer who feels guilty about saying no even if it means not taking proper care of themselves. Having been in these shoes more than once, my advice is to get yourself a button that says, "Stop me before I volunteer again," as a means of gently reminding yourself that you can't be all things to all people. Narrow down your focus to the things which have lasting importance, and give your energy to them instead of scattering yourself to the four winds. Remember that saying no does not mean you are a bad person, it simply means you may not have time right now to truly devote yourself to that activity (be it pleasure or work). Saying no to others, in this case, means saying yes to yourself.

○ *Do I avoid conflict even when I feel deeply about the subject?* This is another point that I get stuck on frequently. I don't want to appear to be the "bad guy" so I will often just keep to myself rather than positively assert my opinion. Holding feelings in can be just as self-destructive as negative language patterns, if not more so. Now is the time to remind yourself that you are an intelligent person who has a right to think and believe certain things. The trick is learning to express those ideas in such a way that you are simply sharing another perspective, not condemning different views from your own.

○ *Do I tell people when they hurt my feelings?* You can't blame people for saying the wrong things when they don't know what issues are sensitive to you to begin with. This is especially important in the family or magical unit where bruised feelings can result in some really nasty tensions until resolved. The best approach is to tell people after the first occurrence that a particular subject really bothers you. At least then they will be able to be more sympathetic about it. Likewise, if they poke fun about something and it leaves that sour taste in your mouth, let them know. You can't expect anyone to change what they are not aware of. From the personal aspect, speaking up when you experience pain is one way of confirming to yourself that your feelings matter and are important. People will not always understand them, and in some cases they won't even respond, but at least you have made a definite stand for yourself, which for many people is a tremendous step forward towards self-actualization.

EXERCISE 2: SORTING OUT YOUR THOUGHTS

One of the greatest mistakes everyone makes in their communications is not taking the time to think before they act. Most predominantly shown during anger, humans have a tendency to spout off everything that has bothered them for years (resolved or not). They say some very painful things in the heat of the moment only to regret it later. Even when we are not annoyed, frequently we express ourselves before the mind has a full grasp of what it is trying to convey. The resulting mayhem of confusion and misunderstanding that can occur is not always easily resolved.

To illustrate, a friend of mine was talking about magic one day and made the statement that his magical Path was on a higher vibrational plane[3] than mine. Superficially, this was not necessarily meant to be an insult, but the way it came across struck me as egotistical and elitist, causing no end of argument between us for quite some time. I found out later that this idea had been inspired by someone else. Even so, if he had considered beforehand the way he shared the information, we could have avoided the whole mess. In this case a little mental organization might have resulted in a statement like, "Someone I spoke to recently proposed that different magical Paths are on different vibrational levels." This is a much less judgmental comment, and one which can be discussed without having a predisposed conclusion.

So when you do have the opportunity to think through what you want to say to someone, consider the following things:

○ *Am I sharing this information just to be involved in the conversation, or is it really pertinent?* Sometimes we try to make ourselves into experts on everything in order to be included or feel important. Unfortunately this type of communication usually makes us look haughty. Remember, in any conversation someone has to listen for someone else to be heard.

○ *Am I speaking in anger before I have the chance to cool down and think things through?* If so, stop and take a few steps backwards. If need be, take a walk or leave the room to consider your options. Be sure to explain to the other person why you are leaving for a few minutes (namely to regain composure), then return to the matter with a cooler head, and hopefully some perspective.

○ *If time has allowed, have I really considered my ideas and organized them so others can understand?* Free-flow writing (see Chapter One) can also be a useful tool in these types of scenarios. Write a letter to the individual or yourself examining all aspects of the problem you are trying to grapple with or the issue you wish to share about. Seal this letter in an envelope for at least twenty-four hours before re-reading it. More often than not, you will opt not to send it, discover different ways to explain what you were trying to say, and actually be able to see the contrast one day and a little emotional distance can produce in your demeanor and outlook. This approach is especially useful for teachers who understand their material very well. Confronting the lesson later from the vantage point of a student can allow for a far more practical and immediately applicable presentation of the subject matter.

EXERCISE 3: CONSTRUCTIVE AFFIRMATION OF OTHERS

Someone once said, and I think very wisely so, that people often do exactly what we expect them to. If we only notice our children when they are bad and never applaud their good efforts, more than likely they will exhibit increased negative behavior because it gives them attention. With teenagers, if we don't trust them to be honest with us, more than likely they won't be, mainly because they feel we wouldn't believe them anyway.

In adults I see this manifested most strongly in the prison magical community. Because of their past, inmates have a very difficult road ahead of them. People outside the walls are not quick to trust their intentions, and rightfully so, but it makes it twice as hard for those honestly desiring change and fellowship to reach out and find a helping hand waiting for them. In many cases they just give up trying and return to the same path they have always known.

So it remains for us to begin to accentuate the positive and try to believe the best in people. To illustrate, when my son is involved in an activity he shouldn't be or is getting too absorbed in the television, I try to redirect the energy towards coloring or reading, then praise him if he takes part in the new project with only a little fuss. I will also spend more time with him during this, to show him that he can get more of my attention by listening than by acting up.

In my work with inmates I have tried to allow them a "trial period" where I put aside everything they have done in the past and see how much effort they are willing to give towards their own future. They are at first shocked that someone would judge them for who and what they are now, not three to ten years ago. In several instances, this approach has made such an impact that the prison system allowed for a change of religious status, and reasonable access to magical religious materials where none were previously available.

These two of my personal experiences help to portray how people, when properly motivated, guided, and given the chance, can (and do) change for the better. So for this exercise, try to positively affirm the one person in your life who really seems impossible to cope with. Perhaps they are always down on themselves or exhibiting other negative attitudes, but whatever the case, build them up (honestly and gently) for an entire week and see what changes occur in their attitudes towards themselves and you. I think you will be surprised by the results.

Author's Note: One word of caution on working with inmates: For every honest one there will be at least one other who is more than willing to take advantage of your good nature. While this does not mean I think we should stop reaching out, I do advise discretion and a healthy portion of skepticism. If you have any questions or concerns about an inmate, contact their facility immediately. Do not enter into any financial arrangements with them unless they are overseen by the director who you have personally contacted yourself (anyone can impersonate a warden). I learned a hard lesson about this which no one else should have to experience. So go ahead and share, teach, write, but do it carefully.

ATTUNED PERSPECTIVES FOR PEOPLE YOU MEET

Every day we are coming into contact with hundreds of people, some of whom could become dear friends or even magical partners. Unfortunately we are not living in a world where everyone can be trusted, so we are left to our intuition and communication skills to help us discern who to welcome into our lives, circles, and families.

In all fairness, I can not say that these abilities, even when well developed, will work all the time. Believe me, I have misjudged a few people in a big way more than once. Even so, development of good opinions through our own natural insight is a valuable tool for all aspects of life, not just magic.

EXERCISE 1: DEVELOPMENT OF SPIRITUAL EARS

When you are listening to others, try to develop the ability to see beyond the surface of their words to the emotion beneath. This attribute can be cultivated by first showing the same interest and caring to others as you would want for yourself in that situation. Usually this helps put people at ease and they are less apt to put on facades for you to dig through.

Next, realize that in some ways each person is like a great symphony of music. Their emotions and energy play all around them, sending out signals, a kind of auric communication, that you can collect and interpret. You may have noticed how some people enter a room about an hour before they ever get there, or how others might automatically change the entire atmosphere of a group simply by entering the scene. This is an outward manifestation of that person's unique energy or music.

Some individuals have the capacity to put people immediately at ease, like a quiet brook flowing through stones, while others are hot and fierce, waking everyone up with the fiery nature of their being. That is why sometimes when you meet someone you might feel itchy or ill-at-ease right from the start. Something in their energy field does not mesh well with your own, thus putting you on the alert. This experience is part of our animal instincts returning to us to warn that a "predator" is near, and to take care.

Don't just shake off these feelings as stupid or unfounded. Instead, take a moment to examine them a little more closely when they occur. The more you allow them to happen instead of forcing them into the back of your mind, the more you will discover your initial assessments of people becoming more accurate.

The next step in developing spiritual ears deals directly with the quality of verbal communication you receive from other people. For a few moments, preferably when you are not at a critical point in the conversation, stop really listening to the words they are saying and listen to the texture just below the veneer. This is most easily accomplished by allowing your mind to drift away from the discussion in no particular direction, and beginning a slow breathing process. When the impression first comes it may exhibit itself as a temperature, texture, sound, or even a picture in your mind.

To illustrate, say someone you recently met claiming to be a "teacher" is sharing about a powerful spiritual experience they had. As you unfocus your mind, you may sense their words as being sticky like honey, or rough in texture as burlap is; you might hear them as static, or taste them in your mouth like bitters. These types of signals are a fairly good indication that this person is not being totally honest with you, and that they are either trying to hide something or have negative motivations. Being aware and sensitive in this instance may very well save you from being taken in by a con who is only involved in the new age movement as a money-making scheme or to boost their own ego.

On the other hand, if their words are cool and calming like silk, unabrasive, and pure to the taste like spring water, you probably have come in contact with a genuine instructor who has nothing but your best interests in mind.

On a more mundane level, after you have finished sensing their words attend the way they present themselves, as you listened to yourself in earlier exercises. Do you recognize any types of hedging on issues? Are they reluctant to stop and explain their terms? Are they speaking to you or at you? Do they try to communicate on a level you can understand, in positive, non-judgmental jargon? By scrutinizing their presentation in this way, the same criteria you used for self-examination is very useful to initial meetings any time in your life.

EXERCISE 2: DISCERNMENT ON OTHER LEVELS

I believe that every person has a basic dominant element and/or animal which is intricately woven into their personality. With regard to the elements, we often speak of people having a hot temperament, or being flighty; in other words, they have the principal traits of fire or air respectively. "Water" people tend to be maternal or healers, and "Earth" people are grounded and enjoy close association with the land.

Animal characteristics exhibit themselves in much the same way. A "cat" person might be a little aloof, sure-footed and very dexterous, while a "dog" person could display a loyal, happy-go-lucky nature. Being aware that these archetypes of human nature exist and developing the ability to identify them can help you tremendously in finding people of common ground, and also in understanding your differences better.

To begin, sit or stand a fair distance from the person in question and unfocus[4] your eyes, allowing their face to become blurry like a foggy mirror. As you relax, you may see this blur shift itself or melt away into a picture, leaving only pure essence. This essence is usually expressed by a symbol. You might discover the visage of a cat looking at you, while your power animal[5] is a mouse or a bird! This would quickly explain any feelings of trepidation or difficulties in communication you may have experienced with this individual. If the symbol appearing is elemental, such as a water fountain when your personality is fire-based, again misunderstanding can occur.

The nice part about this exercise is that it gives you a comprehension of why a particular individual may produce apprehension for you, even though you may enjoy their company. It likewise helps improve the lines of communication because you can approach them already knowing certain tendencies in their character.

One on One Communication

Before we can really develop skills which allow us to integrate productively in groups, most particularly magical ones, we have to build our ability to communicate with one person at a time. There are several "rules" of conversation which are easy to follow, along with the other information shared in this chapter, to give you a strong foundation to start with.

First, try to maintain good eye contact. It shows you are interested and your attention is centered on that individual, not your surroundings. Second, don't rush your words. Speak clearly (don't mumble), presenting your ideas in a manner that reflects consideration, enthusiasm, or whatever is appropriate to that moment.

If you have a habit of tapping your fingers, jiggling your knee, or other inclinations which might be distracting, make an effort to be aware of them. These types of habits are most often caused by nervousness, and tend to make the person you're speaking to even more aware of your tension. Take a few deep, cleansing breaths (in through your nose and out through your mouth) to try and settle down. If it helps, instead of having direct eye contact look just past the person's face to a spot on the wall. This technique is applied commonly by speakers at large functions for the same purpose.

During your conversations, make certain you are not so dominating that the other is hesitant about sharing their thoughts. Likewise, don't be so demure that they feel like you are bored. If discussing spiritual topics, keep your "spiritual ears" attentive and your intuitive senses keen. Remember that not everything someone conveys as "truth" may apply in that exact form to your life or Path. The reverse is true for the information and outlooks you share in return. Keep the attributes of honesty, consideration, respect, and sincerity close at hand, and your personal discourse cannot help but be revolutionized.

EXERCISE: WORKING WITH A MAGICAL PARTNER[6]

You and someone you are comfortable working with in magical realms should begin this activity by creating sacred space for yourselves and trying to ensure some "quiet" time. Before you start, pick a topic of mutual interest that has something to do with metaphysical beliefs.

Next, sit in your circle across from each other. Close your eyes and listen to the rhythm of the other's breath. Match rhythms slowly until you are breathing in unison. Do this for about five to ten minutes. During this time, also try to become aware of the energy around you and your partner and in the room. Taste the air, smell any lingering scents on the winds, notice the breeze and how it moves.

When you are both centered, calm, and attuned to each other's energy, open your eyes and begin to share from your hearts. Usually, if you are properly synchronized, you will find that one of you naturally begins and you will know when the topic has been talked out.

I also suggest that both individuals take notes on ideas which develop during this activity, as they will probably come in very handy in days ahead, if only for reference material.

On a larger scale, this activity is excellent for groups to use before they go into study of a particular topic, or to help them work on a collective Book of Shadows. Breathing in unison is a simple way of getting two or more people working on the same energy level. Because you have to listen so closely, this exercise also helps in learning to be attentive to the auric energy of those around you.

Communication with Friends and Loved Ones

There is an old saying, "You always hurt the ones you love," which unfortunately is often true. When we are upset, stressed, angry, etc., frequently the closest people to us get the onslaught of those emotions whether or not they are the cause, simply because they are there.

How often in your life do you recall hearing the words, "Why are you yelling at me?" or "I know you had a bad day, but could you lighten up a bit?" I have experienced extreme cases of what I call displaced hostility where I physically could not approach a person because their aura felt like a hot brick wall! This is not to say we can't express our feelings, and most of the time our friends will forgive us for being curt once they understand why. However, the hope in building effective communication skills is that this process would also give us greater control over our temperamental nature, and thus impart vastly improved control over our magical energy, not to mention improving our close personal relationships.

EXERCISE 1: OPENING LINES OF COMMUNICATION (SOLITARY SPELL)[7]

When you feel that your connection with a particular person (or group) has been injured because of harsh words or other misunderstandings, this is a nice private spell which you can perform to send out warm, welcoming energy to them. Whether or not this group/person receives this spiritual invitation is really up to them. Remember that magic should not be an attempt to manipulate others towards your way of thinking.[8] Instead, we are simply using it to open a door, with a hopeful prayer that the healing energy will be answered.

For this spell you will need a length of string, a small piece of paper, a green candle in the center of the table to represent healing, two red candles (one each for yourself and the other person), and home-made incense (see Chapter Seven) composed of any of the following: allspice for love and healing, apple for peace, clove for kinship, dande-lion for welcoming, and pine for cleansing any negative energy.

After you have cast your circle, light the two red candles and the incense. On the piece of paper write the name of the individual you hope to reconnect with. Tie the string around this paper and place it across the table from you. Now, in your mind's eye, envision your next meeting with that person being pleasant and forgiving. As you do, pull on the string to bring the paper closer to you. This is a type of sympa-thetic magic[9] whereby the string serves to bridge the gap between the two of you and draw you closer together.

When the paper is finally in hand, place it on the incense to burn and light the central candle from both red ones, blowing them out after-wards. Take your burning paper and incense to a window or door and open it, literally allowing the winds to carry your message of peace to the intended recipient. The incense should be allowed to burn itself out naturally along with the green candle, but you can close your circle before this time if you wish. (Remember, however, that a burning can-dle should never be left unattended.)

This spell may also be used any time you hope to locate a friend who has been out of touch by way of inspiring a phone call or letter from them.

EXERCISE 2: IMPROVING COMMUNICATION IN A MAGICAL GROUP

After being together for a while, any group can find it gets a little lazy about the way they move through their observances. A certain amount of depth of feeling might be lost, small tiffs could occur, or gen-erally speaking, the sharing could become more superficial than it was when they first formed. This is natural. Keeping two people in tune all the time is difficult enough, let alone ten. So from time to time it is good to have a ritual where the entire group signifies their desire to refresh their bonds with each other.

While this exercise more properly belongs in the section on group communication which follows, I place it here because of its similarity to the spell for the solitary given above. In this case, the altar should be filled with one candle per person, and one central larger candle which can represent the unified group. There should also be one long piece of string per person, with all the ends tied securely onto a ring or piece of wood as a base.

After the group has built up magical energy in whatever tradition they choose, each person in turn steps up to the length of strings and shares one thing on their heart pertaining to the whole group. This sharing can have to do with what they hope to see, how they desire to help, what they feel is needed, etc., but it should be a positive, constructive statement. When they are finished speaking, they tie one knot with the entire group of strings in the length near the top to represent their commitment to the whole, then return to their place in the circle. This is repeated for each in turn until the last person knots the bottom.

Knotted String

Finally, everyone takes their candle flame to the central one which has remained unlit until now, and together shares their light with that candle (and through the candle with the group). The individual flames are blown out and a silent moment is observed for everyone to consider the single shining beacon they have created together. At this point it is very effective if someone who is good at leading chants begins a quiet rolling whisper of phrases such as "we are one," "in unity," or "trust and love," which are echoed by the entire group until the chant naturally dies down.

As a note of interest, if the assembly of knots is presented to the leader of your group after this ritual, it can then be used as part of initiations to come, where the new person adds a knot to the end once they have been accepted into the gathering.

COMMUNICATION IN GROUPS

There will always be people you do not like; that is a part of human nature we have to accept. The idea of creative communication is to make the most of time you have with people you can talk to freely. It takes a while to find just the right group, but when you do it is time well spent.

As magical people, we have the inner vision to bring about positive change. All that remains is for us to build faith, accountability, and confidence again; in ourselves and our Circles collectively. This principle is exhibited dramatically by magical groups where each person must be trusted for responsible use of their energy.

The first, best rule of communicating in groups is "never assume." Don't anticipate that people will automatically understand what you do not communicate to them. This is even more imperative for magical associations whose whole ability to function depends greatly on their discernment of each other.

When you are in your gatherings don't be shy about making suggestions. Even if your idea needs modification to work within that setting, it is valid and should be expressed. Meet the response to your ideas with an open mind, remembering that other people have their own perspectives, too.

If you have a proposal but are uncertain of its usefulness, don't disregard the vast storehouse of knowledge teachers can offer. Look to the people around you who have exhibited wisdom in word and deed and seek them out for advice when it is needed. If nothing else, they can give you some healthy food for thought to take along.

It is important from the position of maintaining good lines of communication that your group be as consistent in number as modern responsibility will allow. When the members constantly shift and change it is difficult to preserve continuity of understanding with each other, let alone your magic. To help insure coherence, discuss with your fellows at each meeting when the next, most convenient time and place would be to gather. It is sometimes nice to have each person host a gathering so that no one individual is always left with preparation and clean up. I also suggest you try and find ways to help those with children to attend, even if it means members taking turns watching them.

These types of actions will build stronger bonds between the members of the group because you have been considerate of each situation. Unlike a church, each person is no longer just a warm body filling space, but knows their presence is actually desired.

EXERCISE: HOW DO YOU SEE ME?

This activity can be done in the confines of a study group or magical circle, and is very helpful to learning about other people's views regarding you, and your perspectives of them. Like the exercise given in the last section where everyone matches their breath, this should be done again. When the leader of the group feels everyone is ready, each person takes a turn thinking of one word or phrase which, to them, represents the best in every other person in the circle. If they choose, they can explain why, but this is not really necessary to the productivity of the exercise.

Simple terms and phrases work best. If it is your turn, for example, you might start with Ms. X across from you. The first thing that comes to mind about her is the fact that she seems always happy, so your word for her might be "joyful." The next person in the circle might be "peacemaker" or "good friend," etc. In this way, each person in the circle will receive positive input from all members, and have the opportunity to give the same kind of support in return.

You might be surprised at the intense emotional response this can bring in your fellows, especially if your empathic abilities are being extended. One time when I was working with a young woman in much the same manner, the first phrase that came to mind was "earth mother." Her reaction was astounding. The tension fell from her shoulders and tears of joy filled her eyes as she whispered, "How did you know?" I didn't understand the question at the time, but as it turned out, this woman had been struggling with her desire to move to the country and begin working the land. This well-timed observation helped give her the courage, by way of confirmation, to venture out to fulfill her dream. Likewise, in a well-blended, aware group, the outcomes you experience could literally revolutionize each person's reality into something tremendous and satisfying.

Importance of Touch

Recent studies with babies have shown that children who are not held, touched, stroked, etc., on a consistent basis often develop learning and behavior problems as they grow. They are less peaceful, frequently do not eat properly, and exhibit more frequent disruptions in their sleeping patterns. Another study done on adult males shows that men who are kissed before they leave for work in the morning actually tend to live' longer! These two together make a strong argument for the power and importance of touch to healthy living. It is also a meaningful and influential tool for all types of personal communication.

While words have their place, simply saying that we care is not always enough. The gentle touch of a hand, or a hug, can often get better results than three hours of discussion. Obviously, developing the sensitivity to know when these types of actions are welcome and needed is the most difficult part of the process. Not everyone is comfortable with intimate proximity, and even more people find themselves uncomfortable with physical contact from someone outside their immediate family.

For yourself, you may need to start embracing your friends spontaneously for a while to help get over your fears and become more used to physical contact on a consistent basis. Massage is another means of practicing beneficial touch. I encourage you to begin with friends because you already have a rapport of trust built with them. These people will be able to gently tell you when your timing is off or when your technique needs improvement.

EXERCISE 1: THE BALL OF ENERGY

This activity is designed to help you get used to being physically close to another person and build an awareness of their personal energy space. It is best done with a magical partner, but any willing associate can participate.

Start by sitting knee-to-knee across from each other. One partner places their hands out next to each other, palms up, while the other mirrors this, only palms down. At this point your hands are together, with only a little natural space between them.

Body Position

Each participant should focus their attention on the palms of their own hands. As you breathe, allow your exhaled energy to move down your arms and into the palms. Within a few minutes you should feel substantial heat building up between the hands. When this happens, move them about an inch apart and repeat the procedure. This general process should be duplicated until the hands are approximately six inches apart.

Now a little bit of creative imagery comes into play. You should still feel the ball of heat-energy you have created between the pair of hands quite clearly, but if you unfocus your eyes, can you also see it? Most people get an image of a cloudy gold-red ball. This is a manifestation of personal auric energy which you have created together. When you get very good at this exercise, you can toss the energy back and forth to each other, just for fun! When you are finished you can verbally release the energy for a specific purpose, or place your hands on the ground to allow it to dissipate into the Earth.

The most important aspects of this exercise are first, the fact that you have to sit closely together for an extended period of time, focusing on a common goal. Couples or close friends can even interlock their legs to increase this effect. Second, you have to be aware of not only the energy you are creating, but also the energy of your partner to keep the auric ball growing. Eventually this second point can help you become more attuned to people's personal space requirements, thus helping you to know when touch can be extended and when it will be considered a threat or intrusion.

EXERCISE 2: MASSAGE AND AURIC ENERGY

Most people enjoy a light massage of the shoulders, neck, hands, or feet as a relaxing pastime. These parts are not considered sexual in nature, so most individuals are not uncomfortable being approached this way. However, I do caution to ask first before beginning to massage, just out of common courtesy. There are many things about this person you may not be aware of, not the least of which are injuries that could make your efforts at helping very painful.

Once you do secure permission, begin gently. You can always work the circular movements of your hands more firmly if the person asks, but for the most part a massage for soothing should be soft in nature. This gives you an opportunity to become more comfortable with physical contact without it being sexual in nature. It will perform the same function for the person you are working with.

I suggest for this exercise you start with your eyes closed and senses open. Allow the auric energy of the person before you to guide your hands to where they are needed most. If an area feels strange or somehow wrong to you, ask about it. I frequently find that this is the way I receive psychic information about injuries or sickness.

Next, allow yourself to visualize white light energy pouring from over your head, down your arms, and through your hands. The position of the light mostly has to do with the traditional place people look for God/dess — above! This way, you can add an extra dimension to the massage of subtly healing the little tensions with vibrant, life-giving radiance. Frequently people will comment that the area under your hands feels hot or tingly as a result.

The more you apply this exercise, the more you will become aware of subtle differences in each person's auric energy. You will also become increasingly adept at directing energy where it is needed most and acting as a conduit for it. All the while, you will give a little needed refresher to someone you know and be able to share energy with them on a spiritual level, even if they are not magically inclined! I do not believe this is manipulative, especially if you simply allow the white light to make you more aware of the areas which need attention (like dust shows you where items have been on a table) instead of directing it into the auric field.

Communicating about the Craft

In my position as a writer, my "broom closet" has opened rather dramatically. This has caused me to rethink my approaches regarding how I speak about magic depending on who I am presenting the information to. It is one thing to share metaphysical theory among people who understand the internal jargon, and a whole other matter when you are working with the public at large.

Discussions about your religion usually begin with your family, but I don't suggest having them over dinner where people are likely to choke on a Brussels sprout. In considering how to broach the topic, take a look at their life. Do they watch television shows that have psychics as guests, buy crystals for "decorations," try to be ecologically aware, or even read their horoscope on a regular basis? If so, you might have a bit of common ground to build on. If on the other hand, they are fundamentalists, you may want to reconsider telling them.

One of the easier methods to break the ice is to leave obviously magical books or magazines laying around, specifically on the back of the toilet. Or, if there happens to be a show about the Craft you have on video tape, leave it running and watch what kinds of reactions you get.

Perhaps the most important thing in speaking to friends and loved ones is to remember that everything they know about magic up until this moment is probably what the media or church has taught them. You have become the starting point for a new understanding to be born, so keep a cool head and a warm heart.

Explain the research you have done (hopefully) on the roots of your faith, and what it means to you on a daily basis. Emphasize that this is not a cult or a fad, pointing out the positive nature of Wicca/ Paganism, perhaps most importantly the law of "harm none." Time and patience will be your best ally in this scenario, because the longer you live an urban magical reality, the more people will see the truth in your words instead of depending on preconceived notions. While I do not recommend opening yourself up to everyone you meet, when you do decide to discuss the Craft with others, there are some basic rules of thumb to follow:

1. Keep yourself informed. Anticipate common questions that most people will ask and have intelligent answers ready. Always accentuate the positive.

2. Don't assume the person you are speaking to has any knowledge of magical jargon. Explain yourself in simple, down-to-earth terms they can relate to.

3. Keep calm. Remember your actions speak louder than words.

4. As silly as this may sound, answer each question with sincerity. If you don't know the correct response, say so, adding that you will check on it for them if they wish. Remind yourself that the only exposure this individual may have had to real magical ideals might be happening with you.

5. Remember to show as much respect for their ideas and beliefs as you would hope for your own. Tolerance is a powerful tool towards greater understanding.

6. You have nothing to apologize for. Be firm but courteous. Magic is not a gimmick or fad to get attention, it is a way of life which is important to you and many others.

7. Do not try to share too much information too quickly. Most times it is better to let a little bit digest completely, and then build on that foundation.

8. Wisdom is a good thing to keep close to you. As difficult as it may be, there are times to speak and times for silence. Learning which is which can save unnecessary confrontations, and more importantly makes any conversation more productive.

9. Avoid "cosmic" lingo. Most of the time these types of expressions are misunderstood by common people to begin with, and unless you explain yourself, they will rely on whatever knowledge they have to try and put what you are saying into a system they can comprehend.

10. Know when you are just wasting your time. There are always going to be people who will want to banter about your beliefs just to get you riled up, or in an effort to prove you wrong. In these instances, it is usually best to bow out gracefully and let the matter rest.

11. When attending a public seminar where the "opposition" is speaking, remember:

    ○ Look responsible. Appearance can count for a lot!

    ○ If you are with others, spread out around the room. Good speakers can spot troublemakers if they are seated together, and thus avoid confrontation.

    ○ Take notes. These can prove valuable to asking pointed questions or even just for information to pass along at a later time.

    ○ If you find you have hit a weak spot, keep at it. Rephrase questions until you get the honesty you were looking for. If a question is being avoided, rephrase or redirect it.

    ○ Never get out of control or become rude. This does nothing more than prove their point, and makes your arguments and questions less valid to those in attendance.

    ○ It is not necessary to let the speaker know what group you represent. Your questions are valid whether or not you are a Witch. The idea here is to get answers that pertain directly to the question, not your personal faith.

By following these basic guidelines, you should find that your experiences in talking about the Craft and Craft-related ideology will be generally more positive. Recognize that you will first have to educate people on the truth about magic and its history before any kind of positive perceptions can be born in them. In a land which was supposedly founded on the precepts of religious freedom, the responsibility for proper representations of the Craft is still in our hands. We will not win this battle by quietly standing by the sidelines nor by screaming matches, but by the living of our lives and the power of our words.[10]

WORD POWER FOR MAGIC

In any magical construct, the most powerful words to my thinking are probably "I am" and "I can." If we are able to say with conviction "I am important, I am magical," or "I can make a difference," then the first important step to functional magic has been established; that of belief.

From the time when the human race first looked to the sky searching for the face of the God/dess right up through modern history, we have always reached out for the Divine entity with the vocalized word; in chant, in prayer, in song. No matter the religion or the terms used to designate these activities, there is a common underlying conviction that we will be heard. It is this faith that gives such power to language.

Along these lines, harmonic language work holds great potential to aid healing, increase personal awareness, improve concentration, motivate restfulness, improve discourse, and any number of other important functions to the human state of being, not to mention the magical applications. For example, Ted Andrews (in *The Magical Name*) proposes the use of sounds in the birth name to create types of mantras and music which can, in theory, bring about changes in habits and improve the quality of living from the standpoint of being more centered, attuned, and balanced (see also Chapter One). I believe his proposal holds strong merit. Here, the individual sings, speaks, or shouts certain portions of their birth or magical name to become more closely attuned to themselves, and there seems to be no more personal means of achieving that goal than through the most intimate word to any thinking being — the name.

In considering the power of singular terms, names, or combined words for magical ends, the way the utterances make you feel must be the initial thing you examine. If you don't believe in what you are doing, or are disturbed by the form a spell, ritual, etc., takes, you might as well stop right where you are and save the energy until you can rework things into a fashion more appropriate for your personal magic.

The next item to look at is how to use particular words and phrases in creative manners to bring about magical change. This is probably easiest to examine through various forms of chanting. A casual chant might be something like "I am strong" repeated while the individual is doing other more mundane matters. This is not only constructive use of mundane time, but the repetition of the phrase also helps to build the vibration of vitality within the person and their living environment. I will be discussing a little more of how to employ common household items to emphasize magical work in Chapter Three, but another illustration would be to chant "I am cleansed" while you are vacuuming, visualizing your cleaner sucking up all your negative energy along with the dirt in your home!

Instead of phrases, singular words can also bring very powerful positive results. Before you go to sleep at night, try whispering to yourself the word "peaceful" as you do slow, rhythmic breathing. Say it once with each breath as you inhale, thus literally filling yourself with calm energies along with your breath! In other circumstances, such as when you are trying to concentrate on a project, a term such as "focus" could be helpful. Here are a few other suggestions for similar exercises.

For creative work: flow, skill, vision, imagine

For hard labor: strength, endure, persist

To bring joy: happy, content, satisfied

Before magic: intuitive, harmony, symmetry

For money problems: prosperity, security, abundance

The idea is to choose a term that best represents what you are working toward. As you repeat it to yourself, visualize the kinds of things that might bring you joy, help with finances, etc. See them coming into your life as you release the energy of that word several times a day; while driving in your car, in the shower, at work, and everywhere else you spend a fair amount of time, until each space is filled with a harmonic resonance supporting you, urging you towards that goal.

In this case you have used your own communication skills and command of the language to bring magic with you wherever you go. No place you dwell will ever be the same, and I am willing to bet you won't be, either!

Compassion will cure more sins than Condemnation.
—Henry W. Beecher

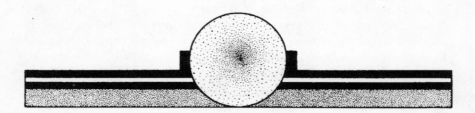

NOTES FOR CHAPTER 2

1. The traditional Eastern idea of Yin and Yang embodies this concept. Here, nothing is just male or female, light or dark in its attributes, but a little bit of both. In other words, men can show great sensitivity, and women can exhibit great strength. There is also the belief in magical realms that the soul often incarnates as each gender at least once to learn the lessons of that specific sexuality.

2. *Past life readings* again refer to the concept of reincarnation. Here the soul, like a thread in the tapestry of time, leaves a mark wherever it has existed. Certain individuals with special vision are sometimes able to trace that thread, and give insights on who we have been before. These readings often help to explain certain irrational fears or feelings. I have a friend, for example, who was always afraid of heights, but never had a negative experience associated with climbing or things of that nature. I did not know this, but when I did a reading for her, the image of a child falling from a ladder in a barn came clearly into mind. It was then that she shared her longtime fear with me. This knowledge has helped her to cope with it more constructively.

3. *Vibrational planes* basically refer to levels of existence. Great men and women such as Ghandi and Mother Teresa might be said to exist in the plane of the Master-Teachers considered closer to returning to a Divine state, while animals are present on the more earthly plane.

4. *Unfocus* is a term used for a meditative technique whose effect is not unlike the childhood activity of crossing your eyes. Instead of focusing our vision on one object, the attempt is made to see a broader panorama, until nothing specific is directly in your gaze. This allows you greater awareness of your surroundings while still maintaining the meditative state of mind.

5. *Power animals*, often referred to as *totems*, are spirit creatures. They may or may not have physical representation on this plane, but come to individuals to act as guides, teachers, and often lend their strength to trying circumstances. Each animal has a different lesson to impart, which is very personal to the recipient. Totems tend to stay with you for a certain season until their work is done, and then another may come to take its place.

6. A *magical partner* is someone you choose to work magic with on a consistent basis in order to learn and grow together on a specific Path. There is usually a strong bond of trust and love between these two people, and they can be life-partners as well.

7. The term *spell* is rather difficult to define. In some ways, it is like a prayer to which actions, symbols, visualization, and other magical techniques are added to help bring about positive results in an appropriate period of time.

8. Manipulation is not something that "white" magicians take part in. It is considered improper to try and force the will of another or the laws of nature for personal gain. Karma (the law of cause and effect) tells us that anything we send out will return to us threefold. This, combined with the rede of "harm none" in the Craft, dictates that we must watch our motivations for working magic.

9. *Sympathetic magic* has been used throughout history for everything from caring for the crops to healing villagers. A common folk remedy up until the turn of the century prescribed that someone with laryngitis should hold a frog in their mouth. After certain prayers were said, they would then remove the frog and ask it to hop away with their sickness. It is from this type of sympathetic magic that the term "frog in my throat" originated!

10. A good resource for information on art, spiritual insight, and tolerance for all positive paths is:

    Aurora Magazine
    120 North Avendale Road, Suite C
    Avendale Estates, GA 30002

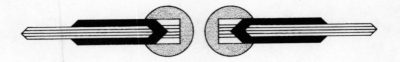

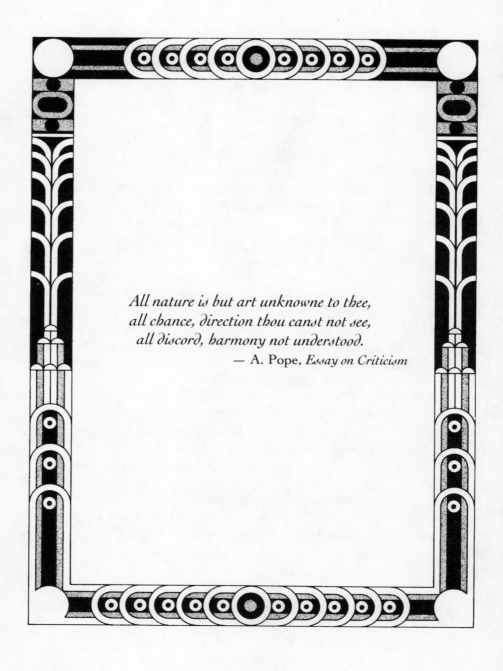

All nature is but art unknowne to thee,
all chance, direction thou canst not see,
all discord, harmony not understood.
— A. Pope, *Essay on Criticism*

Chapter

Sociology and Magic

You Are What You Eat

We can not help but be changed and influenced by the world around us. From the moment we enter this existence, the media, individuals, and culture attempt to dictate how we should act, walk, talk . . . what we should do and ultimately be. In the midst of these conflicting and often negative images, we are attempting to uncover our own Divine nature, which is in itself a difficult task. Yet it is a quest we must finish in order for our magic to be expressed in a positive, creative manner.

This is by no means an easy process, and usually one we don't go through until after we have swallowed a lot of sociological junk food. No matter how hard we may try to be unaffected, our environment and experience play a key role in shaping personality, viewpoint, and concept of spiritual realities. In this respect, we become what we eat. Getting rid of the negative connotations buried deep in the subconscious and starting fresh requires a certain trust in our talents, an honesty about limitations, a sense of humor, and most of all an outlook that does not allow itself to be limited by what is considered to be the normal range of physical senses.

There is much more to the world and the society we live in than the visible. Spiritual undercurrents exist in everything; various types of energy move around us all the time. This energy flow is something most humans are unaware of until it somehow directly affects them. Hence the over-used term "coincidence" is on our tongues for lack of a better word to explain what at first seems baffling.

The ways we express this bit of happenstance are different, but the effects are often similar. We might feel uneasy, depressed, elated, industrious, giddy, sickly, or any other physical and emotional response for apparently no reason. To illustrate, I recently came home from work in a very good mood. It had been a relaxed afternoon with a little laughter to break the tedium of typing. When I arrived, I changed clothes and looked over my mail until another woman picked up her children we were watching that day.

Suddenly, everything changed. My physical energy dropped, my mood became overcast, and for the life of me I couldn't figure out why. Then I realized that the woman who had come by was also carrying a lot of emotional baggage with her, some of which she arbitrarily left in my living room! Once I understood what I was dealing with I could get rid of it, but I should have been more alert to the situation before it affected me so drastically.

Occurrences like this can happen anywhere, at any time, which is why it has become so important to keep our psychic antennas well tuned, and attend to our own spiritual hygiene carefully. People who are not magically trained (and unfortunately many who are) do not realize when they have released energy at random for good or bad. This type of improper "house cleaning" causes problems which can directly affect the modern metaphysicist.

Just as a good physician washes before and after seeing each patient, we need to ground and direct energy which seems to be haphazardly floating around instead of leaving it unattended. Even more so, this should be done before and after rituals, meditations, spells, etc., so we are not guilty of improperly caring for the valuable resources we have to work with. The easiest way to do this is by sitting or placing your hands on the floor, thus figuratively and literally "grounding" the leftover magical static. Another method is to employ smudge sticks, incense, or other cleansing methods (see Chapter Four) as an aid to clearing residual energy. This way your space is as spiritually clear when you leave it, if not more so, as when you entered.

Like the concept of clean, directed energy, there are many things discussed in study groups and privately that leave us with confusing questions because of the ideas and ideals life has written on our hearts. Being a spiritual being sometimes requires us to walk to a "different drummer" while still coping with modern realities; not an easy position by any means.

This chapter and the associated activities are shared in an attempt to reflect on some of the more difficult struggles commonly found in the magical community. They are questions which I see again and again in my mailbox, and ones which are as difficult for me to approach now as they were eight years ago when I first discovered a magical path.

I am by no means a guru . . . I hate wearing white, and mountains in Tibet are too cold for my taste. So what I write here is limited by my experience, and the knowledge imparted to me from others who helped me learn along the way. Hopefully it will act as a vehicle to help you discover your own answers. These and similar issues, once resolved, can support the modernization of magic practically, philosophically, and dramatically.

CHILDREN AND THE CRAFT

It seems the debate over the place children have in magical circles is growing more heated every day, let alone what rights we have regarding the spiritual education of our children. On one level this problem leaves us grappling with our children's freedom of choice. On another level, we have to guard against what a magically reared child might say to their fundamentalist friend at school, and be quickly misunderstood.

In *A Victorian Grimoire* I shared many activities (not all directly related to magic) to help build communication between you and the children in your life, as well as to help them become "good people." Taking this one step further, I would like to pose this option. If we do choose to bring our children up in a magical tradition while giving them the benefit of other viewpoints at the same time, then we must also arm them against the difficulties they may face. This means slowly teaching them how to respond to questions honestly, without openly declaring their faith to anyone who happens to be listening.

Since in all reasonableness this really can't begin until the age of seven unless the child is truly remarkable in their ability to reason, try and keep your terms rather discreetly generic. That way, if a child does repeat your lessons, it will be without the ramifications of fear in uninformed individuals.

For example, my son often dreams of his grandfather (who passed over in 1990) coming to him with messages, which he then communicates in a typical five-year-old vernacular. To help him understand this,

I simply say that Grandpa is like an angel sent to keep him safe. Since in magic we believe in guardian spirits and guides,[1] this is a compromise in terminology which I can impart without feeling hypocritical.

Another more difficult illustration came one weekend when we were camping together. The sky was overcast, everything was damp, and Karl was terribly restless. I jokingly asked him how he would make the clouds go away if he could. Karl shrugged nonchalantly, looked to the torch burning nearby, and blew the smoke in the opposite direction from the wind. Sure enough, not more than a hour later, the sky cleared.

When Karl came to me, pleased with the new weather, I gently reminded him that we can do almost anything when we really believe. I also mentioned that the Great Spirit listened when he whispered that silent wish through the smoke, and helped bring the sun for him to enjoy. This way, if he had chosen to recount the incident to anyone, it was presented in nonreligious terms. These two stories help to show how we can watch our words, yet still give our children small seeds of magical wisdom as the opportunity presents itself.

As the children get older, they will need many mental tools until such time as our society is a little more accepting of magical traditions. First, they need a functional understanding of Christianity and its observances (as well as other world religions). Next, they will need to learn how to answer questions regarding major misconceptions about magic when they arise. Hopefully they will not be put in a situation of having to defend their way of living, but if they are, it is best if they are not surprised by the questions they hear. Let's face it, puberty is difficult enough without someone trying to tell you your mother worships some red-suited evil entity!

I don't suggest hiding your faith from your children to protect them from this. The bonds of trust between parent and child are too fragile, and family religion is too important to just sweep the whole matter under the rug. Instead, instill honest respect in them for other's perspectives, and when they move into their teens discuss what faith, if any, they wish to pursue. Whether or not they embrace magic, try and meet their decision knowing that you have already given them the knowledge they need to make wise choices, and support them.

If the magical path is taken, then there are several ideas I would like to share to make this experience positive for both you and them:

○ Have them help write and choreograph a ritual which welcomes them as a magical member of the family. Give them guidance on choosing a magical name, and use this name when they are working with you in esoteric realms. There is nothing more distracting in a magical circle than to have someone continuously call you by the wrong name.

○ Listen to the simple but often brilliant insight they have. Sometimes we get so involved in doing things one way, we overlook the obvious. The children in our life can grant refreshed vision for the magic of tomorrow.

○ Help them find or create their magical tool[2] collection, and perhaps give them one of your own pieces to get started. It will mean a great deal coming from your hands, as a sign that you trust them to use it responsibly.

○ Encourage some kind of daily or weekly routine of study and practice in their chosen Path, setting aside time to help them. This way you can become an active participant in their spiritual growth, and hopefully steer them away from some of the mistakes you made when you first started.

○ Make gentle suggestions if they might be approaching a particular ritual, spell, etc., incorrectly, and then explain why. Do not discourage creative work on their part, simply guide it so that it is well protected, balanced, and centered.

○ Help them to begin building a magical library aimed at their areas of interest.

○ Share with them the many wonderful associated Craft arts they might like to get involved in. This does not just mean painting or music, but sculpture, pottery, herbalism, dance, and even magical research.

○ Continually emphasize that if they have a question, they should come to you. No question is stupid except the ones that are unasked.

○ If they are having constant problems with individuals, teachers, etc., regarding something they have said or written pertaining to magic, try to help, but don't force yourself on the situation. Children eventually have to find their own solid ground, but that doesn't mean we can't give them a hand to hold for support.

○ Realize that as friendships develop, the way these people react to your home will have a direct effect on the magical child. If their friends are accepting of the Wiccan/Pagan atmosphere many of our homes have, things will go smoothly. On the other hand, if they misunderstand you may see the child shy away from any magical activities until they resolve their feelings. Don't force them in this situation, but give understanding and patience. As trite as it may sound, time does heal many wounds.

○ Finally, let them experience magic at their own pace, not yours. Children have a natural ability to circumvent what we might consider necessary steps in the magical process simply because their imaginations are so rich, and the level of their trust so pure. Don't be overly surprised at the results they can get from even the simplest procedure! You will quickly find they have as much to teach you as you do them.

DEATH AND DYING

The way each individual meets the face of death is unique not only to them but their culture. Throughout the world's religions there is a common belief in life after death, that somehow the essence of our being continues in some form beyond the grave.

Someone once said that death should not be feared. On a purely spiritual level I agree that this should be a wonderful liberating time for the soul. On a more emotional level, however, not so much logic can be found. When we are confronted with our own mortality, the misgivings return to us with a strength we probably weren't prepared to handle.

It has only been a short time since my father passed over. His death was not peaceful nor comfortable, yet he fought to survive. Even when faced with almost nothing that could be considered "quality" living, he still battled the shadows. Perhaps part of the question of death and dying in our society is also a question of life.

My father found he was afraid of the uncertainty, the nagging doubt that his life had indeed been worthwhile and thus worthy of reward. I found that I was afraid of losing him, yet wished that he would go quickly to avoid all the suffering. It was an interesting dichotomy and one which brings to bear the living will[3] and the idea that we have a right to leave this existence with our dignity intact. The quest for immortality has lost its flavor in the reality of old age, sickness, and loneliness.

While I agree it is wrong to willfully cut short human life, exercising a God-like prerogative, I cannot help but wonder if it is just as wrong to unnecessarily prolong it. When we do, are we keeping that person from fulfillment in another reality?

We cannot prove that there is life after death, even with all the accounts of near death experiences. Likewise, we do not know if plants, animals, and insects have souls. Somehow I can't help but hope that mosquitos do not. These types of questions are what faith is for. It helps us to find some peace of mind in that part of the unknowable we call God/dess. In any culture, any tongue, the questions do not change, only the names and words used. Who are we? What is the true meaning of our life? Why are we here? Throughout history humanity has turned to religion for the answer and could only pray they were right.

It is no less so for those of magical Paths, no matter how modern our mindset. Reincarnation or not, there is a sense of loss and confusion which occurs during the process leading to death. Many of the more delicate questions are ones which have to be answered in our own hearts. The final one, though, of how to let go, magic can help with.

EXERCISE 1: HEALING RELATIONSHIPS

All too often serious sickness in the life of someone near to us suddenly makes us aware of things we never apologized for, of haunting pain never quite healed. It's a shame that it requires such drastic circumstances to make us aware of these things, and one can hope that such occurrences are less frequent for those living a magical lifestyle, but if you do feel the need to mend your bridges at times like these there are several ways to go about it.

The first step is to forgive yourself. Everyone makes mistakes, and now you have the opportunity to rectify some. Instead of wasting energy berating yourself, put it to good use. You will need a lighted green candle for healing, some type of salve (recipes in Chapter Six), an item which represents the other individual, and a piece of paper. On the paper, write everything down that brought about the division of understanding. As you do, allow any residual anger or pain to pour out through your pen onto the page.

When you are done and have resolved to leave that negativity behind, catch the paper on fire and let it burn completely, then take the ashes out of the room to move them and your negative feelings physically away from you. Next, take out the item which represents the person with whom you hope to heal communications. Cover your hands with the salve and hold the item between them, pouring love and compassion into the item as you work in the salve on your hands. In your mind's eye, it helps to actually envision the face of the person to whom the magic is directed, and even see yourself talking with them. When finished, wrap the item in white cloth for protection and keep it in a safe place.

The final step is perhaps the most difficult, that of actually approaching the person. More often than not, though, you will find they are as eager as you to put things to rest. Most people near death want that peace of mind, too, and if by the Fates[4] they do not pass on, you can carry on your refreshed relationship not only in your memory, but in reality.

EXERCISE 2: LETTING GO

For both the person near death and those that must remain, letting go is the most difficult part of the cycle. Those that are leaving us feel a responsibility to those they love, and we feel the emptiness of our world without that shining spirit as part of daily experience.

My best friend experienced this with her mother. I remember her sharing with me how she felt the only reason her mother managed to fight death for so long was because she was worried about her daughter's welfare. I saw something very similar in my father the night before he died. So I tried to find a way to tell him it was okay to go, that we would be fine, and to have a peaceful transition. It was through a veil of tears that I acted, but for that one brief moment I was closer to him than I had ever been in my life.

The way each person approaches "letting go" may vary, because it is deeply personal. I will simply share with you what worked for me. From this, perhaps you can find some basis for creating your own transition rites; a way to bring serenity to your heart and the one you love.

I began by sitting at his bedside and moving myself into a more meditative frame of mind, trying to look at him with the eyes of spirit instead of flesh. It seemed as I did that a grey-white cloud hung over his body, which felt like his spirit. It was vital and alive, unlike the body below. I reached out a hand to stroke the energy as I would a child who was frightened, and in my mind I kept repeating, "go, be at peace, we'll be fine" and other similar phrases.

I can't tell you how long I sat there, or when I knew to leave, but something happened in the silvery veil that told me my father understood. It wasn't anything that can be quantified by words, just a feeling, a moment of empathic knowledge that left little question in my mind of what was to come. When I returned home that night I told my husband that my dad would be leaving soon. As it turned out, it was only a few hours later.

I should warn those who try this or a similar process to brace yourself for feelings which will not be easy to cope with. On the other hand, the tranquility of heart and soul I left with that night was worth the struggle. I realized then that letting go of my father also meant freeing myself; that he would always be with me in some ways, but life, like the river, needs to keep flowing. Perhaps the Psalmist put it best when he said, "A time to laugh, a time to weep . . . a time to every purpose under heaven."

ELITISM, OR ONE HUNDRED ONE TRUE RELIGIONS

One of the greatest dangers facing our world today is one which rarely comes directly to mind — elitism. Groups and individuals who establish themselves as superior and wholly correct in their ideology are a threat to freedom on all levels of existence. The direct result of such factions is to stunt growth by offering bondage to fear instead of creative thinking and learning.

The anxiety the elitist mindset creates acts like a cancer on the mind and soul of those taken in by the shiny outward images, instead of the bleak inward reality of people promoting their own ideals for their own benefit. These are the individuals or groups who gather at book burnings and movie bans, and who lobby to censor the media to suit their own narrow visions of right and wrong. In the past, spiritually aristocratic attitudes brought about atrocities in human history such as the Witch hunts, concentration camps, and the burning of the library at Alexandria with no more remorse than that with which one might tie a shoe.

So how does elitism effect the urban magician today? The way we handle this problem could mean our liberation or demise. On one level the factionalization of religion will always bring about certain contentions. However, when these struggles evidence themselves in our private lives through threats to our health or the welfare of our families, it is time to make a stand. That is what civil liberties groups are for. If you or your family have been harassed, lost a job, had admittance to various organizations denied, or even perhaps had a child taken from your home because of religious beliefs, you have the legal right and means to fight back.

While it can be difficult to fight against an uninformed individual or group, continuing to be a "silent" minority simply encourages difficulties. Magic then is viewed as secretive and therefore questionable. When concerns about your faith begin to infringe on personal rights, you will need to meet the occasion with strength, honesty, and integrity. Some of the groups which should be able to provide you with good council on these matters, if needed (please send a self-addressed, stamped envelope), include:

> The Pagan Parents League
> CEM Box 1652
> Bethany, OK 73308

The last contact I had with this group was about a year ago, but as of that date, they were working on an informational pamphlet for parents as well as recommended spiritual activities for children.

> W.A.R.D.
> Box 5967
> Providence, RI 02903

Directed by Joyce Siegrist, High Priestess of Coven Rosegate. Confidentiality and privacy respected. Concerned specifically with fighting for religious rights within society. New members welcome.

> W.A.D.L. National Headquarters
> Dr. Leo Louis Martello
> 153 West 80th Street, #1B
> New York, NY 10024

A long established, politically active organization with chapters throughout the U.S. They should have multitudes of information and resources to share with you.

National Alliance of Pantheists
Thomas Paine Chapter — Rev. Ron Parshley
8612 Fishlake Road
Tampa, FL 33619

Ron has been a public figure in the Florida area, actively speaking out for Wiccan/Pagan rights for many years now.

Universal Federation of Pagans
Box 6006
Athens, GA 30604

A newly created organization still in the fledgling state. However, the Church of All Worlds is at the base of the organization. With Otter G'Zell[9] and Rhuddlwm Gawr mainstaying the foundational process, this could prove to be a significant force for the future. The Church of All Worlds is also responsible for the production of *The Green Egg*, which has a useful pamphlet on Wicca vs. Satanism (a descriptive who's who).

Circle Network News
Box 219
Mt. Horeb, WI 53572

Has continuing updates on legal issues pertaining to magic around the country. Circle Sanctuary has seen its fair share of persecution, so they should have valuable insights to share.

Jack Armstrong
2237 West Morse Avenue
Chicago, IL 60645

Director of the Heartland Pagan Association and occult consultant to Chicago Public Libraries (just to name a few).

Isaac Bonewitz
Box 1022
Nyack, NY 10960

First person in history to receive a degree in ritual magic. Teacher on Pagan-related subjects since 1970, and consultant to police on occult-related crime.

Witches League for Public Awareness
Box 8736
Salem, MA 01971

Several pamphlets available on Witch's League Statutes, Witchcraft and the Law, etc.

Peter Pathfinder Davis
Box 85507
Seattle WA 98145

Consultant to the State Attorney General's office and
Department of Corrections. Served many years in political
functions from police commissioner to mayor. Priest of the
Aquarian Tabernacle Church.

W.P.P.A.
Box 1392
Mechanicsburgh, PA 17055

An association of magical newsletters promoting a positive,
professional image for same. Silver RavenWolf, the director,
has listings of hundreds of Pagan/Wiccan journals and
descriptions for up-to-date information on magic around the
country.

Occult Public Education Network
492 Breckenridge
Buffalo, NY 14213

A media networking organization set up to improve public
awareness and tolerance of alternative faiths.

Witching Hour Network
Box 24067
Cincinnati, OH 45224

Affiliated with WAIF radio, this is a new networking service
for magical people.

Within the magical community, elitism exhibits itself in another way. It
is part of human nature to want to be right. On the other hand, sometimes it's easier just to let someone else define our spirituality, then
blame mistakes on them. Modern magical living requires us to be
responsible for our own actions, tolerant of other's Paths, strong on religious freedom issues, and aware of frauds. It is a tough juggling act
which we are only starting to learn about.

No matter how old[5] your tradition is, who you were initiated by,
or how long you have been involved in magic, now is the time to move
out of an ivory tower rationale. The amount of energy which has been
wasted between warring magical factions in the last decade alone, if

applied towards positive ends, could probably stop a small army. Moot points of doctrine are of very little importance when we consider the larger picture of the welfare of our whole planet. Isn't it time we stopped being our own worst enemy?

From another perspective, the elite mindset makes it twice as difficult for the serious seeker to find a group they want to work with. They are either put off by the attitudes they perceive, or get so discouraged by the lack of response that they give up and practice as best they can without the advantage of training.

Elitism does not grow or promote growth, it simply stagnates like a swamp. If you have suddenly found yourself immersed in this mire, ask yourself in all honesty if you are fighting over a point to prove others wrong, or to prove to yourself that you're right. Consider how important this issue is in the greater scheme of things. The egotistical mud-slinging really isn't necessary, and usually only serves to give the media something else negative to latch on to regarding the Craft as a whole.

I share these reflections not in an attempt to point fingers at anyone, but hopefully to bring a fresh perspective. I am only one person in millions just like you, looking for my divinity through the mass illusions society has given. I am praying to find a better way for magic that allows us to see past the point of "how it's done" to "what it can do." If my bluntness in this regard serves as a motivational nudge towards this end, all the better.

It is long past time we woke up and realized by uniting our vision and talent we have tremendous capacity to help bring about positive change in our world. But it won't happen while we're arguing over whether or not widdershins[6] dancing is appropriate to a Circle and if an altar can be placed in the West.[7]

My hope for the urban magician (and all humanity, for that matter) of tomorrow is that s/he will embrace the motto of the Universal Federation of Pagans[8] and incorporate it into every mystical moment of their life: "Unity through diversity." This doesn't mean losing our individuality, not voicing opinions, or throwing out the baby with the wash water. It simply suggests that we learn to focus on the really important issues, keeping a level head and balanced ego. If you find it difficult to gain perspective in a particular situation, to help with this try returning to the exercises on this in Chapter One. All our "rightness" will count for little if we destroy the Earth before we ever have a chance to discover the truth.

MODERN MORALITY

I am quite certain our ancestors would be shocked and angered by what they would perceive as "loose" moral standards of our society. To a certain degree, I would have to agree with them. Some of what the revolution of the 1960s fostered was not "free love" by any means. There was a price tag to it; that of our respect for our own bodies.

With the increasing pressure on teens to have sex at even younger ages, and the message from the media that certain physical actions are not only acceptable, but desireable, we are faced with some very difficult philosophical questions for modern magical people. How should we view divorce? Abortion? Open marriages? Infidelity?

The question of what is moral and what is not is a very personal one. My major bit of advice on any of these subjects is not to make any rash or quick decisions. Once done, these types of actions are irrevocable. Responsible living is at the center of our ideals which means being responsible with our judgments, considering how they will affect not only us, but the lives of those we touch. In other words, don't jump in the pool before checking for water, and even then make sure the sharks aren't out.

When you do make a decision and discover later it was the wrong one, there are magical means to help bring resolution. To these ends I have included a forgiveness spell, a separation ritual for divorce or parting of long-time significant others, and some herbs believed to protect against infidelity.

EXERCISE 1: FORGIVENESS SPELL

When two (or more) people have been angry for a while, it is sometimes difficult to get past personal embarrassment and tackle an apology. Even afterwards, a certain amount of distrust and tension linger in the air. This eventually dissipates over time, but to help the process along all people involved can perform a spell in their own home.

It begins by placing an item on the altar to represent all other individuals involved. If the altar is not in plain view, then move the item to where it can be easily seen every day for an entire week. I feel this spell might be best performed during the new moon, which rests quietly between the phase which allows us to cultivate forgiveness (waxing), and one which can release anger (waning).[10]

You will also need a red candle to represent the love and understanding you hope to bring to the situation. Each time you pass the item and have ten minutes or so you can spare, light the candle and focus your attention on the symbol you have chosen. Pour out all your feelings, both good and bad, into that symbol. At the end of the time, whisper the word "forgiveness" three times, then blow out the candle.

After a week, the individuals involved should gather to burn or bury their symbols together, showing the earnest desire on everyone's part to put the past behind and start fresh. From this point onward the situation should not be spoken of again. It has literally died and been buried so that a new understanding could grow in its place.

This spell may be altered to help an individual cope with personal guilt simply by allowing their object to represent themselves. In this case they may want to hug it each time they pass by, and continue to whisper words of forgiveness to the icon. The rest of the working can be followed alone, discharging the guilty feelings into that image before it is burned or buried.

EXERCISE 2: SEPARATION RITUAL

No matter how good our intentions or how hard we try, sometimes couples, friends, or groups separate because of differences which go beyond the level that even love can mend. When individuals recognize that the season for their association is past, but want to refrain from the heated exchanges which all too often result from intense emotional stress, a separation ritual can be a positive magical aid. It gives the people involved an actual physical and psychological release, and often helps heal some of the pain in the process.

For the ritual you will need a fair length of twine or string, a green candle on the center altar for healing, a white candle of peace, plus scissors for each person involved. The leader of the ritual, after creating the magical space, begins binding all individuals participating in the rite together by the lengths of string. As an aid to the visual effect, the leader may even want to chant in a quiet tone, "These strings symbolize your connections to each other, the bonds we sometimes place on each other, the expectations, the good, the bad," until the binding is finished. The individuals should not be so constricted that free movement of the arms can not occur. Then moving counterclockwise, which is the direction of undoing, each person in turn cuts away their strings, saying to all others, "I release you in peace, I release myself." Then they turn their back to the circle, representing the end of their connection. When everyone has done this, the leader might wish to close with some thoughtful words and a blessing to all. Please note that whoever leads this should be an impartial party, sensitive to all members involved.

If possible, each person should either leave from a separate door or individually to improve the affect of the rite. During this ritual, be prepared for tears. They are an honest release and necessary to the healing process. Remember during this time, though, that endings are also new beginnings. Through this ritual you have given both yourself and the other individual(s) involved the chance to start fresh without bitter memories to haunt you.

EXERCISE 3: HERBS OF FIDELITY

While I believe that good lines of communication, trust, and consistent tending will help this issue take care of itself, there are some traditional herbs which have been used for ages to help keep faithfulness alive in any relationship. They are not meant to be used manipulatively, so before trying any of these please consider your motivations, then apply the magic with care and love.

While your partner is sleeping during a waxing moon, sprinkle basil over your body. This is said to help develop stronger devotion in both people. If you present a red clover to your loved one, it is a request for a pledge of fidelity. Therefore clover can be an excellent spell component for any matters of love and trust.

Make a sachet of caraway seeds, lemon peel, nutmeg, and magnolia for love, tenderness, loyalty, and purity of intent. This may be carried close to you, or left in your partner's drawers to help inspire positive romantic energy (and keep the clothing smelling good at the same time).

PREJUDICE

I consider myself a liberal-minded person, so it bothers me tremendously when I find that my initial reaction to people is sometimes tainted by prejudice. It bothers me even more when these feelings are so intense that I have trouble separating the image from the reality. For example, although I have friends and acquaintances from other cultural backgrounds, I find that my world for the most part is monochrome. Where I work the majority of people are white, and the groups I am part of seem to be the same way. I didn't set out to have this seeming segregation occur, but it has.

I am sure part of this has to do with the affinity people have for others of the same cultural background. However, I feel we are missing many opportunities for diversity because of preconceived notions and images, some of which are very subtle. To illustrate, if you see a mixed race couple, do you assume they are dating or just friends? Most people I asked said that honestly they would think first in terms of a friendship, simply because mixed couples are still not that prevalent in our society.

One way to discover your personal prejudices are to make a list of similar questions such as: When I see a child of another race, how do I expect them to behave? Do I sometimes cross the street or walk faster when someone of a different race is nearby, even if they seem harmless? When I am riding a crowded subway, do I get nervous for no reason? Your answers to these questions should reveal the impressions you have developed without knowing it. It is good to remember that the Great Spirit doesn't look at our skin or listen to our language, but seeks out our heart and honest intentions.

EXERCISE 1: SENSING THE MUSIC IN PEOPLE

Since the first step towards mutual understanding is to get past the superficial, our knowledge of meditation, visualization, and other magical techniques comes in handy to seeing a person for what they are.

In the section on healing in this chapter, I shared a little of what I call the music in people. If you have ever seen written scores, you know that each note and its placement on the page are important to the harmonic impression the music will ultimately have. Think of the spirit in each individual along the same lines, each having a range of notes which describes their nature, and which when played with your own can create harmony or discord.

The basic technique can be much like those used for spiritual "ears" and discernment as discussed in Chapter Two, only this time you are trying to set aside any preconceived ideas of what to expect from this person and going to a more spiritual insight, so that you can react to them accordingly.

As I mentioned before, during this exercise you may not actually hear the music. Perhaps you will get a textural sense like one thread amidst a great tapestry, visual images like puzzle pieces working together, or even taste their basic essence, but whatever the sense that comes to you, try to be aware of your initial response to it. Did you enjoy the sounds, sights, etc., or did they make you uncomfortable?

While you will not be able to overcome all your prejudices overnight, taking the time to be aware of them and at least making the attempt to be less judgmental will help greatly in your future experiences with people. First we recognize the problem, then put an honest effort into solving it, along with a little spark of magic to bring everything out of the shadows and into the light.

SEXUALITY, SENSUALITY AND MAGIC

Our "liberated" society sends us many conflicting signals on what is considered beautiful, holy, spiritual, sexy, etc. We toss around many of these terms like banners of declaration, but I wonder how many of us, including myself, truly incorporate the deeper meaning of these things into our lives.

For a healthy magical reality, I believe we must first return to the idea of the body as a sacred thing for both men and women. Much of our self esteem has been torn away by pressured sexual activity at too young an age, and the lingering notions that a man must be active to be virile and a woman cannot be active to maintain her honor. These are trained reactions that we have to change in order for our lives to get back in balance.

In *A Victoian Grimoire*, I shared a little of how the Victorian people treated their physical natures with a kind of reverence, one that accepted life as a God-given gift. While they may not have been liberal in their assessment of women, this particular point is something to learn from. Our bodies are ours, and we are the ones who must decide what is healthy for us sexually and socially. This is not a matter for culture or even magical traditions to dictate, but our hearts.

Thus, if some of the activities or advice of this section seem a little prudish, it is not meant to be. I simply urge caution and forethought in all physical and emotional encounters. We, like our ancestors before us, are facing new times with new diseases which cannot be ignored. "Harm none" must apply to ourselves if it is to have any meaning.

Since love is the most powerful force on the earth, romance and sex can be incredibly magical in nature. It is because of this and the deep feelings that come into play during physical encounters that I encourage prudence. Our bodies are holy; they are the tools we have been given to learn with, grow with, and eventually share. The sharing, though, should be when we are ready and can thus give much more of our being to the person we choose.

Clad or Unclad

One of the first issues which brings sexuality into focus is the fact that certain factions of Paganism and Wicca prefer to perform certain rites unclothed. Despite the notions of fundamentalists, this is not for a sexual purpose, but stems from a deep abiding belief that such actions give a closer connection to the natural world, and rid us of materialistic associations. Even so, the action itself can make many people uncomfortable, especially those who are more shy.

The decision of a group to work with or without clothing affects the whole group, and therefore should be done by general consensus. I also feel that certain allowances should be made if the entire group is not in accord. For example, perhaps your people can choose for themselves which way they prefer to enter the circle, both robed and unrobed being acceptable. As an alternative, you can announce ahead of time which rituals will be skyclad (in the nude). At no time should anyone be forced to work magic without clothing if they do not feel comfortable with it. The God/dess cares little about what we wear, it is our hearts and minds S/He's interested in.

If you or your group have skyclad gatherings, certain preparations can help bring the proper frame of mind to make this state most effective. To begin, it is nice to have separate changing rooms available where people can think about the act of "taking off the world" while they undress. This can be accomplished even at camping events with a bunch of 2 x 4's and bulk fabric. When finished this assembly looks a bit like small closets, the veil between the inside and out marking the difference between everyday life and the magical world.

In this scenario, when the ritual is about to begin a chime or bell is rung and everyone steps out, aware they have crossed the threshold to the magical circle. The idea here is that you walk into the closet clothed with the mundane, but emerge without those burdens as a new magical being. Here your old self has fallen with the garments to the floor, and you are refreshed with the power granted to you as a child of the universe.

Notes on the Great Rite[11]

Perhaps the most important aspect of sexuality as it affects modern magical rites comes to us through what is commonly called the "Great Rite." Here the individuals involved draw themselves into communion with the God and Goddess in order to personify them in sexual union. This joining is believed to create the most powerful and sacred form of sympathetic magic, and is most frequently employed only in times of extreme need.

In times past, the Great Rite was performed to help insure the harvest or protect the area from extreme weather, and other circumstances which could mean the life or death of many people. Today there are still certain instances when a couple (or group) might wish to enact this rite, but it is by no means sex for its own sake. This ritual is executed to raise pure, magical power which is then directed for urgent situations. Therefore it should be treated and approached with the appropriate respect.

For many of us the issues of sexuality and religion have been kept separate all our lives, so when we consider how or even if we should enact the Great Rite today, it brings to bear many of our other feelings about sex itself. First and foremost, we should remind ourselves that sex is a gift from the God/dess to be enjoyed, appreciated, and celebrated. This is a source of incredible positive energy that, when applied with the proper attitude, can bring about impressive results.

On the other hand, because the power of magical binding is so transformational I do not recommend the use of the Rite without serious consideration. It might best be done by either married or unattached individuals so that other more difficult social situations don't occur as a result. When performed by two well-trained, loving magical adults, this can be one of the most powerful experiences that they or the coven will ever experience.

If a situation arises where you or your group are considering this magical rite, make sure there is private magical space prepared for the couple to work unhindered by any sense of embarrassment. Have low, slow drums to sound, or quiet chanting as an accompaniment. All members participating should meditate beforehand, reaffirming their attitudes and goals.

For those who do not feel comfortable with this approach, the athame, wand, or sword when combined with a ritual cup, horn, or cauldron can symbolize the physical rite in place of an actual one. In magic, we recognize that tokens can become what they symbolize in a spiritual sense,[12] so even this act should be performed with no less reverence. Remember that your observances are symbolic of a higher purpose: a celebration of the soul, hope for plenty, an appreciation of nature's gifts, and the creation of new spiritual life.

Magic for Conception

Besides in our love for each other, another beautiful manifestation of our sexuality is through the giving of life to a new soul. When two people wish to have a child, I can think of no lovelier way to try than by a combination of physical and mystical efforts through a small, private magic circle.

The couple should prepare the ritual chamber with bright, creative colors and sprigs of herbs such as parsley, myrtle, and yarrow, all believed to help bring conception (especially if picked on Midsummer's Eve[13]). They will also want to assemble a small altar in the room, with a seed starting to send out a shoot in the center.

On a physical level, the couple should heed the suggestions of their doctors regarding rest, diet, and even remaining chaste for a while before the attempt. The woman especially needs to be aware of her cycle, but at the same time try not to get nervous about the whole affair; it is perhaps the most natural thing in the world. Remember to turn off your phone and ask your friends to give you a little privacy so that nothing can distract you from focusing on your desire.

On a magical level, a waxing to full moon is best to help encourage fruitful labors. Eating basil, pomegranates, and cucumber is believed to increase fertility, and a pinch of mandrake and jasmine somewhere near the bed is said to ensure sexual prowess! One note of caution: If you have pets eliminate the mandrake; it can be deadly.

Beforehand, a nice long bath with lemon and lavender should help calm both people down. A brief meditation may be done where the two bring their breath into unison and make an effort to become attuned to each other's energy and physical rhythms. Slow, tender massage with herbal oils can also be very beneficial. When lovemaking is finished and the couple is rested, they may then take their seed and plant it in a stoneware bowl full of rich soil. Next to the seed, each of you should place a little crystal which you have charged[14] with personal creative energy. Then continue each day to tend it with loving care, allowing nature to take her course.

If pregnancy does not occur, this rite may be reenacted any time you wish to try again. Any number of things can cause delays, so try not to become disheartened. Keep in close touch with your physician and trust in your magic.

As a note of interest, couples who cannot have children of their own may also employ this spell to help the adoption process along.

SUMMARY

Our modern reality has presented us with many confusing questions that touch frequently on our spiritual natures. Because of this, the urban magician is being called upon to blend the esoteric and the mundane into a new harmony. In this way, our existence can reflect the growing awareness that we and this Earth are not just things of a physical nature. As the caretakers of this planet, we need to approach the individual inhabitants and the world itself as three-fold entities (body, mind, and spirit), confronting all the associated problems. As we reclaim our heritage as magical beings and turn negative images into positive learning, the world around will begin to reflect this transformation. To these ends, we can also help by allowing our inner world to express itself in every corner of our lives. So it was in history that the saying "As within, so without" was born. Let's make it live again today!

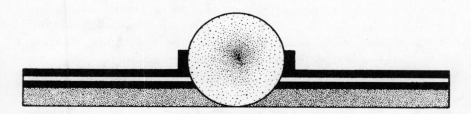

NOTES TO CHAPTER 3

1. *Spirit guides* are non-physical entities who are believed to come to individuals to help them in life, not unlike the Christian idea of guardian angels. Except in this case, the guide may actually communicate to the individual in some manner, sharing insights into spiritual and mundane matters.

2. There are a wide variety of tools commonly used for modern magic. These devices are by no means necessary to the effective working of magic, they are only aids. Just as a plumber can do the job better when well-equipped, these items are believed to help the Pagan/Witch achieve the state of mind necessary to bend energy towards specific ends. The tools include a cup to hold water, an athame or ritual knife to scribe the circle and cut magical herbs, incense to match the purpose of the gathering, candles, symbols of the Divine, and a number of other personal items as chosen by the participants. A good source (send detailed description for price quote) for custom clothing and hand-made toys for adults and children alike is:

   Sunny Creations
   c/o Kroldart
   1801 24th Avenue
   San Francisco, CA 94116

3. A *living will* is where an individual indicates by legal documents that they do not wish themselves resuscitated or maintained by extraordinary means if death should occur. Many hospitals are now keeping these forms on hand as a release of responsibility, most specifically for terminal cases.

4. In traditional mythology there were three Fates, one who measured the thread of life, one who sorted the direction of the

threads, and one who cut the thread at death. These three are similar to the threefold Divine seen in the Wiccan Maiden, Mother, and Crone, or Christian Father, Son, and Holy Spirit. Actually, this theme is repeated in many religions and cultures.

5. From what we can tell by history, magic in one form or another, even if not termed by that name, has been around since the great days of Egypt, and even long before then. Always transforming and changing to meet the needs of the times, very few magical traditions are the same today as they might have been two hundred or more years ago.

6. *Widdershins* means counterclockwise. Some factions of Wicca do not approve of the use of this form of dance, thinking it is somehow negative in implication. I see it basically like the use of the waning moon, where you employ it to banish or decrease.

7. Most magical traditions place their altar in the East, the place of the rising sun. However, since the layout of my home does not allow for this luxury I put it where it would fit, and if I need to face East during the ritual, I do so.

8. The Universal Federation of Pagans is an interesting group with many solid ideas for the future of magic. The address for further information can be found in this chapter.

9. Otter G'Zell is also the founder of the Church of All Worlds and one of the first people to pose the idea that the Earth is a living entity unto itself.

10. The phases of the moon have been used as magical components or focal points for hundreds of thousands of years. From planting and harvesting various types of foods to when certain types of rituals, spells, etc., are performed, the symbolism of the growing and shrinking lunar sphere has been intricately woven into our traditions. It is also important to note that the Goddess is most frequently associated with the moon, which is also considered aligned with the intuitive nature, maternal instinct, healing, etc.

11. May have also been called the *Rite of Joining,* if it had a name at all. From what I have been able to gather, magical people of days gone by, especially country folk, did not always feel a need to "title" all their holiday observances. They simply followed their instincts and the seasons, creatively applying the know-how taught by their families to new circumstances.

12. This belief is similar in nature to the mysticism in the Christian Church which believes that the communion feast is actually transformed by divine power into the body and blood of Christ.

13. *Midsummer's Eve*, or June 22nd, is believed to be the most potent time to harvest magical herbs.

14. Like a battery, various objects (specifically crystals) are believed to be able to hold energy. This is best evidenced by the quartz crystal today. In magic, we often use items like crystals as spiritual energy retainers for use in various rituals, spells, etc. If, for example, I wanted to use rose quartz in a particular ritual to symbolize myself, I might carry it close to my heart (in a pouch) for a week, then place it in the light of a full moon (for creative energy) for three days before the ritual is performed. This way the intentions of my magic are reflected by the energy brought to the crystal.

AS WITHIN, SO WITHOUT

Creating a Magical Living Space

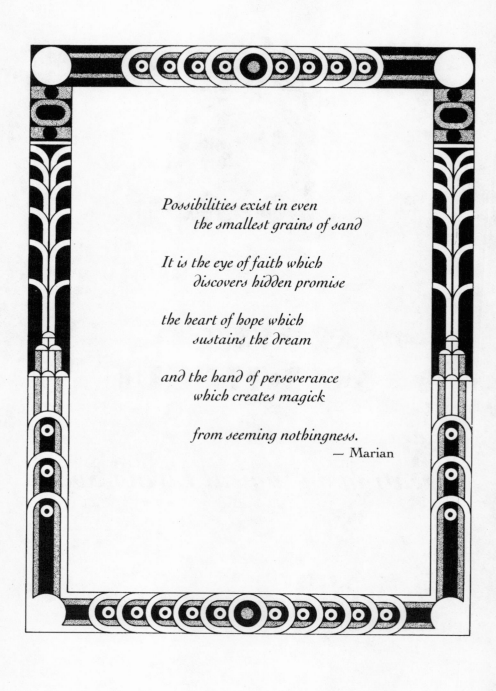

*Possibilities exist in even
      the smallest grains of sand*

*It is the eye of faith which
      discovers hidden promise*

*the heart of hope which
      sustains the dream*

*and the hand of perseverance
      which creates magick*

from seeming nothingness.
— Marian

Sound, Light, and Mood Magic

In common things that round us lie, some random truths he can impart, the harvest of a quiet eye, that broods and sleeps on his own heart.

—Wordsworth, *Ode to Dejection*

I firmly believe that having an emotionally healthy living space is very important to spiritual progress. Once we have built our inner magical foundations, rediscovering self-worth and confidence in the process, we can then allow this new understanding to pour outward. With this in mind, it stands to reason that the energy we put into the places where we spend most of our time should reflect the best of what we are and what we hope to become.

There are obvious limits in all our lives as to how explicit our public expressions of magic may become. Thankfully, there are subtle ways to change ambience which do not require neon signs or bumper stickers stating, "Witchy person, I break for occult shops." While I am not a great advocate of hiding my faith, there are many circumstances in life which require the more subtle approach.

Like you, I have friends and family who are Christian, some of whom are uneasy (to say the least) with this "magic thing" even though they have known me for many years. When they are invited to my home, I want them to be comfortable. So the question that immediately comes to mind is how I can change my living, working, and playing surroundings to encourage spiritual growth while maintaining a certain amount of privacy when needed.

Because this book centers many of its ideas on the urban magician and since not everyone has a yard anymore, this chapter is confined to things which can be done indoors. For ideas on creating outdoor magical environments, turn to Chapters Five and Six on the magical ecologist and creative herbalism.

FINDING A HOME

Whether you choose to live in an apartment, rent a room, or actually own a house of your own, you can make the place where you spend most of your free time very magical in nature. Through rituals, items, and a little creative effort, you have the ability in your own hands to transform this structure into a "home" brimming with the warmth and comfort the name implies. The first step in this process is that of finding good raw materials to work with. In the same way you need the right ingredients to bake a cake, you need to consider what ingredients are necessary for you and your family to be comfortable wherever you settle.

Before you go out looking for a place to live, you may want to do a little folk spell to aid your efforts. Take the petals of any flower you would like to have at your new residence and place them in the palm of your strong hand. Hold them tightly and envision the kind of place you hope to live in. Pour that image into the flowers, then take them outside before you leave and blow them into the wind. This energy, once released, will help guide you to something reasonably close to your goal.

No matter the locations you look in, in order for our personal space to reflect magical ideals you need to first approach the setting from a different perspective. Remember that buildings, land, and objects can collect all kinds of energy, not all of which is good. When you first enter a place to consider it as a potential home, try to keep your senses keen. When you walk through the door do you feel immediately comfortable? What do you know (or can find out) about previous owners/tenants? Why are they leaving? Basic information like this in our rather transient society can be helpful in finding a home which really suits not only your pocketbook but your intuitive sense, as well.

One method for "checking out" the general energy of a home works very well for me. I stand outside the door for a minute, take a few deep breaths, and focus my attention on the surroundings. I listen for the sound of a friendly bird, the bark of a happy dog, and/or children's laughter. These are the feelings I take with me inside. Once through the door, I stop again to consider if my attitude has immediately changed, or if the joy and peacefulness carried over. If the sensations remain, it is a positive sign that the house is pretty clear of negativity.

I also watch how the light and shadows play against each other throughout the house/apartment. For one thing, good natural lighting is proven to be emotionally healthy. On another level, you will find that if the spiritual atmosphere of the home is dark no amount of windows will help until you do a good psychic cleansing (see below).

If you happen to have a friend who is adept at sensing spirits, it might not hurt to bring them along to see what they can tell you. I live in a city with older dwellings which tend towards ghostly roommates. For the most part this isn't a problem, but it never hurts to be on the safe side. If you do decide to move to a dwelling with a few more occupants than expected, it is important to introduce yourself to them. While it may seem a little odd, spirits can improve the atmosphere of a home or make it miserable, depending on how they feel about you.

For example, while I was traveling in Scotland I stayed at a beautiful home in Inverness. Everything was pristine, yet the only place my new husband and I felt safe was in bed. During the night, the door to our room opened and closed by itself several times, once separating us. Paul and I aren't normally skittish about such things, but we did leave earlier than planned the next morning. While reviewing the particulars in the car we realized that the ghosts did not like the owners of the home and were trying to scare away their business so they would move! Just out of curiosity, we checked back a year and a half later. Sure enough, someone else was listed as the owner of that cottage!

Now, not all ghosts dislike those who come into their domain (especially people who are already sensitive to spiritual matters), but they can't just be ignored, either. Alive or not, these entities are part of what makes up your living space, and they should be treated with respect. Usually the ghost will let you know the things it likes and dislikes in little ways, like straightening pictures or moving items to a spot more than once. Try and watch for these things so you can respond. For the most part spirits stay closely connected to one object or part of the house, and as long as you give them a little leeway there, they will be content.

Besides spiritual occupants, another thing to watch for in prospective homes is what kind of land the structure stands on or around. If you hear that your potential apartment building stands on an old church-yard or grave site, you probably have already discovered a certain amount of discomfort when viewing the place. Holy ground[1] does not appreciate disrespectful change. Mind you, we can't always find out these kinds of details in advance, so again I encourage you to trust your instincts.

My last bit of advice for house hunting is to take your time. Unless you are under a deadline, it is worth reading a few more ads and doing a little more driving to find a place you can feel good about. Remember that this is the place that you want to work personal magic in, where you will be sharing time with friends, and where you will have your shelter from storms that life brings daily. Make sure before you sign anything that your higher senses[2] agree with the decision.

WITHIN THE HOME

Once we finally settle on a place to live, there is a nesting instinct in all of us which wants to make this new haven uniquely ours. We want to express ourselves and personal taste throughout the decor, when money allows, so that our private time is permeated with things which not only bring joy, but act like a mirror reflecting the individual to the world.

Decorations

Perhaps the strongest way personality evidences itself is through the way we decorate. We are very fortunate today to have a wide range of talented magical artists to quite literally color our world. From paintings and sculpture to pottery and woodworking, fresh images of the Divine are now frequently seen alongside of those from lore to share their grace with our hearth.

Even preferable for those not open about their faith is the fact that much of the mythical art is coming into fashion. No one today thinks anything of the occasional dragon or chalice showing up on a poster or carving in your home. If you just happen to place the dragon some-where in the South and the chalice in the West, all the better![3] It is through this type of creative decorating that every part of your home can reflect the magical tradition you follow.

Those of shamanistic callings might lean towards images of animals and trees to surround themselves with. People involved in Dianic traditions[4] could choose statues and paintings of important women in history. Basically, you need to look at your dwelling with a creative magical eye. To give you some ideas, here is a list of items which might be used to represent the four compass points, major magical elements, or God/dess images in your home:

East (Air): a spray of feathers, a yellow-white flower arrangement with feathers, an incense burner, potpourri, scented candles, an air conditioner, fans (electrical and paper), wind chimes, paper or model airplanes, any representations of birds and winged animals, wind instruments, flutes, magical wands, staves, bellows, light curtains which move with the breeze, small silver bells (to announce the winds).

West (Water): cups, bowls, seashells, a humidifier, hot tub, hose, wash tubs, decorated sea nets, depictions of sea animals (especially fish), a cauldron, blue-green candles or fabrics, pieces of coral, miniature boats, driftwood, sand sculptures, bells constructed from divers' tanks, stones collected at the shore, a water filter, floating candles, fire extinguisher, water-associated plants,[5] an aquarium.

South (Fire): red-orange candles or fabrics, firewood and kindling, matches, a lighter, fireplace, a bright sunny window or sun catcher (to reflect fire into the room), a salamander, cactus, red-toned flowers, sunflowers, ashes mixed into soil for plants, warm cozy chairs, any decorative blade (such as an antique or ritual sword), heaters or wood-burning stoves, oil lamps, portraits of arid places and native desert animals.

North (Earth): any potted plant, crystals, brown or green candles and fabrics, bonsai trees, a loose change dish,[6] images of animals and natural settings, a pet's bed or food dish, a globe, herbal storage areas, anything made from plant or mineral matter, wooden frames, carved candle sticks, dried flowers, brass vases, silver platters.

Center (Spirit): pure white candles and fabrics, any creature or item representing myth, legends and the world of the imagination including books about same. Depictions in various art mediums of dragons, griffins, unicorns, faeries, elves (and the like) all work well.

God/dess Images: posters or paintings of various men and women of myth, carvings, cups and wands as male/female representations of

Divine aspects, calendar art, greeting cards, pewter statues (for various fantasy gaming systems), the yin/yang symbol embroidered on pillows or table covers, pictures of the moon and the sun,[7] silver and gold candles or fabrics,[8] old-fashioned scales with tokens[9] on each side to illustrate sexual balance.

This list is really very limited in nature. There are literally hundreds of things around us every day we can use as symbols with magical meaning to us. As you can see, only a few of them might be recognized by someone really looking for their mystical connotations. What is most important is that the icons you use have personal meaning and make your environment more positive for magical living every moment of every day. In addition, you can bless and charge[10] each item for protecting their area of the house. This way, as you look around, the images which fill your heart and mind are those which will inspire growth and bring peacefulness.

Lighting, Color, and Music

If we examine colors, shades, and light intensities in combination with sound on a personal level, I believe we can not only improve psychic-spiritual techniques for healthier living, but perhaps eventually medical approaches, as well. We have all heard phrases such as "music is a universal language" or "what you need is fresh air and sunlight" spoken casually in a wide variety of circumstances. The fact that they are statements, not questions, is important for the Wiccan/Pagan thinking process. If music (or sound) can communicate specific things to the conscious and unconscious mind, and degrees of light and color grant a heartier attitude, then these two things incorporated into our home can be of tremendous help domestically and magically.

The dramatic effects sound, light, and color can have on the human state of mind have been shown to us again and again through scientific investigation and history. In religion, the use of chanting, mantras, prayer, worship, and song is an almost universal means for the human mind to reach upwards in an attempt to communicate with Higher powers. A study of various cultures reveals in the use of war cries the belief that these words or sounds can ensure certain amounts of prowess and frighten the enemy. In Ireland, keening (or wailing) is employed as a way to expedite the mourning process, and the cries almost seem to rise up to announce the arrival of the soul to the spheres.

The use of color to reflect mood is no less predominant in human nature. For example, green is almost universally regarded a color of growth and healing. However, the pea-green paint which hospitals have been known to employ is anything but comforting (except on the level that it helps motivate the patient to want to leave)! Children naturally respond more positively to bright, cheery colors over black and grey. Depending on the culture, you might wear white or black to signify death.

So in choosing colors, lighting, and sounds for our living space, we need to keep in mind the function of the rooms, how well the colors will reflect natural light, and how these things can affect us on an emotional or spiritual level daily. Some basic color, light, and sound correspondences which can be used in magic follow below. When you apply them, keep in mind that certain colors and sounds might have different effects on you because of the unique individual nature of the human soul and its life experiences. Ultimately, this should act only as a guide. Please follow your intuitive senses over any list.

Color	Correspondences	Sounds
Crystal white	Sincerity, purity, protection, centering, divinity, healing, transformation, transcendence	Singular sounds such as a gong or bell to center on
Bright red	Vibrant energy, fire, intense emotions, inspiration, sex, vitality, life's blood, healing, purification, deserts, change	Dynamic music, drumming to heart beat, crackling fires, lightning, fierce storms
Fiery orange	Autumn, stimulation, spirit, will, theory, abstracts, intuitive sense, alertness	Passionate music, sounds at dawn and dusk, birds after a storm
Golden yellow	Attraction, charm, confidence, power of the sun, trust, convictions, summer, fruitfulness, the beach	Rock and roll, bright and clear sounds, children playing, birds at sunrise

Pastel yellow	Air, spring, rebirth, psychic work, creativity, new projects, goals, breezes and meadows	"Oldies," soft rock or upbeat instrumental music
Forest green	Growth, sustenance, fertility, material needs, connection with nature, the body, courage	Classical music, anything with wilderness sounds, low bells or drums
Ivy green	Feelings, belief, sorrow, coping with pain, healing	Hushed music, silence, a churchyard bird
Midnight blue	Ocean and stars, midnight, wishes, dreams, hopes, aspirations, magical studies	The "blues," crickets, planetarium music, the beach at night
Sky blue	Patience, understanding, tranquility, hopefulness, improved situations	Most "new age" music, sounds of spring, wind chimes, church bells
Violet	Spirit, power, love, honor, ancient wisdom, midnight, enchantment, mystery	Impassioned opera, owls, magical songs

By way of example, let's say you want to magically cultivate some patience in your life. You review this list and see that sky blue is a good color to aid that desire. So you might begin to wear more items which are sky blue, perhaps burn that color candle in your home to remind yourself to be more forbearing, and can even incorporate the information into a spell for patience by working your magic outdoors, with new age music playing under a bright, clear sky. A second illustration of this would be that you use a white candle to focus on during visualizations of white light for protection, while sounding a Tibetan prayer bowl to aid your awareness. The idea in both cases is to allow the subconscious message of the color/sound to empower your spell or ritual for more potent results.

Another example I have of how this type of information can be used in the home came to me recently from a friend who, in an inspired moment, tossed some glitter into his custom blue ceiling paint. Now at night when he lights a candle and puts on some soft music, the visual impression is similar to laying out under a starry night sky, and the effect for meditation or magic is no less exquisite. It is as if, for a few moments, the entire room is transported outside and the universe is at your doorstep.

I don't expect that everyone reading this is going to repaint their ceiling, but the concept is one worth remembering. When you come home at night, turn on some favorite music which lifts your spirits, leaving the television noise to rest for a while. Use natural light, candlelight, or soft-white bulbs which are not harsh on the eyes. Candlelight especially gives everything a warm, comfortable glow. Surround yourself with colors easy on the mind and spirit, yet vibrant enough to rekindle your energy. Take walks in the sun, or stop by bright windows to breathe in a little warmth. Encompass your life with blossoming beauty and you cannot help but discover magic as the seed.

Magic for Every Room

Each room of your living space has a unique character which can be used symbolically or be amplified by magical means.

Since I am a hearth-and-home Witch, to me there are few places better for magic than the kitchen. Here everything you need is in one place, for the most part, and easily accessible. It's also easier to clean up!

Say you want to bake cakes for an upcoming ritual. Isn't it best to do so in a kitchen which has been prepared and enchanted specifically for the magical cooking process? In this instance I might clean my kitchen a little more carefully than usual, paying close attention to the implements I want to use. To this activity I could add a charm while I cook such as "Light flow through me, life flow through me, fill my cakes with prosperity," or a visualization of white light saturating the room to give the whole area that special magical spark from start to finish.

Obviously your visualization and incantations should change to suit whatever magical outcome you are working for. If you are holding a circle for healing, your words might be something like, "Better than wealth, renew _____'s (insert appropriate name here) health," and the color of your light energy would be a crystal green, that most often associated with healing work.

And what about other areas of the house? The bedroom is the perfect place for any magic pertaining to rest, health, and peacefulness. Try lying on your floor or bed, and visualizing the entire room nestled safely in a cradle. Begin to feel the soft movements, hear the song of the wind as it rocks, and allow the visualization to shift you into uninterrupted slumber. The rocking motion is very comforting and may be shared as part of a guided meditation for healing (see also Chapter Ten on exercises for body, mind, and spirit).

I do most of my meditations that specifically pertain to tension release in bed. That way, if they work I will fall asleep and stay asleep. I also recommend this type of meditation for people with chronic pain as it can often help bring drug-free rest.

The bathroom might be best for spells and rituals of cleansing or healing. While I am in the shower I like to use the visualization of light-filled scrubbing bubbles absorbing all my tension, sickness, anger, etc., in the form of dirt and washing them promptly down the drain. The warm water aids the effectiveness of the visualization by helping to loosen muscles and generally make you feel fresher. You may also burn a little homemade lavender, basil, ginger, and lemon incense (recipe in Chapter Seven) to bring peace, purification, health, and banish negativity, respectively.

The dining room is a good place for spells regarding communication and fellowship. Here you may sit comfortably with one or two other people and share in a casual ritual of sharing bread. Breaking bread has been known as a sign of welcome and hospitality throughout history. When you and someone else wish to encourage the special energy of your friendship, you may do so by following this basic rite or creating one more personal to you.

You will need one candle for each person participating, plus one central pink and yellow one (the colors of love and communication). The bread for the ritual might be best homemade, or if not that, blessed beforehand. I suggest an onion dill bread as a good choice to encourage blessing and stability in the relationship. The yeast in the recipe for this (see Chapter Seven) becomes an activating ingredient to help the magical power rise!

The ritual itself is done in silence, or with only a few words as inspiration dictates. After creating sacred space, each person takes off a small piece of bread, gives it to the other, then lights the central candles from their own. All candles should be allowed to burn together as a symbolic celebration of both the individuals represented and their shared unity. Afterwards it is nice to have a private meal together, reminiscing and enjoying each other's company.

A study or studio is a good area of the home for intellectual and creative magical pursuits. For this exercise you will need bright-colored construction paper and a paintbrush, marker, or crayon of a favorite hue. Before you start, consider for a while what your goal is, then close your eyes and visualize it. If you are working towards your degree, see yourself with the paperwork in hand. If you are endeavoring to write a book, envision the manuscript in finished form at a bookstore.

Once you have the image of your goal firmly in mind begin to try and draw it on the paper, if only in symbolic form, with your eyes closed. Not unlike its method of working with runes, our unconscious mind has its own way of translating desires into icons which can be used productively in magic. When you feel the picture is finished, open your eyes and look at it closely. Note the curve and space of each line, not with a critical eye, but one which appreciates the feeling underneath.

Now all you need to do is use this little item as a book marker, tape it to the refrigerator, or put it in your sock drawer where you will see it at least once a day. It will make you smile and remind you of your objectives. On deeper levels of thinking it will help you become more confident that your dream can become reality, and self-reliance is one of the most powerful forms of magic I know.

The cellar, not surprisingly, might be used for times when you feel you need foundation or grounding. Perhaps your thoughts have been scattered and your energy unfocused and you really want to get back in balance. The cellar, because it is built into the ground, helps bring an immediate affinity for the Earth. Sit here (on a rug, if your floor is cold), and visualize roots growing out of your body into the floor below, and beyond even that. Allow yourself to sense the cool soil, the moisture, the security of having those roots. Continue in the meditation until you feel more like yourself and ready to keep one foot on the ground.

If you do not have a separate bedroom, use your sofa. The kitchen table may be substituted for the dining room, the front porch for the cellar, and a reading chair for a studio. By working in such a manner you allow your environment to reflect your magical goal, and vice versa.

I also feel that by performing spells and rituals in all rooms of your house you are effectively helping to transform it from normal wood and plaster to mystically charged fibers. Like a giant battery, your home will slowly absorb the personality of your magic. After a while, this energy will surround you like rich soil in which you can maintain your spiritual roots.

House Blessing and Cleansing Ceremony

Considering the violent nature of the world we live in, periodic blessing and cleansing of our homes becomes very important to the urban magician. Most people who are magically trained also tend to be more sensitive to changes in energy patterns. By taking the time to do our spiritual house cleaning on a regular basis, we can help avoid a lot of negative residue that otherwise might go unnoticed until what I call "sticky build up" occurs.

Just like dust on your dining room table, everything that goes on in and around your home can lodge in your walls, chairs, jewelry, art objects, etc. You know the old expression "If these walls could talk"? For the psychometrist,[11] or anyone who is open to receiving such information, they literally can and do just that. How often have you walked into someone's home and known immediately by the atmosphere that the people living there recently had a fight? The excess energy from these kinds of situations lingers long after unless people do a very good job of psychic cleaning.

The easiest form of prevention is simply sticking to a routine. If you do your vacuuming once a week, why not bless and protect your house at the same time? Or if it doesn't seem to need magical reinforcement that frequently, repeat the procedure once every season just before your celebrations (March 22, June 22, September 22, and December 22) as another way of commemorating the turning of the wheel.[12] Just like the magical habits you keep for yourself, those you create for your home are equally important.

There are many ways in which you can cleanse and bless your home. One simple method is to use a combination of burning sage and cedar to help release negativity. Another is to employ white light visualizations to literally paint the walls with protective energy. Herbs, such as basil, dill, and marjoram, when hung in bundles or placed in pillows are believed to bring protection, blessing, and love to the home (see recipe in Chapter Seven). Not only that, but they release their light, spicy scents into the house to keep the air continuously fresh.

Most people will add some type of verbal spell or prayer when blessing or cleansing simply to declare the intention of their energy. Short, rhymed verses are best for easy remembering. A version of one that I use goes, "Bonds of power, bonds of light, grow strong, protect, defend, let all darkness take flight." I repeat this phrase in every room as I blow incense into it or as I perform the visualization. If you find you are not comfortable openly expressing these kinds of phrases, simply remember to keep the goal of your magic firmly in your mind while you work, saying a quiet thank you to the God/dess when you close.

Again, it is not so much a lofty word or fancy means that will create effective magic for your home, but a strong will, focused mind, and a heart full of love.

Welcoming New House Members

I don't know what it is about our home, but it seems that we frequently have people staying with us for extended periods of time. If you find this is the case for you as well, and the people staying with you are magically oriented, you may wish to have a welcoming ritual to help make them feel part of the family. This ritual is also excellent for families who adopt a child or become foster parents, or even to receive a new pet with only minor adjustments appropriate to the situation.

Before the ritual you will need to purchase a small token gift for the new member of your family. This gift should be reflective of their personal taste and their new role as a part of the household. For my pets, I get small identification hearts with our phone number on them. For long-term guests, we usually purchase an oriental sake cup or earthenware goblet for them to keep and use when sharing wine with us.

Next, you should cast a magical circle with the newcomer outside being brought in by a sponsor (another member of the family). Once the circle is formed, an opening is made for them to enter. The effect is even better if they can come into the circle from outdoors. At this point, the gift is passed to each member of the family who, in turn, shares a little of how they feel about and hope for their new housemate. These insights should be positive and focused towards making the individual or pet welcome.

Finally, the gift is passed to the leader of the ritual who will explain its significance to the new member and present it to them. A group hug is appropriate at this point, followed by a sumptuous meal and fellowship. Since life sometimes places us in circumstances where we have large numbers of people sharing our home, this type of ritual encourages responsible actions on all people's parts, and helps strengthen the bonds between those living under the same roof.

House Reclaiming

Ah, your house guests have left, your roommate has finally moved out, and you want nothing more than to feel like your living environment is really yours again. I know the feeling well. Some people have very dominant energy which seems to loiter around the house long after they have gone. Likewise, if the parting was not a pleasant one for whatever reason, there is the excess negativity to cope with.

I recently experienced this myself with a friend whom I had to ask to leave after living with us for nearly six months. It was terribly awkward and not without a certain amount of bruised feelings, but even so it was necessary. After the turmoil, I looked around my home and felt almost like a stranger in it. I had rearranged space to make room for this individual to the point where my house no longer really reflected myself or my family.

So over a two week period I did what I call cathartic cleaning. Everything got moved, reorganized, polished, blessed, smudged,[13] redecorated, and laundered. It was an exhausting experience, but incredibly satisfying both magically and emotionally. On the final night when everything was finished, I waited until my son went to bed, lit the candles on my altar, burned some favorite incense, listened to music, and enjoyed a glass of homemade wine with my feet up. There was immense pleasure in looking around at what now seemed to be a totally new house. The fervent nature of my cleaning poured fresh energy into the whole living space until it simply brimmed with almost visible healing light.

While this particular method may not work for you, especially if you are not a neat freak, it is important during these times to find something that does help you reclaim your space. Try buying a new rug, setting up or moving some art around, putting out different colored candles, bringing in live flowers, or any other activities which will help turn a seemingly stale environment into a fresh, magically alive sanctuary.

AT WORK

Unless you happen to be independently wealthy, you probably spend anywhere from twenty to fifty hours a week in a work-related atmosphere. Here, you are expected to maintain a certain professional demeanor, perform various tasks consistently, be courteous even when you want to yell, and very frequently hide your magical nature under a more mundane veneer.

I know for me this last part has been the most difficult to manage because it makes me feel a bit hypocritical. I'm sure other people experience the same discomfort I do when discussions of religion, holiday observances, and the like come up. Many times you don't know what to say, if anything at all, for fear of misunderstanding and even possibly losing your job. It may be illegal to fire someone for their religious status, but in many companies the true reason for separation can be easily hidden beneath mounds of paperwork.

So the majority of magical people spend approximately 23% (40 hours of a 168 hour week) of our personal time weekly in an environment which is anything but spiritually conducive. While there is a fair amount of satisfaction to be gained through a job well done, and especially being able to pay our bills, there are ways to improve the climate of your work place to covertly reflect a little more of your metaphysical focus.

Decorations

The most obvious way to start subtly changing the area where you work is through small embellishments. Live plants, baskets of potpourri, cards from friends, dry flower arrangements colored to suit the season, photographs, posters, nature calendars, and other ornamental objects can give your work area that little extra spark to help the day go better.

Obviously if you work in a factory these items may have to be restricted to your locker. Even so, when you open that door the immediate emotional response to seeing warm, friendly items is very healthy.

I have a shelf above my computer complete with a seashell (for water), pinecone potpourri (for earth), a hanging-style plant (to represent air), and a white candle for fire. To look at it you wouldn't think twice about the magical connection with the computer books interspersed, but I know what's there and why. Consider what items you can keep near you at your place of employment for the same kind of effect.

Protective Magic

Another recommendation for the workplace is to do protective visualizations in the main areas you spend your time, just as you do in your home. I usually use a white light dome or bubble to encompass my desk and files. An alternate version of this imagery places a mirrored coating on the outside of the dome to reflect any malevolent intentions or energy back to its source. In this way I can maintain a certain amount of sanctity in my work area without being manipulative in my magic.

Protection can also take different creative forms, such as a little sachet filled with apple peel for peace, bay leaf for protection, camomile for success, cloves to hinder gossip, and dill for mental clarity. This can be tucked inconspicuously into any drawer, filing cabinet, or even simply carried in your wallet or purse. Or, something even less noticeable, a little salt sprinkled on the floor encompassing your personal space can, in fact, signify a magical protective circle, salt having been used throughout history in the common and magical sectors for cleansing and protection.

Becoming Invisible

Another means to help you cope with your work environment is to become imperceptible periodically. When you find that for whatever reason you feel too much in the forefront of conflict, try this exercise for three days in a row. When you become adept at it, you will be able to use the practice in the work place without anyone being the wiser.

If you can, go to a nearby zoo and watch a chameleon. Notice how easily it changes its colors and adapts to suit the surroundings. Remember this unique ability for your visualization. Start by sitting comfortably in a position that you might be in at work. When you feel settled, take special notice of the areas in your body which feel tight. Purposefully try to relax them one at a time. Imagine a white-green light moving like sparkling air to each area that is tense and let it wash that anxiety away. At this point you should begin to feel very peaceful.

Try to see yourself in your mind's eye as you sit even now. Note every detail of the room, the lines of your body, and even your personal auric energy. As you do this, allow yourself to slowly start looking blurry and out of focus until your skin, hair, and entire body are just another part of the room, not individual to itself. Change your coloration to match your surroundings, even the air . . . you are melding into the room and slowly becoming invisible. This does not mean that you will actually disappear from view, it simply acts like a veil of energy which makes you less noticeable to those in the vicinity. As your visualization abilities improve, you may also discover a new oneness with any surrounding you happen to be in. If so, you are doing this exercise correctly. The nice thing about this particular activity is that it can be altered slightly for different effects. For example, if you feel the need to be more grounded, go out to a place where there is rich soil and work towards the image of yourself as a beautiful plant growing there, or even as a part of the soil itself. If you are angry, go to a well, fountain, or other water source to "cool off," becoming as calm and fresh as the water is.

Difficulty with Other Employees

Finally, if you do find that even with all your other magical efforts you are still having co-worker problems (which are likely to occur almost anywhere, thanks to human nature), there is a little folk spell you can use which I really like. You take a piece of their stationary or scrap paper from their work area and write their name on it. Fold this paper in thirds, then in thirds twice more. When you are finished, hold the paper in your hands and visualize the face of the individual clearly in your mind. Project that image onto the paper, then wrap the paper with white and red string for protection and binding. Next, place it in a container of water in the freezer to literally paralyze (or at the very least slow down) any unprovoked bad intentions on their part. Please note that this is not a spell which wishes any harm on the other person, but simply acts to reflect their negative energy back to them off the surface of the ice. In some instance I have known this spell to work so well that the individual gets transferred into another department or decides to leave the company altogether!

ON THE ROAD

Our society has become one of mobility. To go more than a few miles at the turn of the century meant a long outing. Now we can traverse hundreds of miles in moments, thanks to airplanes. This mobility in itself creates problems for the modern magician in that it is not always easy to carry magical tools along. Most specifically, ritual knives are not looked upon highly by the airport authorities. For that matter I have recently discovered that you are not even allowed to transport home-made ritual wine on a plane due to certain food and drug laws. With this in mind, I began to consider how we could transform our modes of trans-portation to reflect magical Paths without getting arrested in the process.

Magic for Safe Travel

Fortunately, simple spells for travel require no tools and no out-ward evidence to be productive. In contemplating spells for safe travel, also keep in mind the vehicle as a mechanical object. Somehow the vehi-cle should figure into your spell or ritual work, even if only on a sym-bolic level. It may be physically impossible to walk up and lay hands on your airplane before a flight to bless it, but it is easy to do so once your are inside, or for that matter, before you ever reach the airport by using a toy airplane to represent the real one!

A safe travel charm can be produced by using a paper or cloth bag filled with a bay leaf for protection, camomile for success, dandelion to represent your wishes, lemon for joy, and pine needles to repel negativ-ity. On the outside of this bag scribe the rune of protection (Y), and then close it up and keep it somewhere safe in your vehicle. For a car, the glove compartment is best. The charm does not need to be large to be useful. If you are traveling by bus or train, simply carry it with you. Planes present a minor problem for this approach due to airport secu-rity. I suggest you carry your herb pouch in your luggage in this instance so your herbs are not mistaken for illegal substances.

Other procedures to help protect you and your vehicle while in transit are to use white light visualizations similar to those for your workplace, or to use a little rhymed verse. For the latter, consider first your vehicle. When voyaging by plane, use this as the prime rhyming word. For example, "God/dess be with me on the plane, that where'er I travel, safe I'll return again."

Poems such as this are easy to remember and can be changed to suit your circumstances. Most often the incantation is repeated three times over the vehicle (or symbolic representation) while holding an item you intend to carry with you. The item can be anything from a lit-tle charm, piece of jewelry, your wallet, etc. A minor variation on this technique is to grasp a handful of leaves during the spell, then take these outside and release them to the wind in the direction you will be traveling to carry the magic safely to your destination.

Biking and Walking

When you can, there is no better way to reflect your magical ideals to the world than by respecting the earth. Biking and walking when you might normally drive to the corner store are great ways not only to get some exercise, but reduce pollution. During Buffalo winters this is difficult, but as soon as the warm weather comes I take every opportunity to enjoy the slow routes within reasonable distances. During the journey I take the time to listen to the birds, talk to the occasional stray animal hungry for a little love, pick a dandelion, and even hum a song or two. It is a marvelous means to reduce tension and get myself centered again. I also enjoy sharing these times with my son, husband, or a friend. You would be amazed at how much you can learn about someone when there is no television around to distract conversation.

Once during a private jaunt, I was walking down the street when a fat, red robin swooped down to the ground beside me. He chirped my way merrily, to which I replied, "Good morning to you, too." About two seconds later I stopped in my tracks, realizing that not only had I heard the bird's song, but understood it. I happened to be so relaxed and aware of my environment at that moment, that the feeling from the bird's chirping was translated directly to me as if it was perfectly natural. Come to think of it, it is! This was truly a magical moment, and one which shows what incredible things can happen when we slow down a little and really appreciate the simple beauty of life.

Portables

Another way we can make any area we go to a little more magical in nature is to carry items along which will help transform the locale. This approach is serviceable for any of the circumstances I have shared about in this chapter, but probably most useful during travel when we want to have a few goodies with us, but not be overloaded.

WALLET/PURSE/POCKET ITEMS

About the easiest things you can carry in a wallet, purse, or pocket are coins, crystals, small charms, and pictures. Coins can be very useful in magic, especially since they have dates and countries of origin. I carry an Athenic silver piece dated the year of my birth because my power animal was once a snow owl, native to Greece. The little gold-tone pill box I keep it in usually adorns my altar, but I often take it with me on trips for increased positive energy. In much the same manner, you can place any small item in your sacred space to absorb beneficial magical energy that can then be taken with you anywhere.

One word of caution; don't be overly analytical about exactly what you decide to carry. Many people have unusual "good luck" tokens. I have been known to carry an Inspector Gadget doll around because my son was trying to share something special with me. The simple adoration stored up in that toy makes me smile whenever I see it, thus it has become a symbol of joy and harmony wherever I go. You, too, may discover you have odd little things like gum wrappers, pieces of ribbon off a treasured gift, remnant threads from a well-loved blanket, etc., which can easily be transported. Don't ignore the positive emotional impact their association can have just because you feel a little silly. At home and abroad your wealth is not measured by what items you carry, but like the Gift of the Magi, the heart-felt meaning behind them.

CLOTHING

Someone once said, "Clothes make the man." What we wear does make a difference to how we feel, act, and even how we speak. When I am dressed in frills I am much less apt to sit on a desk or casually lean on a wall as I might be in a pair of jeans. The subtle messages our clothing sends to our minds can be useful to the modern magician. If this were not the case, we probably wouldn't bother with magical vestments such as robes.

So when you travel consider having a few pieces of special clothing you can take with you. If you are staying at a hotel, there is no reason why you can't wear your magical robes in the privacy of your room. Perhaps you have a blouse, shirt, or other piece of apparel which is special to you. Why not bless it, and set it aside specifically for those times when you're going to be away from home? This way you can put on a garment, which to most people around you appears to be normal clothing, and literally surround yourself with warm, wonderful magic!

JEWELRY

When I went to my first open Circle (meaning anyone was welcome to attend without express invitation from coven members), a friend of mine walked up to me and jokingly said, "Girl, you're almost naked!" I had a befuddled look on my face, feeling quite covered in my full-length, bell-sleeved robe and replied, "Excuse me?" She laughed and went on to explain, somewhat lightheartedly, that a Witch without some decent jewelry is basically unheard of.

Interestingly enough, there does seem to be a love of sparkling bangles and bobbles in the Pagan/Wiccan community, most especially those which depict magical symbols such as pentagrams, mythic creatures, god/desses, moons, and stars. These trinkets are then usually blessed and charged with some appropriate energy for protection, peace, etc.

A good illustration of this comes from my best friend who is both an astronomer and a Witch. She happens to love the fact that she can wear such jewelry and have people think it is because of her occupation instead of her religion. There is no reason why others of us in the magical community can't follow her lead. Remember that a symbol does not have to be directly related to magic to make it significant to you. Because of this, a pin or necklace fashioned like musical note for a bard, a paintbrush for the Craft artist, or a quill for a writer all could function perfectly well as part of the portable magical regalia!

I have found for the most part that few people even notice my pentagram when I wear it. Those who do seem to have some small knowledge of what it means. With other pieces of jewelry, unless you say something it is rare that people will ask why you are wearing a specific item. This is especially nice when you are traveling among people you don't know very well.

SUMMARY

By this brief introduction, you can begin to see how almost everything you experience in life can be met with a fresh, enchanted perspective. From protecting and cleansing your home to taking extra care with your travel plans, metaphysical techniques can move with you, become a part of you, and slowly develop into a valuable component for every bit of your reality. From within your living space to the great outdoors, you have the power to transform each moment into something really special; a magical memory.

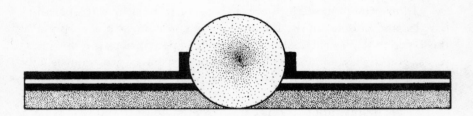

NOTES TO CHAPTER 4

1. *Holy ground* is generally considered any place which has been con-
    secrated for specific use by someone recognized as having that
    authority, normally a member of some clerical order.

2. The term *higher senses* refers to those intuitive abilities which go
    beyond the normal range of sensual input.

3. Each direction of the compass is associated with certain attributes
    in magic. Here, the south is associated with fire, so symbolically a
    dragon can represent it. Likewise the cup for the west is indicative
    of water.

4. *Dianic traditions* are ones specifically for women, frequently aligned
    with liberation groups and women's studies. The focus here is on
    reclaiming positive feminine attributes, concentrating on strong
    Goddess images, and the importance of women's networking.

5. *Water-aligned plants* are basically those considered to have this as
    their dominant element. Good examples might be water rushes,
    sea lily, kelp, and cat tails.

6. In the traditional Tarot decks, the coin is a symbol of the earth ele-
    ment, presumably because the metal ores used to make them came
    from deep within the land. Thus, using a change dish to symbolize
    earth in the home begins to make more sense.

7. The masculine and feminine aspects of all things, including the
    Divine, can be represented many ways. Most often the moon is
    indicative of the female intuitive senses, and the sun is the icon for
    strong male energy.

8. As above, gold and silver are the colors most frequently associated
    with the moon and sun, so they can be used for sympathetic mag-
    ical goals or inconspicuous tokens for the home.

9. In considering what to use to represent the male and female on your scales, try to find items which are equal in weight, thus strengthening the image of balance. A good illustration is to use a seashell for the feminine side, and a bright bit of pyrite for the masculine.

10. *Blessing* is the moving of Divine energy to an item or person to grant special protection, care, and love, and a method of consecration, sanctification, and bestowing of grace. *Charging* is using your mind to send energy into an object for use at a later time. Not unlike "plugging in" a battery except this is accomplished through deliberate psychic focus.

11. *Psychometry* is the ability to read the energy in objects. This means the psychometrist may be able to describe who gave it to you, what the occasion was, what feelings are associated with the item, etc. In some ways psychometry works similarly to what happens when you close your eyes after staring at an object for a while. You can still see the object in your mind, and even describe it in detail. Comparably, the psychometrist simply tunes into the leftover images of energy on the item in question.

12. *Turning of the wheel* or *wheel of the year* refers to the seasons and major celebrations of Wiccans/Pagans. For more information on this, turn to Chapter Eleven.

13. *Smudging* is the process of sending an item or individual through the smoke of a smudge stick, traditionally made out of cedar, sage, and lavender to help relieve negativity. This type of tradition is very old, possibly growing out the May Day traditions in Europe.

Listening to my sweet pipings . . .
The wind in the reeds and the rushes
The bees in the bells of thyme
The birds in the myrtle bushes
The cicadae above in the lime.
— Percy B. Shelley, *Hymn of Pan*

The Magical Ecologist

The Earth has music for those who listen.

— Shakespeare

More than any other problem facing our world today, the issue of ecological decay stands out as a beacon to remind people of their connection to the land. For the modern magician, our responsibility to the Earth seems to likewise be moving to the forefront of our thoughts, as well it should.

Unlike people who simply go to church occasionally to appease their image of God, someone approaching life from an honest magical perspective will quickly find that this ideology can not be confined to one day of the week. Accountability for our actions includes not just the way we handle interpersonal relationships, but also how we treat the world we live in.

I must confess that it has only been in recent years that I have begun to actively learn and practice ecologically sound activities in my home. Part of this was due to lack of information, but even a greater portion had to do with pragmatics. The difficulty lies in finding practical ways we can help the earth within the constraints that urban living often places on us. I am fortunate to have a small yard, even though our house is in the middle of the city. This gives me the opportunity to work the soil and stay close to nature on a regular basis. Not everyone is so lucky.

On the other hand, most people do have access to open areas where they can at least refresh their attunement to natural cycles. Because of this, I will be spending a fair amount of space in this chapter discussing various gardening techniques and other "outdoor" ecological aids alongside of things which can be done within any home environment to show our Earth respect, and make it more magical.

OUTDOORS

Nature is lavish in her gifts and opportunities for learning. All around us every day is a microcosm which reflects the lessons of the universe. With the hectic schedules many of us face, sometimes much of this beauty gets overlooked to the point where it is now in danger of being lost to pollution.

The goal of the magical ecologist must first be one of reconnecting with the land. We can not hope to help the healing process along if we are not aware of the cycles our area exhibits. Learning the habits of the birds, listening to the signals in the wind, and sensitivity to the seasons is very important in building our respect for the amazing living entity Earth is.

Consider for a moment that this planet has not only housed and fed the human race, but also thousands of types of plant and animal life for millions of years now. Out of that time, it took technology only about the last century to disrupt the delicate balance to the point where it is uncertain as to how much can or will be salvaged in years to come.

Alfred Lord Tennyson once wrote, "My robe is noiseless while I tread the Earth." Perhaps it was a quiet veneration that he spoke of, as if to make even a disturbing noise would break the fragile loveliness. It is this same considerate manner with which we should begin to approach our surroundings. Even if it is only ten feet of lawn, sharing a little extra loving attention and magical energy with that space is a good first step.

Remember that even a small bit of grass houses insects which feed birds, birds which pollinate flowers and sustain other animals, and so on up the food chain. All things are connected in the great web we call life. As we learn to tend the strands carefully, they will be strengthened and nourished, extending outward from the space we call home to our greater home, the Earth.

Magical Gardens

Perhaps one of the best first steps a magical ecologist can make towards helping to care for the Earth more is to work directly with it. Planting, harvesting, and weeding serve for more than just an education in gardening. By cultivation of vegetables, for example, you are giving the Earth more oxygen, enriching the soil, and feeding yourself!

Magical gardens can take three basic forms. First is a garden which you set up specifically to grow items you use in magical work. This might include herbs (see specifics in Chapter Six), berries for dyes or wines, and flowers for anointing oils.[1] Obviously, what items you include will vary according to personal needs and traditions. If you happen to live in an apartment, consider window sill cultivation as discussed in the next chapter.

To decide what to plant in your magical garden, review your magical recipes to see which items are most frequently used and will grow best in your area. If you are uncertain as to the correct climate for any item, simply call your local nursery or hothouse. They will be happy to provide you with information along with appropriate gardening supplies and helpful hints.

In thinking about my own magical needs, I came up with a rather extensive list, many items of which can be considered herbal in nature. Because of this close intertwining between magical gardens and herbalism, more specifics on planting and tending "herbal" gardens can be found in Chapter Six.

The second type of garden is one which houses many items for mundane and magical use, but which has been cultivated according to magical ideology. This approach would carefully consider the added dimension of planting and harvesting by phases of the moon and astrological signs. Other methods employed might include adding some blessed crystals to the soil, planting garlic around the perimeter for protection, and sprinkling a little camomile on the earth to bring success. Camomile in tincture form also helps discourage certain types of bug infestations!

As mentioned above, planting and harvesting cycles are of great importance to this variety of gardening efforts. Fortunately, planting by the moon and various signs of the zodiac is something which our ancestors knew well, and left many hints on.

The word *zodiac* comes from the Greek and means a circle of animals. Originally it was a way for ancient people to measure time, and as a trading map. Since these cultures were based heavily on agriculture and barter systems, the knowledge of natural rhythms, animal care, and planting times was a matter of life and death.

The list given here is year 'round in nature. Obviously if you live in a four season climate, your approach will have to vary. Even so, awareness of the associations for each sign can help you with your personal magical approach. For example, you may not be able to plant in February, but since Pisces (February 19—March 20) is a good sign for root crops and flowers, consider what foundations you need in your life, or what you hope to bring into full blossom!

Aries: March 21—April 19

Barren sign, but good for turning the soil, weeding, and cultivating. Excellent time to bring in root crops or fruit. A good time spiritually for magic dealing with cleansing or development of skills.

Taurus: April 20—May 20

A hearty sign, good for growth and planting any round- or bulb-bearing plants including turnips, potatoes, onions, etc. Productivity abounds!

Gemini: May 21—June 21

Not a time for planting; let your land lie for a while. Weed out unwanted plants or insects, mow your lawn to help stay its growth. If you plan to harvest fruit or root crops, do so during the third or fourth moon quarter for best results. Rid yourself of negative habits and get proper rest.

Cancer: June 22—July 22

Very fertile sign. Buds and grafts are good to cultivate now, along with any necessary irrigation. Rye, wheat, or any field crops do well during this phase. Excellent time for any creative endeavor.

Leo: July 23—August 22

Good for harvesting, if nothing else. The driest time of all signs; weed your garden again and get rid of any items you don't want there the following season. Consider the attributes you wish to bring in your life.

Virgo: August 23 — September 22

The best time to plant flowering vines such as honeysuckle and morning glory, but not a good season for vegetables. Also a good season for daffodils, endive, iris, and tulips. For magic, a time of fruitful workings, spells related to success and financial stability.

Libra: September 23 — October 23

Any above-ground crops, including flowers and vegetables such as cauliflower and broccoli. Magic relating to bringing things to the surface, specifically secrets or mysteries, and finding lost items.

Scorpio: October 24 — November 21

Another very fruitful sign. Berries, flowers, vegetables, and grains can be planted bountifully. Also a good sign for irrigation. Spiritually, allow energy to flow in and through you now so you can grow. Take extra time for studying a specific aspect of your Path until it blooms within you.

Sagittarius: November 22 — December 21

Not a time for transplanting, although you may want to begin canning, especially jelly and pickles. Garlic, potatoes, leeks, and other robust plants do well now. Focus on spells associated with conservation, grounding, and personal control.

Capricorn: December 22 — January 19

Very much an "Earth" sign, but more arid than Taurus. Beets, onions, and other root crops are productive, as well as any fertilizing attempts. Excellent period to work with grounding, centering, visualization, and meditation techniques.

Aquarius: January 20 — February 18

Time to harvest your fruit or root crops. Another good sign for cultivation and getting rid of pests. In your own magic take a break and enjoy the culmination of earlier efforts.

Most gardeners realize that lunar gardening is not a cure-all for problems in their land. Planting success does depend greatly on the soil, sun, moisture, and numbers of other factors, including a little luck. However, our ancestors believed that growth and yield could be increased if certain tasks were performed when the moon or astrological sign was correct.

If you wish to try this approach, the first thing you will need is a good astrological calendar, one of which may be obtained from Llewellyn. Two others that I know of are published by Astro Computing, *Planting by the Moon;* and Starlog Press, *Raphael's Ephemeris.* All three of these are produced annually.

The next thing to decide is exactly how elaborate you want your moon gardening techniques to become. While many people might follow the simpler rule of planting above ground during waxing moons and below ground during waning, this is not always a perfect practice. Just as each month of the year has governing astrological signs, each day of the month will likewise be influenced by these factors. So, by again consulting your astrological calendar and the information given above, you can combine the best of both systems.

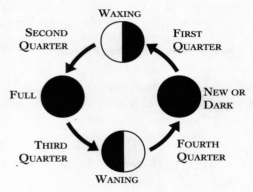

Phases of the Moon

The first quarter of the moon is a time to plant for abundance, especially with flowers. When combined with the sign of Scorpio, it grants extra sturdiness to plants. Many green vegetables such as asparagus, Brussels sprouts, cabbage, and celery, along with herbs and flowering plants, do well when planted in this quarter.

The second quarter, as the moon moves toward fullness, is a time to begin to think of your round plants. Peas, peppers, pumpkins, tomatoes, watermelon, especially if planted in Pisces or Cancer, will bring good yield. For flowering vines, employ Virgo. Garlic or other "hot" plants such as onion may be planted in Sagittarius.

The third quarter, while the moon's light wanes, is good for below-ground planting including beets, carrots, potatoes, radishes, and all flowering plants with a bulb base. Excellent also for most fruit trees, sage, strawberries, and sunflowers.

The fourth quarter is the time for rest. Turn your soil, pull weeds, and give both you and your garden a break from hard work. Perhaps harvest a little mint, make a cup of tea, thank the Earth for her bounty, and enjoy the fruits of your labor!

The third garden is one which is specifically set up to help direct and augment the Earth's natural energy in a beneficial manner. It might take the form of a medicine wheel or magical circle in that it would be aligned to the four directions, although the design is really up to the individual. This particular category of garden would also be best set up near or on a ley line, which is a strong magnetic energy field produced by the earth.

Major ley lines are pretty well charted by those who study sacred geometry,[2] but other minor lines of energy can be discovered in many areas, including your own backyard. Some people use dowsing[3] as one way to find just such a line of earth power before they construct their garden. This method is reasonably sound if you are adept at the procedure, but for the novice it might prove less than successful.

An alternative is to go out to the area where you hope to plant, and close your eyes. Take a deep, centering breath and allow yourself to feel the life all around you. Let your feet move naturally to a spot where you are drawn (if you can safely continue to keep your eyes closed, do so). Mark this first spot with a stone or other item. Now repeat the procedure, moving to a second spot. The line between the two marks the strongest energy line in your yard which can be used to center your garden over. If this ends up being in a really awkward section, try and work the land as close to it as possible without completely disrupting walk space.

Another thing to consider with regard to the energy lines is whether or not you would like to erect adjacent dolmans. Megaliths in various forms have their roots in antiquity, but their usefulness for modern magic remains. Here, you can use large stones placed carefully along the lines of energy to help direct that earth power and even augment it. At Callanish in Scotland and Stonehenge in England, the stones mark a circle along with other midpoints and an entry way. Many of these stones seem to have astronomical significance.

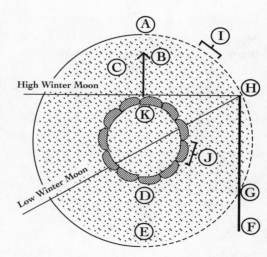

In this drawing adapted from astronomer Gerald Hawkins' work of 1965, we see how Britons could have used Stonehenge to sight the following:

A. High moon
B. To the heel stone
C. Solstice sunrise
D. new moon
E. low moon
F. Winter solstice sunset
G. high moon
H. low moon
I. 56 holes counting off the lunar year
J. 30 archways for one month
K. Full moon

Stonehenge and the Moon

Smaller single or groups of stones have been used throughout the British Isles to mark everything from ancient Druidic worship sites to the boundaries of farmer's fields. Anyone who visits these places cannot help but immediately notice the special energy in the land, and the almost lifelike nature of the adorning rocks. This is the effect you would hope to achieve with your own dolman arrangement. Some traditional styles for dolmans are shown below.

Stonehenge (England)   **Ireland**

Callanish (Scotland)   **Wales**

Traditional Standing Stone Styles

After you have decided where the garden will be and the ground has been prepared through weeding and tilling, the next step is to decide what you want to place in the four major directions. In some instances, the variety of choices may be limited by the amount of sun which reaches your garden space, but for the most part you have open reign on creativity. You can use flowers or vegetation in various colors to represent the four elements, or items such as bird baths, standing incense burners, strands of bells hung in trees, and stones to symbolize Water, Fire, Air, and Earth, respectively. In *Victorian Grimoire,* I detailed a crystal mandala garden in much the same manner, only here various kinds/colors of stone were used to mark the perimeter of the circle.

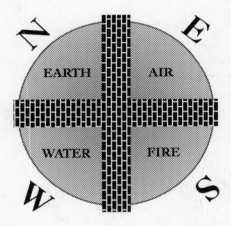

Magical Garden

Something this simple allows the area to be used later for outdoor magical functions. In fact, most of these gardens can be used during fallow periods for personal or group magic. If constructed properly, they can even include walkways or dance alleys for use any time of the year.

Again, your intuitive nature should play a key role in where plants, objects, or walkways are placed on your land above anything written in a book. With this particular magical garden, you do not have to worry about having a pristine *Better Homes and Gardens* arrangement. The goal instead is to have everything in the area look almost as if it grew, unaided, right in that spot. Thus the final outcome is something which really reflects harmonious sensitivity to the land and your own special magical attitudes.

Chemical Free and Companion Gardening

All three magical gardens are best created employing chemical free gardening techniques, again as a way of showing respect for the environment. The other advantage to this is that your plants will not have chemical additives to hinder the magical process or your health.

Thankfully, even modern science has begun to recognize that many of the older gardening methods had a lot of wisdom entwined in them. Various plants were placed together, not by happenstance, but to discourage insects. Likewise, many other procedures known by our ancestors as well as those devised by environmental groups today can be employed for the magical gardener wishing to really make a go at a chemical free cultivation.

Companion gardening is the science of using specific plants in combination with one another to encourage certain type of insects for pollination and discourage those which destroy the yield. It also studies what kind of nutrients various plants remove or replace in the soil, so that the earth can continue to be refreshed.

For the purpose of this book, I would like to look at plants which aid the growth of other plants (Chart I), and those which can deter pests (Chart II).

CHART I

Companion	Enhances
Cucumber	Sunflowers and other vining plants
Basil	Peppers and tomatoes
Camomile	Cucumbers, onions, most herbs
Chives	Roses, carrots, tomatoes, peas, lettuce, chrysanthemum lettuce
Dandelion	Fruit trees
Dill	Cabbage, onions, lettuce
Garlic	Roses
Marigold	Potatoes, roses, tomatoes, cucumbers, squash
Mustard	Beans and fruit trees
Onions	Beets, lettuce, cabbage, berries

Sage	Cabbage, carrots, tomatoes, marjoram, berries
Tansy	Most berry bushes, roses, cabbage
Tarragon	Vegetables
Yarrow	Aromatic herbs

CHART II

Pest Type	Repellent Plants
Ant	Cucumber peel, peppermint, tansy
Aphid	Aromatics, chives, garlic, mustard
Cabbage looper	Dill, garlic, onion, pennyroyal, sage
Carrot fly	Lettuce, rosemary, sage, wormwood
Potato beetle	Catnip, nasturtium, onion, tansy
Cucumber beetle	Catnip, marigold, radish, rue
Flea beetle	Peppermint, tansy, tobacco, wormwood
Japanese beetle	Catnip, chives, garlic, tansy
Leafhopper	Geranium, petunia
Mouse	Wormwood
Mole	Narcissus
Rabbits	Garlic, onion, marigolds
Slugs	Rosemary, garlic, fennel
Mites	Coriander
Squash bugs	Petunia, spearmint, radish, tansy
Tomato hornworm	Dill, borage, opal basil

To take this one step further, you can use various plant and herb combinations in powder or tincture[4] form to help repel insects in your garden. Catnip, coriander, nasturtiums, tansy, marigolds, rue, onion, garlic, tomato leaves, sage, thyme, and many other strong-scented herbs are said to help this process. Basically, the tincture's aroma disguises the plant to its normal predator as something else. The general rule of thumb is the stronger the smell, the better the success. Determining exactly what to use may be a trial and error process, but also look to your garden and see what the bugs are staying away from for a good indication.

Likewise, plants such as dill, anise, spearmint, daisy, savory, and thyme help attract beneficial bugs to your garden. These insects catch other parasites instead of your harvest!

Composting and Fertilization

Composting household waste is an excellent way to enrich your soil. The only difficulty arises with various city statutes which may make such efforts illegal in your area. The reason for this in most urban settings is the concern over rat infestation and associated disease. Please check with your local housing authority regarding the specific composting rules for your community before you begin.

Early in my research in this area I quickly discovered that natural items which can be used for fertilizer are also welcome in your compost pile. For some reason I had never made the connection before, but since ultimately the use for compost is as fertilizer, it makes sense.

Below I have given a brief list of some of the items commonly considered good for your soil. If you are placing them in compost, try to break them up into small pieces so that they will mix and decompose into their component beneficial aspects more quickly. I also suggest taking some precautions against animal visitors snacking at your pile, such as good fencing or use of a large barrel with a secure lid. Collect your ingredients all summer and move them into the soil late in fall. This gives them time to become well incorporated. You may also use your winter remains come spring just before planting for an extra boost. I do not recommend placing into compost anything which has been treated with preservatives or other chemicals.

ITEMS FOR COMPOST

Potash	Hardwood
Lime	Coal ash in limited amounts
Bones or bone dust	Meat scraps (ground)
Coffee grounds	Egg shells
Fish	Greensand (a marine deposit)
Animal manure	Leaves
Grass clippings	Sawdust
Seaweed	Hair cuttings
Peanut shells	Fruit (overripe or cooked)
Herb bits	Oak bark
Vegetable ends	Leather (natural scraps only)

Another interesting method of enriching the soil is through combining certain fresh ingredients into a tincture which is then allowed to saturate the soil. Nettles brewed with dandelions, yarrow, camomile, valerian, and oak bark are believed to be excellent for this type of procedure. This tincture can also be used to water plants occasionally.

Other Tips

○ *Don't litter.* It sounds simple, but many times we forget out of habit. If you can, keep a little garbage bag in your car or other areas where you might be tempted just to toss aside trash.

○ *Pick up litter.* It only takes a minute, but it is one which is well worth your effort. If the litter happens to be a can or other item which can be recycled, try to find a way to get it to an appropriate receptacle. Obviously this is not always possible when wearing three-piece suits and carrying a briefcase. The rule here is when you can, do! Don't get lazy.

○ *Walk or bicycle whenever possible.* Each time you choose this over your car you are giving precious moments of life back to the Earth.

○ *Take the time to really enjoy your environment.* The more you get out into natural settings, the more you will discover that they are worth fighting for. While we may have to give up a few conveniences along the way, consider a future with no daisies or bird songs, then see how important those amenities seem.

○ *Be observant.* If you see something which may indicate gross neglect of environmental law, report it to your local Environmental Protection Agency. In most states there is an environmental hotline which is toll free. You can't help if you don't get involved!

○ *Educate.* Your friends, your family, your children. Many people don't know how to even begin to help. Give those around you the gift of knowledge, showing them that the main tools they need come with their standard physical equipment; two willing hands!

○ *Reuse.* Take a couple of days to look at the items many of your neighbors throw away. Can you think of uses for them? If so, write them down and share your ideas! The major problem with the American public is wastefulness. I recently applauded my vet for employing a plastic pet vitamin pail as a planter in their office. This is only one small example of how many things we toss into our trash could be reused (see detailed list in this chapter). The key is to look at everything you come across with a creative, concerned eye.

○ *Replace.* If a tree is taken down in your neighborhood to make room for a road or walkway, plant two trees to replace it. Trees provide oxygen, help to give valuable nutrients to the earth, furnish homes to many animals, and help keep rich topsoil from being washed away. Begin to live in thankful reciprocity with our Mother.

○ *Keep informed and involved.* In the next section is a complete list of organizations and businesses which can help you get started on earth-aware living styles.

INDOORS

The most difficult obstacle to overcome for most of us is simply learning what various ecological terminology means, and then exactly how to put this knowledge to use daily. Many of us, including myself, have been left in the dark, trying our best to recycle with newspaper and bottles, but this is only the beginning. We need practical, day-to-day means to convert our throwaway society into one with a refreshed respect for everything acquired.

I know, for myself, being a Kitchen Witch made me even more desirous of finding ways to creatively reuse what might normally be thrown away. Much to my surprise, there were many more items in my home than I suspected which would prove useful for magic and "normal" living. The benefits of reusing and recycling are not just environmental, but also exhibit themselves through savings in your family budget. Below are of some of these items and the applications I found for them, but I am quite certain you can think of many others, more personal in nature.

Aluminum foil	Small pieces as cat toys, reuse larger clean scraps, good for children's athames if wrapped over wood or cardboard, neat-looking lightning bolts and sound effects for "fire" festivals
Books	Contribute to a local library or school, take to a paper recycling center, keep for your children (A really neat storage area for personal magical items can be made by hollowing out the center of a non-descript book, lining it with cloth, and securing it with a bit of satin ribbon)
Wine bottles	Get appropriate-sized corks and use to hold your ritual drinks, candle holders, bud vases, rooting bottles, juice mixers
Dry bread	Bird feed, bread crumbs, "egg in a basket" breakfasts (cut a hole in center and cook your egg in it), animal treats; to refresh stale bread, put it in a damp paper bag in a warm oven for ten minutes
Metal cans	Rinse and recycle; if you sand the edges you can make tin-can telephones for children; may be cut down when small pieces of metal are needed around the house; bottoms for makeshift candle holders
Fruit bits	Conserves, wine, tarts, jelly, bird treats, compost; rinds may be used in incense, as a spell component, for teas and tinctures or scented oil; cut different shaped pieces and hang from a window or off Yule tree for scent

Buttons	Holiday decoration creations, makeshift tiddlywinks for children, drainage stones for plants, poker chips
Cardboard	Use in soap making, projects for children, packing delicate packages, doorstoppers, levels for knickknacks, picture backing, cloth covered for gift-giving, to absorb excess grease, protect floors from chairs, emergency candle guards, kindling
Milk cartons	Frequently used by schools for projects; at home can be used as candlemolds, scrap container; decorate with cloth for little gift boxes; some areas now recycle the gallon size
Towels and other cloth	Used to wrap gifts and as rags; bird feeder bottoms; magical pouches; quilting; school art departments; wrapping your ritual soap
Plastic containers	Those with lids may be used for storing just about anything including noodles, rice, leftovers, buttons, etc.; great drums for children; ballot boxes; planters; parts for costumes (especially helmets); storage for meat grease to be used in soap
Glass jars	Storage, especially for herbs (can be labeled with tape); cut a slit in top for a coin bank; reuse for canning
Spice jars and shelves	Small amounts of expensive items such as amber, crystallized marshmallow root and mandrake; shelves are all-purpose
Old rugs	Wash and use in the cellar for pet beds, camping, meditation, etc.
Old pots/pans	Instant drums, cooking gear for festivals, non-food herbal preparations
Soap ends	Used to help put lacing through small holes, collect to remelt and mold, put in jar with lots of water for liquid soap
Bits of string, yarn, or thong	Children's projects, to tie up gifts, securing storage bags, loops for Yule decorations, cat toys, holding hair in place, fastening curtains temporarily, emergency shoe laces

Herb tea bags	Recycle paper cover; remaining herbs can be used as a base in incense, potpourri, and certain magical oils preparations (mix with olive or saffron oil in a dark jar set in the sun or under a sun lamp for at least 30 days)
Vegetable and herb pieces	Soup stock, compost; some herb ends such as garlic will sprout if planted
Wooden boxes	Homemade soap molds; go carts; refinished for a traveling magical equipment box by adding a handle, latch and hinges; sanded and padded for pet beds; bookshelf

The Recycling Household

Examining garbage can be very educational. Research has shown that 41% of our trash consists of waste paper, 18% yard clippings, 8% glass, 9% metal, 7% plastic, 8% food waste and 9% miscellaneous items. Of these items only 10% are recycled; the majority of the rest is taken to landfills. In one year, this is enough garbage to fill a fleet of trucks which would reach halfway to the moon!

Obviously, this is a serious problem. Recycling is one way all of us can help. Recycling means separating, processing, collecting, and ultimately using items thrown away. The good reasons for recycling are many; it reduces landfills, costs less than incineration, protects our environment, and offers a means of conservation by reducing our dependence on raw materials.

Training yourself and your household to think in terms of recycling will not be easy. It will take time and patience to learn new ways of handling waste products and how to think before we buy. Magical ecology requires not only the spiritual effort, but physical follow-through to really make a difference. Generally speaking, paper, yard waste, metal, aluminum, motor oil, glass, and plastic are all recyclable. To be able to apply this in your home, however, you will need to make a spot to separate out your items.

It is best to rinse everything you use before separation for obvious sanitary reasons. Next, consider your home space. A closet with shelves, small bins under your sink, an area in your cellar or any other small niche can be the perfect storage area for recyclable items until they can be taken for curbside collection or to drop-off centers and waste companies.

During the process of trying to educate myself in these matters, I found many helpful hints which I think you can easily apply in your home:

○ Buy smart. Get non-aerosol bottles, bulk food, recycled paper products, and biodegradable items. When you shop, take your own paper or cloth bags. Avoid wasteful packaging and minimize the use of disposable products.

○ Stones or bottles filled with water can help decrease water usage in your toilet. Do not, however, use bricks as they can contain harmful minerals which will leach out.

○ Before throwing away your plastic rings from six-packs, snip them so birds and other wildlife don't choke on them. Even better, buy loose aluminum cans and recycle them.

○ Many fuel companies offer free energy audits to show you areas in your home which can be improved by insulation. In New York, National Fuel offers interest free loans specifically for refinements in this area.

○ Turn off lights when not in use, or when possible, go to candle power! It's romantic and very magical. Change conventional light bulbs for compact fluorescent ones to reduce CO_2.

○ Borrow items instead of buying them.

○ Reduce your junk mail by writing the Direct Marketing Association, 6 East 43rd St., New York, NY 10017. Ask them to remove your name from their lists.

○ Showering generally uses less water than a bath.

○ Look for companies which offer safe cleaning and pet products for the home. Some that I am aware of include:

Lotus Light   Co-op America
Box 2   2100 M Street NW, Suite 310
Wilmot, WI 53192   Washington, DC 20063

Granny's Old-Fashioned Products
3581 East Milton
Pasadena, CA 91107

Ecological Do-it-Yourself Kit

Another practical and budget-minded means of being ecologically aware in your home is to learn how to make a wide variety of items instead of buying those which are produced commercially. If enough people begin to do this, it can serve many objectives. First, because you are directly decreasing your patronage of certain companies, it cuts down on pollution and chemical wastes from factories. Second, it allows you to know exactly what types of goods you are using in your home or giving to your family, including their ingredients. Third, it should eventually decrease the cruel use of animals for product testing, much of which is unnecessary. Finally, it allows you to blend what ever type of magic you desire into that product, or into your life while you make it.

To illustrate, there are some wonderful recipes for ink which could be ritually prepared[5] and scented with oils for use in a Book of Shadows. Or, if you are making glue for your children, you could use it as a magical opportunity to build stronger "bonds" in your family through visualization or chants while you create.

I have spent a fair amount of time poring over a combination of contemporary sources and antique books to find recipes[6] which have no harmful ingredients and which are reasonably easy to put together at home. These recipes, generally speaking, are not for food items as those are readily available to you through other sources. Instead I have focused on commonly needed utility goods such as silver polish, wood stains, dyes, incense, etc.

It may take a while for you to collect all the components to do this type of cooking on a regular basis, and it does take a little extra time, but the rewards of a healthier home and planet are well worth the effort.

RECIPES

Air Fresheners

Besides using incense to clear the air in your home, there are other methods which can help to keep it smelling fresh. One of the easiest is to warm a bit of wax over a low flame and add to this a heady portion of scented oils that you like. As you let the wax cool, be sure to place a string in the center so you have something to hang it with. This wax can then be placed in a sunny window to release its scent as it is warmed. When the freshener looses all aroma, keep the wax for candle making.

An alternate version of this is to save your citrus fruit rinds and dry them. String them together and place them in front of an open window where the winds can move their crisp fragrance through your home. On a magical level, lemon is considered an excellent cleanser for negativity. When you find the rinds have lost all scent, they can be refreshed with essential oil or ground and kept for a base for incense.

BAKING POWDER

1 oz. tartic acid
6 oz. cream of tartar
2 ¾ oz. bicarbonate of soda
4 oz. flour

Use your homemade baking powder in any spell which you want to bring "active" energy to.

BOOT WEATHERPROOFING

Take one pint of caster or linseed oil and mix it over low heat with 4 ounces beeswax and ¼ cup of coloring (wax colorings can often be found at hobby shops). This can then be rubbed onto boots to clean, waterproof, and preserve their texture.

BRASS CLEANER

Brass can be cleaned effectively by mixing one pound of soft soap with one cup each of vinegar and turpentine. This mixture should be applied with a soft cloth.

COLOGNE

A good cologne for men can be prepared by taking one pint of alcohol and adding to this a slice of orange rind, rosemary, slice of lemon rind, and touches of cinnamon and ginger. Let this sit in a warm window for two to three weeks, strain, and use. Feel free to change the herbs to suit personal tastes.

DEODORANT (POWDER)

Mix one cup each corn starch and baking soda to which one cup of orris root and two teaspoons each powdered orange peel, lemon peel, sage, and lavender have been added. Apply as needed.

EGGS (TO PRESERVE)

Eggs may be kept anywhere from five to eight months if you rub the shells with salted butter or dip them in boiling sugar water. You then place them in dry grain, salt, or sand (small end down) and store in a cool, dry spot.

For magic, this technique might be employed in any spell where you are trying to safeguard or protect something. In this instance, a symbol of what you hope to guard should be placed in sand or soil on your altar until the problem has passed.

FACIAL

Simmer two cups of rose hips and four pieces of candied ginger in ¾ cup of water until the rose hips are mushy. Strain the mixture, adding ¾ cup of sage honey to the liquid. This should be brought to a slow boil over thirty minutes. Refrigerate to store. Application to the face should be done in a thick layer and allowed to dry. Remove with warm water, then rinse your face with a cool splash. Makes about eight masks. This facial is also quite edible and makes a good jam or syrup for a sore throat!

FLEAS

Many magical people have pets, but the fleas that go with them are unwelcome company. To aid this problem, sprinkle your pet's sleeping area with tincture of pennyroyal. Next take a string or soft cloth and saturate it with the same mixture. This should be tied around the animal's collar and refreshed every twelve to fifteen days.

It is best to begin this procedure about three weeks before the flea season really begins in your area, and continue until after the first frost for best results.

FRUIT (TO DRY)

Slice your fruit into thin bits and lay them on a fine mesh (not touching each other). Place a tight netting over the entire fixture and leave it, turning the fruit regularly for even drying.

FRUIT (TO KEEP LONGER)

Place oranges, apples, lemons, and even sweet potatoes in dry sand. This will help you retain them fresh for up to five months.

Fruit juices can also be preserved by warming them to 140 degrees and sealing them in air-tight vessels. This will keep them from fermenting.

GLUE

Take powdered rice and mix it with cold water in equal quantities. Add to this another portion of boiling water until the texture you desire for the glue is reached (you can add more rice powder if needed). Next, take this entire mixture and boil on the stove for one minute. This yields a colorless glue which is excellent for setting crystals into wands and staves.[8] You may add some finely-powdered herbs during the boiling process for more magical effects.

HAIR CONDITIONING OIL

To one pint of alcohol and four ounces of almond oil add two drams of bergamot oil, one dram lemon grass oil, and two drams of lavender oil. This may be used after washing as needed.

HAIR SPRAY

Simmer one lemon and one orange in three cups of water. Strain, store, and refrigerate in an old (well cleaned) glass cleaner bottle. Make fresh every few days.

INK OR RENOVATING DYE

1 lb. log chips
1 lb. turmeric dissolved in rainwater (for one week)
1 dram gum arabic
2 oz. bicarbonate of soda
2 oz. powdered nut galls (optional)

Simmer all for one hour over a low flame; strain. At first this will be steel blue in color, but will slowly turn black and may be used to touch up faded spots on clothing, shoes, and will work reasonably well as a fountain ink.

For magical books, you may wish to add a few drops of essential oil (your choice of scent) to the ink. This aroma will last for a very long time on your pages.

IRON RUST CLEANER

Warm lemon juice, salt, and cream of tartar in equal proportions on the stove until well incorporated. Cover the item with this solution and rub with a rough cloth. Excellent especially for any iron magical tools such as a pentagram.

LEMON SYRUP

To one pint of water add one dozen lemon peels and bring them to a boil. Add the juice from your peeled lemons and a pound of sugar. Boil this together for ten to twenty minutes until it has a syrupy consistency. This can then be stored and used in cooking. To make lemonade, add one or two tablespoons to cold water and stir!

MOTHS

If you find these little creatures nibbling on your stored items, try making a mixture of one ounce each camphor, pepper, tobacco, flour of hops, and salt mixed with four ounces of cedar chips. This can be tied into small sachets, sprinkled into the corners of closets, etc.

PERFUME BAGS (FOR CLOTHING)

To three ounces orris root add a half ounce each clove, nutmeg, mace, caraway, and cinnamon. Tie in small bundles and place as desired into drawers.

To make magical perfume bags, decide on the purpose of the scent and check the herb list in Chapter Six for items which will have a pleasing aroma and the correct magical significance. The proportions are the same. These bags, once made, may be given as gifts or carried to bring that special energy with you.

PLANT FERTILIZER

To one gallon of warm water, add one ounce nettle, two ounces comfrey root, and one ounce kelp. Use this until the water is gone, then refresh the herbs.

POLISH

To one pint linseed oil add one pint old ale, one egg white, one ounce alcohol, and one ounce vinegar. This makes a fairly good polish for most wood surfaces.

ROACHES AND ANTS

Many techniques of keeping these creatures out of the house have been devised by clever minds, including sprinkling onion water or cayenne pepper around the area where they come in. Another method is to take a half pint of cornmeal and molasses with Borax blended in and leave it where they appear. They will eat this mixture greedily until dead.

SEALING WAX

One pound rosin, one ounce each of tallow and beeswax, and the coloring of your choice can be mixed together over a low flame. This mixture can be used to seal bottles of magical oil by dipping the cork or cap into the wax while hot and placing it directly on the receptacle.

To make this useful for letter-type sealing wax, you will need a wick and a small square mold which has been greased and sprinkled with water. Lay your wick in the center, pour in the wax and let it cool. Usually it will pop out of the mold easily if hit solidly on the back. If not, run some hot water over the container and repeat.

SILVER CLEANER

Take soft pieces of cloth (such as felt) and cut them in six-inch squares. Next, on the stove prepare a tincture of two ounces of carbonate of ammonia boiled in one pint of water. Once this is cool, dip the cloths in the liquid and let them dry. These may now be used any time you need to clean your silverware, jewelry, etc.

SKIN CONDITIONER

Stuff rose and geranium petals into a bottle, cover them with glycerine (available at most pharmacies), and close the bottle tightly. In three to four weeks it will be ready for use. Just put a few drops in your wash water.

SKIN CREAM

Four ounces of almond oil and a half cup each of orange flowers, lemon grass, lavender, and a hint of cloves. Warm these together over a low flame until the scent is well incorporated. Next add one half cup white wax and two tablespoons aloe gel, if available. Take the entire mixture off the heat, and continue to stir until it reaches a creamy consistency. Store in an air-tight container.

Scents may be changed simply by substituting different herbs as desired. Take care that the flowers or spices used are not physically irritating. This type of cream may act as a substitute to anointing oils for those people who have sensitive skin.

SOFT SOAP

Take one half pound of lye, one gallon of water, and two pounds of tallow or vegetable grease. Boil these together until the solution turns clear. Add one more gallon of water and mix well. This will be very ropey in consistency. Allow your soap to cool and store it in a good container. Once prepared the mixture can be diluted as desired.

Soft soap may be scented for ritual baths,[9] if desired, simply by adding spices, ground flowers, and/or essential oils after your boiling process is completed. Approximately two cups of herbs will saturate the soap with a light aroma which improves greatly with age.

STAINS (WOOD)

Burnt umber boiled with linseed or other oil makes a nice dark stain. Try substituting other barks or roots for different color levels. Polkberry, carrot, pomegranate, turnip, and other vegetable/fruit juices may also be added to bring out tints of red, orange, etc.

TOOTHPASTE

Mix one tablespoon baking soda to one teaspoon salt, a cup of water, and a few drops of mint or other flavoring. Apply in small quantities to your tooth brush.

VINEGAR

To make your own cider vinegar, open a batch of cider and leave it with a cloth cover (I suggest the use of cheesecloth found in many hobby shops, brewing supply stores, and even a well stocked supermarket) in the sun for three to four weeks. To this, allspice, clove, mustard seed, garlic, dill, and/or coriander may be added for pickling.

Additional Environmental Information

As I began to study more in this field, I discovered numerous interesting facts about not only what we use, but the "little things" all of us can do every day to help stop the blatant waste of so many of our resources.

- ○ Use your own cup at work instead of the throw-aways.
- ○ K-Mart and other collection centers offer $2.00 for any junk automotive batteries which will be given to Exide for environmentally safe recycling.
- ○ Some states have a toll-free number for suspected environmental crime.

○ Don't allow balloons to fly free in the atmosphere. Animals sometimes mistake them for food and die from the ingestion.

○ Recycling one ton of paper saves 17 trees, causes 35% less water pollution, 74% less air pollution, and 65% less energy than making paper from virgin pulp!

○ Every year cars and trucks generate 300 million gallons of used motor oil. All but 10% of this is properly disposed of. This 10% can be recycled at about ⅓ the energy it takes to refine oil from crude. If you wish to recycle your oil, keep it in a clean plastic container and take it to a service station.

○ One acre of trees can absorb as much as four tons of carbon dioxide. Plant a tree!

○ Nitrous oxide and hydrocarbons from industry and automobiles are accountable for more than five billion dollars worth of crop destruction yearly. Begin to lobby for a national commitment to alternative energy sources such as hydropower, windpower, and solar and geothermal energy.

○ Use your scrap paper. Keep it near the phone, for grocery lists, give it to the kids — if it has a clean side, don't just toss it out.

○ Try and organize recycling efforts in your community, specifically with your office or school system. If bins are established where clean paper (no waste products) is thrown and collected once a week, you will be surprised at how much accumulates.

○ The U.S. and several other industrial nations are trying to phase out the use of chlorofluorocarbons (used to propel aerosols) by the year 2000; however, slower developing nations will probably continue to employ them. You can help decrease the use of these toxins by finding alternatives to air conditioning, repairing leaks in your refrigerator, using pump sprays instead of aerosols, and halon-free fire extinguishers.

○ The present rate of extinction for animal species is between four and six thousand annually. This is mostly due to habitat destruction, illegal poaching and loss of genetic diversity due to decreasing numbers. To help, you can learn about those endangered species in your area and get involved in survival efforts. Also watch for consumer reports on products tested on animals and avoid purchasing these or items which are made from endangered species.

Groups to Contact

The following is a brief list of organizations which can offer you practical guidance in your efforts to recycle, reuse and renew the Earth. Do not hesitate to write or call them with your questions.

The only word of caution I have is that not every group which claims to be fighting for the environment is what it seems. If you plan to donate time or energy to any organization, do a little checking first. This can frequently be achieved through the Better Business Bureau or your local library, just to be certain the association has integrity.

1. E.P.A.
   Office of Solid Waste
   401 M Street SW
   Washington, DC 20460
   Recycling Hotline: 1-800-424-9346

2. National Recycling Coalition
   1101 30th Street NW, Suite 305
   Washington, DC 20007
   202-625-6406

3. Coalition for Recyclable Waste
   17 E. Church Street
   Absecon, NJ 08201
   609-641-2197

4. Co-Op America
   Box 14140
   Madison WI 53704
   608-256-5522

5. Earth Care Paper Products
   2100 M Street NW, #403
   Washington, DC 20036
   202-223-1881

6. Environmental Defense Fund
   257 Park Avenue
   New York, NY 10010
   Recycling Hotline: 1-800-CALL-EDF

7.   Environmental Action Foundation
        1525 New Hampshire Avenue NW
        Washington, DC 20036
        202-745-4870

8.   National Wildlife Federation
        1400 Sixteenth Street NW
        Washington, DC 20036-2266

9.   Earth First
        Post Office Box 7
        Canton, NY 13617

10.   Rainforest Action Network
        301 Broadway, Suite A, Dept. P
        San Francisco, CA 94133-9846

11.   Global Re-Leaf
        Post Office Box 2000
        Washington, DC 20013

12.   Conservation and Renewable Energy
        Inquiry/Referral Service
        Box 8900
        Silver Spring, MD 20907
        1-800-523-4108

13.   Citizens for a Better Environment
        647 West Virginia Street #303
        Milwaukee, WI 53204
        414-271-7280

RITUALS AND SPELLS FOR EARTH HEALING

Once our homes reflect the magical Path of choice, and we have begun to really work towards living in educated harmony with the planet. The final step for the magical ecologist is to weave some of their spells and rituals specifically for Gaia.[10] The Earth has an undeniable spirit, referred to down through time eternal simply as "the Mother." It is towards this injured, struggling spirit that our focused energy should be directed in Earth-healing rites.

While it is good to physically recycle and be mentally aware of the way you move through this sacred world, the essence of the Earth can not be ignored. The great gift of magic is that it gives us the tools necessary to return substantial power to this spirit and wrap it with a rehabilitating balm of light.

To create Earth-healing rituals, we first need to consider some of our components. A symbol of the Earth can be almost anything natural. In the Tarot, a disk or pentacle is used because they are round. Other good choices might be a picture of the Earth from space, or the cloth Earth models sold in various nature stores.

The best type of incense to use is anything picked, dried, and ground right from the land, such as wildflowers, bits of wood, and leaves which correspond somehow to the four natural elements (a leaf being air, lily of the valley being water, wood being earth, and perhaps a bright yellow dandelion for fire, for example). When you collect these items, please be sure to do so with thanks and a respectful attitude.

Whatever else you use in your homemade rituals is really up to you. I have outlined three ideas below which you can try out and adapt for individual or group application, but sometimes in your relationship to Gaia you might find the personal approach more pleasing. Your connection to this world is exceptionally private in meaning. It is from the deepest portion of your heart that words, songs, and rituals can come to move over the land with gratitude and new life.

Adopt a Tree

This exercise takes one year. Go to a nearby park or woods, or even your own backyard, and find a tree that looks a little bit like a Charlie Brown Christmas tree. In other words, it needs some tender loving care. Name this tree "Earth." For the next year, at least once a month, take offerings to this tree of crystals, natural fertilizer, or other items you feel are important. Hold as many of your personal rituals here as possible.

Hug the Earth-tree, tell it how you feel, sing joy-filled songs, and dance on the land around it. Meditate with your back against the tree and feel your connection to the planet. For this entire year, your job is to serve your image of the "Earth," giving it as much loving attention as you can.

I think you will find through this activity that not only will the tree become more healthy, but a new appreciation for your world will be born in your heart.

Healing Visualization

Go again to a quiet natural spot where you can sit on the ground. If this is not possible, sit on the floor of your cellar or a room close to the land. If you are outdoors, few if any tools are really required. Inside, however, it might help to have green and brown candles burning (the colors of earth), and some type of earth-symbol to focus your attention on.

As you sit, place the palms of your hands down next to you to connect as directly as possible to the Earth's energy. Breath deeply, turning your mind to the pulse of the world just beneath you. Feel it breathe and sigh with each wind; hear its heartbeat through the birds. Once you feel very attuned to the ebb and flow of the natural forces, begin to visualize a white-green light pouring out from your hands in all directions. Continue to allow this divine healing light to move through you, out to the world.

In your mind's eye, you should try to see the Earth from space, and the light you are creating slowly encompassing it, feeding it, refreshing the lakes and streams, cleaning the air, bringing new life to the animals. At this point you may want to begin a quiet chant such as "Earth be one, Earth be healed, by this spell your strength is sealed." Other similar verses can be created by speaking for each part of the Earth such as trees, land, birds, animals, water, etc.

When you are finished, leave that area and take a walk to enjoy your natural setting. Refresh yourself as you would the Earth.

A Pledge

Once a year (or more frequently, if you choose) it is good to have some kind of ritual where you renew your magical pledges, and your promises to the planet. Exactly what you decide to say can vary each year according to the new understandings which have grown in your heart. By way of example, I have written one pledge that I use, which I encourage you to change and adapt to be more personally meaningful.

I pledge to greet each day as a new beginning
to walk with respect on this Earth
to live in peaceful reciprocity with nature
to see the best in my fellow humans
I pledge to give some time each week to reclaiming the land
to renew the animals and plants humanity has stripped away
to learn the old ways, close to the soil
to heal, to nurture, to grow.
I pledge to live a magical life each day, each moment
to try and meet needs spontaneously
to serve with loving hands and heart
to work in perfect trust
So mote it be.

Do not enter into such a pledge without thought. This is a serious commitment you are making to yourself, to the God/dess, the four winds and your own world. It should be one made through contemplation and love.

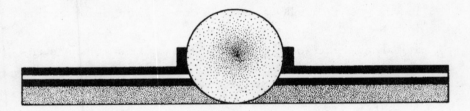

NOTES FOR CHAPTER 5

1. *Anointing oil* is used to help bring increased awareness during meditation and/or bless the participant of a particular ritual. The practice is not at all dissimilar to the anointing by a priest in Christian traditions, except that the individual may anoint themselves, if desired.

2. *Sacred geometry* is the study of the patterns of the Earth, specifically the energy lines which create certain archetypal patterns in all of nature. The hope is that by studying these patterns, we can learn more about our world and how best to live in harmony with it.

3. *Dowsing* is an old system of divination which usually employs a forked branch or other type of rod to discover water, lost items, etc.

4. The basic proportions for a tincture are four ounces of herb steeped in eight ounces of alcohol for about two weeks. This bottle should be sealed and left in a dark area. I have also had reasonable success with combinations of fresh and infused herbs to which alcohol is added, then left in sunlight.

5. Items can be ritually prepared by a number of methods which may include, but are not limited to, working during certain moon phases, reciting spells and incantations, chanting, harvesting the ingredients during specific times of the year, and visualization.

6. Using older sources is very helpful to this type of work since our ancestors did not have many of the modern conveniences which have caused much of our pollution. However, since these people did not have the advantage of medicalization or modern science, some of their ingredients were hazardous to physical health or the land, too. The blend allows for better balance.

7. Wines are often used in ritual as the "fruit of the Earth." Sharing in wine is a type of fellowship, and is done in gratitude for the gifts from the land we have been granted.

8. It is always better to use homemade stains and glues on any magical item you are making. Chemicals and magic do not usually mix well. Likewise, anything that you make yourself will have more of your personal energy in it, and therefore will be more effective for your rites.

9. *Ritual baths* are often performed as a outward means of cleansing a person in preparation for a ritual. Just as a surgeon is careful to wash before work, it is good to "wash away" the mundane world and negativity of the day before starting on magical pursuits.

10. *Gaia* is another name for the Earth spirit, considered the mother of humanity.

PERSONAL POSTSCRIPT TO CHAPTER 5

I am very discouraged by the trend in supermarkets and various businesses which makes the price of recycled goods or earth-safe products much higher than those produced by other means. To me, this dissuades the consumer from initially trying the goods, let alone continuing to purchase them, especially if they are on a tight budget.

Many of us want to help reclaim our planet, but in order to do so, some of the world's basic business philosophies must change to reflect the growing awareness that this may be our last chance to salvage the Earth. There must be a willingness to invest in more ecologically safe machinery (and tax breaks for companies who do so), an understanding of the problems of consumers who face difficult choices, and most of all a desire in businesses to put the welfare of our planet before an executive's often disproportionate expense accounts and salaries.

This will not happen overnight, and not without many voices from the community raised together to the ears of our politicians. We need to support those companies, to the best of our ability, that reflect ecologically safe, concerned practices. We also need to participate in community activities to bring these concerns into the eyes of our leaders frequently, until they know we will not stop shouting until our voices are heard.

So, to both the consumer and business person, this is my personal challenge to you to get involved. Find out what you can to ensure this planet's natural resources will be around for our grandchildren and great-grandchildren to enjoy for a very long time. If you can, dedicate a certain amount of your time each week to a constructive activity aimed towards this goal, even if it is just picking up litter.

While I know this invitation towards ecological action may sound a bit radical, it comes to you from my heart. The world we live in has many beauties and wonders. When I look to my son, I can't help but speculate how many of them might be gone when his children are born. This is why I have begun to take a more vigorous stand on environmental issues; I want to give this planet to our children in better shape than when we first acquired it in our generation.

Mother, Earth of singing ken
chant the wards, protect this glen
hum low your song with drum and fife
bring the White Hart[1] back to life.

— Marian

Chapter

Creative Herbalism

Give me a spark o' nature's fire, that's a' the learning I desire.
— Robert Burns, *Scottish Poems* (1786)

n preparation for our future, we are quickly discovering how much valuable information on viable alternative lifestyles has been left to us throughout history. Even for the modern accomplished herbalist, having a working knowledge of the foundations of this art is extremely useful. Many techniques and recipes we presently employ have come to us from sources far older than just granny's cookbooks. The more we explore these avenues, the more valuable information is uncovered which, when combined with modern knowledge of toxicities, can be applied with surprising results.

HISTORICAL OVERVIEW

While herbalism has its roots deep in antiquity, its long-reaching effects on humanity are felt today. We have seen interest in natural medicine and non-chemical health aids growing steadily over the last hundred years, delayed only slightly by medicalization at the turn of the century. Even then, books such as *The Family Botanic Guide* by William Fox, M.D. (1907) was in its 18th edition. These types of guides typified the Victorian atmosphere which seems to be rekindled presently, and included not only what is considered traditional herbalism but hints on clothing, ventilation, recommended foods for the sick, and animal care. They also contained constant references to the much older texts of Culpeper, Hippocrates, Galen, and Paracelsus.

The earliest foundations of herbalism, as traceable through written history up to its predominant uses in the Middle Ages, is truly a wonder to read about. I say "predominant" because it will quickly become apparent in this reading that "folk medicine" was central to the living of the people who trusted old-wives tales, superstition, and magic as a means to improve their life. It was, in this respect, a kind of science to them.

Perhaps better called the history of economic botany, herbalism has been employed by wives, warriors, charlatans, doctors, and dreamers of all ages. It is important to remember, however, that we are exploring documented history versus that of oral tradition,[2] which would tend to indicate that the fascination which humanity has had with the natural world began almost as soon as the mind could comprehend a "tomorrow."

The oldest written records of herbalism date back to Egypt, China, and India. In China, the Emperor Shen-nung Pen-ts'au compounded and self-tested 365 preparations (of which all but 51 were herbal-based) as early as 3737 BC. The first translation of this Chinese material came in 1596 as the *Materia Medica of Li-Shih-Chen*. This contained over 12,000 prescriptions, 1074 analyses of plant substances, 443 animal substances, and 354 mineral substances, and is still considered useful today.

In Egypt the ideas of medicine and magic were united into a more "metaphysical" system of cures. The earliest papyruses date to 2000 and 1000 BC, but refer to older texts and oral traditions frequently. There is strong evidence to believe that the hanging gardens of Babylon may have housed herbs for embalming.

In India, herbalism was known as *Ayurveda*, the science of life. It was believed that Ayurveda was originally taught by the gods to a handful of human disciples, who then placed this information in the *Vedas* (Hindu scriptures) for the general populace. Later versions of this work introduced the belief of balanced diet, exercise, meditation, and good environment as also necessary to healthy living (see also Chapter Ten).

There are many colorful figures among early herbalists, not the least of which is Hippocrates, perhaps the most widely recognizable to the modern mind. He was a famous Greek physician who practiced around 4 BC, and is celebrated for directing medicine towards a science and away from magic. He also formulated the code of ethics still used by physicians today. Many of his herbal remedies, described in two books from 3 BC, are still employed by contemporary practitioners because of their simple wisdom. Hippocrates' work was foundational to all which was to come in the Middle Ages.

Next to follow was the Roman scholar Pliny the Elder, who worked on 37 books of natural history in 1 AD. He was very dedicated to his studies, as history notes him even dictating to his servants from the bathtub in order that the writing be complete. Many of Pliny's cures ventured close to the realms of folk medicine as well, because of the incorporation of unusual items such as axle grease and ass's milk.

Besides these men who laid the foundations, the two most impressive figures by far in the Roman empire were those of Galen (130-200 AD) and Dioscorides (first century AD). Galen wrote a recipe book of 130 antidotes and medicines. Dioscorides, a contemporary of Pliny, traveled with the Roman legions and used the knowledge he collected to write an herbal which attempted to describe the plants of the Mediterranean and their functions. The work assembled by these two men was considered the authority for all herbalism until well into the sixteenth century.

Next we come to the Middle Ages, where perhaps the greatest repository for learning herbal arts lay in the monastery. Most monks were content to copy the older works for posterity, but there were a few who boldly included their own notes on gardening in various texts.

An example of this comes to us from Walahfrid Strabo (807 AD) in Switzerland. In a poem translated as "The Little Garden," he wrote a celebration of the art of gardening, including information on cultivation, planting and harvesting! As a side note, the Plan of St. Gall from 820 AD showed the ideal Benedictine monastery complete with the medicinal garden near the infirmary and the kitchen garden for culinary herbs. The tradition of the "kitchen garden" persisted well into the 1900s, not only in Europe, but also in the United States!

The amount of time the medieval people dedicated to herbals may at first seem disproportionate to the modern mind. However, we must remind ourselves that this was a staple to these and later peoples, used for dying, inks, paint, incense, food preparation, and much more, not to mention the medicinal applications.

Greco-Arabic Herbalism

From 641 AD to the fall of Alexandria in 1096, the monasteries continued to provide copies of the works of Galen and Dioscorides. Folk healers were also predominant, using lore, pragmatic know-how, and Pagan ideals combined for their healing arts. It is interesting to notice that even the Christian Church adapted some superstitions regarding the use of herbs placed at the door or as amulets to protect against evil during this era. This odd blend of magic, herbalism, and Christianity is often best evidenced in certain rites of curing found in older texts.

In *Anglo-Saxon Magic* by G. Storms (pg. 165, 1948 edition), the following edited text occurs:

> *Take goose fat and viper's bugloss, bishops wort and cleavers. Pound them together well, squeeze and add a spoonful of old soap. Scratch the neck after sunset, and silently pour the blood into running water, spit three times, then say, "take this disease and depart with it." Go back to your house by the open road, and go each way in silence.*

The editor of this book then notes that it was not uncommon to end such a speech with "In the name of the Almighty Father, Son, and Holy Spirit, Amen," or by reciting the names of the first disciples. Thus the basic herbal is mixed liberally with folk traditions, and a bit of prayer on the side for good luck! While most monks would have never admitted such consortation with magic, the ones trained for healing would most likely not hesitate to use mandrake for its ability to drive away elves causing a sickness, the roots of this tradition being so commonplace by this time that it was "standard" procedure.

Greco-Roman medicine was collected and studied by Arabic physicians, who had pharmacists as early as the ninth century. And like the monks, the Arab peoples employed astrology and various "magically" related rituals as part of their healing techniques, especially that of preparation of medicine. After the Crusades, these beliefs and supplemental knowledge were brought back to Europe and added to the wealth of herbal approaches already growing there.

When the clever Arab spice traders met the Europeans, they quickly recognized a lucrative atmosphere full of magic, omens, and Witchcraft, ripe for harvesting. They used their wisdom and cunning to spread even more fantastic stories about their spices (laden with a heavy portion of folk tales) to raise the value of their trade. So talented were their efforts that the Muslim hold on the spice trade did not diminish until sometime in the fourteenth to sixteenth centuries! No matter the Arab intention, however; the common people employed the magical significance of herbs for boon and bane as needed. Parsley was taken to prevent drunkenness, anise for nightmares, basil for hatred, and laurel to invoke the gift of prophesy.

At this point, the conglomeration of magic with medicine made it difficult to sort out one from the other. The common person may have used ingredients because of their proven effectiveness. More than likely, though, word of mouth played a stronger role. Here, effectiveness was mingled with sympathetic magic symbolism, where a liquid or parts of an animal known for strength would be given to one who is weak. Or if the stars and planets were correctly aligned for virility, an herb would be harvested and prepared for the same patient. The four major directions, winds, and especially moon phases were likewise considered before treatment. In this instance, bark is most potent when taken from the east side of a tree, where it meets the sun, and plants to cure lunacy must be used when the moon is waxing to be most effective.

It is interesting by comparison to notice that despite Hippocrates' early efforts, this was also when we see the first significant separations between "herbal science" and folk medicine. The crude but delineated medical community regarded folk medicine and magic as either amusing or a threat to the strength of the medical community, and thus their profits! This feeling spilled over into the organized church, causing many a healer to be banished or killed for their efforts. On the other hand, the criticism of folk healers did not lessen the medieval love of herbs in the least.

Marco Polo's travels in the 1200s helped increase interest in the East and spurred trade routes for more exotic spices, which quickly became in demand. By the end of the fourteenth century spices and herbs permeated all classes of medieval life, and were often used as a commodity more valued than actual money. Extraordinary changes also occurred in diet with the influx of Oriental products such as dates, citrus, almonds, rice, and sugar.

In the 1400s, Portuguese ships opened the trade route to India and beyond, followed shortly thereafter by Columbus' exploration of the New World yielding the love apple (tomato), Jesuit bark for quinine, and tobacco.

The period from 1558 to 1603, during the Reign of Elizabeth I, is considered the greatest age for herbal books. In Germany, Otto Brunfels and Lemand Fuchs published herbal texts which were unequaled in quality. Fuchs' *Historia Stirpium* focused on perfect plant specimens, featuring 500 woodcuts and well-spaced text, the latter being unusual for the period. Brunfeld displayed plants realistically (wilted leaves and all).

Another herbalist of great popularity, Rembert Dodoens of Belgium, put together a book first appearing in 1554, then later translated into Latin in 1583. The English title is *Rams Little Dodens*. He, like Brunfeld, furnished his artists with fresh plants for painting and watched carefully over their work.

In England, the herbalists coming on the scene were proving almost as spicy as their subject matter. John Gerald first published his herbal work in 1597, which actually was a rewrite of *Dodens*, in part! To his credit, however, Gerald also included information on exotic plants, of which he personally grew over 1000 species, and added the rich English flora, fauna, and associated plant lore.

Late in the medieval period we have John Parkinson and Nicholas Culpeper's books, 1640 and 1649 respectively. Parkinson became the apothecary to the King, while Culpeper became one of the most widely questioned herbalists of history. This was mostly due to the publishing of certain questionable "eyewitness" accounts to prove his theories.

In retrospect, Fuchs' work probably marked the end of the herbal texts as had been known up until that time. Science was now on the horizon with Copernicus, and humanity's relationship to the universe would never be the same. Herbalism had taken a far more botanical turn which helped bring the earliest forms of popular medicine to humanity in the late 1800s. From this point forward, the magical essence of herbalism would be kept alive by the folk healers and oral traditions which are being recovered slowly today.

Thanks to this and the advent of the printing press, without their knowledge many modern herbalists are often quoting or using recipes whose first expression came with Pliny, Aristotle, and Hippocrates. We now have the opportunity to reclaim much of this wisdom, lore, and symbolism and apply it in practical ways, not only for magic, but for our physical health and the betterment of our world.

A MODERN HERBAL

As mentioned above, an herbal was usually an illustrated book of plants which were commonly used for simples, or cures. Interestingly enough, the herbal did not just contain spice-type "herbs" but barks, flowers, berries, roots, and numbers of other items in combination with each other. So while we call it herbalism, the overall magnitude of this art is far more reaching than just our kitchen spice shelf.

In the last hundred years, many of these healing techniques have slowly been uncovered as having real scientific foundations, thanks to intense scrutiny by various academic minds. Even so, the superstition and lore so closely tied to herbalism has never quite left us, nor should it. This dimension adds a richness for magic that the modern herbalist can be most thankful for.

While there have been many excellent books published on herbs and their uses, for this text to be useful to you consistently I felt a brief overview of commonly used plants for health and magic would be appropriate here. This is by no means complete, and I always suggest when making any preparation to compare your recipe with two other sources (if possible) to find the most frequently mentioned ingredients. Research of this nature can often alleviate dangerous mistakes in proportions, and hopefully will provide the most effective blend.

I urge you to remember that herbalism is not a cure-all. If you are ill, using herbal teas may indeed help you, but that does not mean you should ignore the advice of your doctor. Likewise, magical herbalism is only another tool to help direct and guide energy to your intended goal. Please use it wisely.

In the listing given below, you will note the following abbreviation: *G/P/E*. This stands, in order, for gender of the plant, the ruling planet, and lastly the commonly ascribed elemental correspondence. In the instance of ruling planets, I found that some sources differ in opinion. Where there is a discrepancy I have noted both options for your reference.

For the most part, this information helps the magical herbalist to know more specifically what types of spells, rituals, etc., the herb is useful for. However, since the study of astrology as it relates to plant lore is very extensive, I will not go into details here. Instead I suggest if you are interested in studying these particulars, you obtain any of Scott Cunningham's herbal books, especially *Magical Herbalism*, for further research.

THE HERBAL[3]

ALOE

G/P/E: Feminine, Moon, Water.
Magical attributes: Beauty, protection, success, peace.
History/Uses: Discovered 2000 years ago, aloe has always been known for its healing qualities. It's original uses of treating wounds and maintaining healthy skin are still viable today. It may be applied right from the plant or in gel form for burns, and is an excellent additive for soaps and creams as a conditioner.

ANGELICA

G/P/E: Masculine, Sun, Fire.
Magical attributes: Psychic self-defense, inner vision, ritual baths, healing incense, longevity.
History/Uses: In the Middle Ages, angelica was believed to bloom on May 8th, the feast of St. Michael, and thus was given into the care of the angels. A decoction of roots or seeds will aid an upset stomach, and relieve insomnia and headaches (one teaspoon plant to one cup water). Culpeper believed this plant should be harvested when the moon was in Leo for greatest potency.

ANISE

G/P/E: Masculine, Jupiter or Moon, Air.
Magical attributes: Protection, purification, awareness, joy.
History/Uses: In the sixth century BC, Pythagoras prescribed anise in the treatment of epilepsy. A better and still employed recommendation came from Hippocrates one century later, who advised it for coughs. Pliney suggested that it made a good breath freshener in the morning (it does), and that if a person kept it near their bed, anise would prevent bad dreams. This might well make anise the perfect amulet for a child's room. Finally, anise is a digestive aid when taken as a tea, which may be why it often appears as an ingredient in wedding cakes!

BASIL

G/P/E: Masculine, Mars, Fire.
Magical attributes: Protection, love, wealth (if carried in your wallet), healing relationships, courage, fertility.

History/Uses: In Italy, a pot of basil on your balcony means you are ready to receive suitors. In India, the herb is dedicated to Vishnu and is given to the dead to help ensure their entrance to the afterlife. As a medicinal herb it is good as a tea for calming the nerves, settling the stomach, and easing cramps. In tincture form, it also makes a good hair rinse for brunettes.

BENZOIN

G/P/E: Masculine, Mars or Sun, Air.
Magical attributes: Harmony, vision, prosperity, purification; any spells having to do with mental functions.
History/Uses: Benzoin is a resin of balsam usually found in powdered or gum form and is available at your local pharmacy. It has been used most predominantly as a scent fixative in incense or oil preparations, but in tea form can also be employed as a skin cleanser.

BLOODROOT

G/P/E: Masculine, Venus or Mars, Fire.
Magical attributes: To draw love, vitality, healing incense.
History/Uses: Bloodroot was an official botanical drug between the years of 1820 and 1926, after which time it was found to have certain negative side effects. In small quantities when used by a qualified herbalist, it still has value in tincture form to treat wounds. However, it is best suited to making dyes for cloth from its deep red sap.

BROOM

G/P/E: Masculine, Mars, Air.
Magical attributes: Protection, purity, divination, wind spells.
History/Uses: During earlier times, this herb was actually used to form crude brooms for the home, making it the perfect utility plant for cleansing magical spaces. It has little medical value due to toxicity, but the tops can be used for a fine, natural yellow dye, and decorative bundles are often presented at Pagan weddings to promise joy to the new couple.

CATNIP

G/P/E: Feminine, Venus, Water.
Magical attributes: Cat magic, familiars, joy, friendship.
History/Uses: Catnip was known 2000 years ago. Its flowers and leaves have often been used to treat colds and insomnia. The scent of

catnip was believed by certain peoples to aid in fertility, and as an incense it may be used to consecrate magical tools.

CAMOMILE

G/P/E: Masculine, Sun or Venus, Water.
Magical attributes: Good as a meditation incense, for centering, peace; sprinkle in your home for protection, healing.
History/Uses: Meaning "ground apple" in the Greek, camomile's use dates back to Egyptian times when its fragrance made it a popular aromatic. Camomile is an excellent herb both internally and externally for calming. In tea form, it is also a good hair rinse for blondes. Plant camomile in your garden to be the guardian of the land, and you will have certain success.

CINNAMON

G/P/E: Masculine, Sun, Fire.
Magical attributes: Spiritual quests, augmenting power, love, success, psychic work.
History/Uses: Cinnamon is one of the frequently mentioned herbs in the Bible, having been used in Egypt for embalming and in the East to purify the temples, bringing improved concentration or focus. Medicinally, it is recommended as a skin astringent and digestive aid in tea form. It is an excellent aromatic and makes a good anointing oil for any magical working.

CLOVE

G/P/E: Masculine, Jupiter or Uranus, Fire.
Magical attributes: Dispel negativity, protection, money, incense against gossip, vision.
History/Uses: This intense aromatic was introduced to Europe by traders in the fourth to sixth centuries. It has a mild antiseptic quality for toothaches, or in tea form it is an expectorant for colds. Most commonly, though, the clove has been employed to ward off moths and disease because of its pungent nature.

COMFREY

G/P/E: Feminine, Saturn, Water.
Magical attributes: Safe travel spells, money, healing.
History/Uses: Known as the "great healer" as far back as 400 BC, comfrey has been known to slow bleeding, aid colds, ease burns, and for

seemingly hundreds of other applications throughout history. Its name comes from the Latin meaning to "knit together." As a poultice or a tea, comfrey may be applied to bites, sores, and cuts. It is also a good ingredient for lotions to soothe sunburn. Comfrey is high in protein, and may be steamed and eaten as a green.

CORIANDER

G/P/E: Masculine, Mars, Fire.
Magical attributes: Protection of home, peace, good in ritual drinks, incenses for longevity and love, security.
History/Uses: Coriander has been a predominant herb in the perfume and cosmetic industry, having been cultivated for 3000 years. It is one of the predominant herbs in the Hebrew Passover ritual and considered to insure immortality by the Chinese. If added to wine, it makes a serviceable love potion for two consenting parties.

DANDELION

G/P/E: Masculine, Jupiter, Air.
Magical attributes: Divination, welcoming, messages.
History/Uses: Dandelion was first seen in twelfth century medical journals in Arabia. By the sixteenth century it had been adapted by British apothecaries as a valued herb for anemia and appetite increase, for which it is still used. Dandelions are high in vitamin A, potassium, and calcium, making their leaves good for a healthy salad. The ground root can act as a coffee substitute, and dandelion flowers make a lovely wine. It is said if you rub your skin with dandelion juice, no home can refuse you hospitality.

EUCALYPTUS

G/P/E: Feminine, Moon, Water.
Magical attributes: Healing, cleansing, protection.
History/Uses: Eucalyptus comes to us from the Pacific Southwest, and was popular in the nineteenth century because of its sturdy lumber. The oils from the tree's roots, leaves, and bark are useful in treating colds, acting as an expectorant. Eucalyptus is also a mild insect repellent.

ELDER

G/P/E: Feminine, Venus, Water.
Magical attributes: Sleep, prosperity, luck, fidelity, protection from lightning.

History/Uses: The Romans used elderberries to dye their hair and for jams. The wood of the elder is often used to carve pan pipes, the berries for wine, and the fresh leaves may be made into a poultice to relieve the pain of hemorrhoids. You can alleviate the ache of a bad tooth by chewing on an elder twig; the flowers, when steeped in cider vinegar, are a good inhalant for colds.

FENNEL

G/P/E: Masculine, Mercury, Fire.
Magical attributes: Purification, protection, healing, money.
History/Uses: The ancient Chinese believed that fennel could cure snake bites, and the Romans used the herb frequently in salads. Fennel comes from the Greek word meaning "to grow thin," and is sometimes employed as an appetite suppressant and digestive aid. If you place a bit of fennel in a keyhole, it is said to keep ghosts away. Fennel was one of nine sacred herbs of the medieval people, believed to cure the nine causes of disease.

GINGER

G/P/E: Masculine, Mars, Fire.
Magical attributes: Power, success, love.
History/Uses: Back to Egypt in the time of Cheops, people were making gingerbread; 4400 years ago, the Chinese were importing this herb for the same reason, and to act as an aid to indigestion or colds (tea form). Carry the root of ginger in your purse to ensure prosperity, or make it into a fine drink for summer days (see Chapter Seven).

GINSENG

G/P/E: Masculine, Sun, Fire.
Magical attributes: Love, wishes, beauty, desire.
History/Uses: Mentioned in China as early as 5000 years ago as a stimulant, tonic, and agent for prolonged life. It is used today by Russian astronauts to prevent infection in space. It is also a mild painkiller, and improves blood circulation. In tea form it helps to relieve stress and moderate heart disease.

GARLIC

G/P/E: Masculine, Mars, Fire.
Magical attributes: Protection, healing, good weather, courage.

History/Uses: Garlic comes to us from Asia. It was distributed daily to the workers at Cheops to give them strength and protection for their sacred work. The Greeks call garlic the "stinking rose" due not only to its smell but general usefulness to cooking and medicine (as with the rose). In Sweden, people sometimes place garlic around the necks of livestock to protect them from trolls. Generally speaking, having garlic in your diet serves to lower tension, ease colds, and improve circulation. Garlic vinegar can be used to disinfect wounds and sooth rheumatic pain (made from one liter of vinegar and ten cloves of crushed garlic steeped for at least ten days).

HAWTHORN

G/P/E: Masculine, Mars, Fire.
Magical attributes: Happiness, prosperity, protection, to attract faeries, protection from lightning.
History/Uses: The history of hawthorn is rich with lovely folklore. At wedding feasts in Athens, guests often carried a sprig to ensure joy for the new couple. In Rome, a twig of hawthorn was often attached to the cradle of a newborn to protect it, and in the time of the Crusades, a knight would offer his lady a bit of this tree with a pink ribbon tied to it as a token that he would live, hoping for his return to her. In Christianity it is believed that the crown of thorns was made out of hawthorn. The therapeutic properties of this tree are no less magnificent. It is a great regulator of blood pressure and has excellent sedative effects. The infusion proportions are one teaspoon of fresh petals per cup of water twice a day (or just at night for insomnia). It is said where oak, ash, and hawthorn grow together, you can see faeries!

LAVENDER

G/P/E: Masculine, Mercury, Air.
Magical attributes: Sleep, long life, peace, wishes, protection.
History/Uses: Romans used lavender in their bath water, the name deriving from the Latin for "to wash." Early healers used lavender in oil or tincture form to heal sword wounds, burns, and snake bites. Modern study has shown lavender to have strong antiseptic qualities. Mild infusions (three tablespoons to six cups of water) make a good sedative, headache treatment, and digestive aid. This also acts as a tonic and may be used for colds, chills, and the flu. Lavender is an excellent aromatic, usually mixing well with other floral scents, and has its origins in India.

LEMON

G/P/E: Feminine, Moon or Neptune, Water.
Magical attributes: Purification, love, blessings.
History/Uses: Mentioned by Virgil for sweetening of breath and steadying of the pulse, the lemon is recognized widely today as an anti-septic and hypotensive. Even so, for a long time it was used mostly to deter moths and as a preventative to food poisoning. For chills and sore throat, the juice of a lemon mixed in a glass of honey and warm water taken three times daily should help. For nose bleeds, apply a small piece of cotton soaked in lemon juice. Lemon juice also makes a good skin cleanser, hair rinse for blondes, and cleaning agent for brass and silver. In the home, sachets of lemon rind deter moths and keep the air smelling fresh.

MARSHMALLOW

G/P/E: Feminine, Moon or Venus, Water.
Magical attributes: Love, protection, dispel negativity.
History/Uses: Marshmallow derives its name from a Greek word meaning "to heal," which would indicate that the ancients regarded it as a panacea. The people of the Middle Ages also believed that if you rubbed yourself with the juice, it would keep away snakes. Also known as "mallow," it was mentioned in the Old Testament as a substitute for meat and was grown in the temples to Apollo at Delos. Internally, a tea of the flowers (best collected in July) helps break colds and eases con-stipation. Externally, the root is good for most skin treatments, and may be given to teething infants to soothe sore gums.

MARIGOLD

G/P/E: Masculine, Sun, Fire.
Magical attributes: Prophesy, legal matters, the psychic, seeing magi-cal creatures.
History/Uses: In the time of King Henry IV, it was suggested that his subjects fill their gardens with marigolds because they kept flowering well into winter. The homeopath today, however, is much more grateful for their remedial qualities. For internal use the flowers are prepared by infusion and recommended for the flu, fever, rheumatism, jaundice, and painful menstruation. Externally, buds are made into compresses for the treatment of burns. In England and Germany, the flowers are also used in soups, to color butter, and as a hair rinse.

MINT

G/P/E: Masculine, Mercury or Venus, Air.
Magical attributes: Money, healing, strength, augment power.
History/Uses: The mint is perhaps one of the most useful herbs known. From its lovely aroma to use in cosmetics, wines, and foods, it seems to have almost endless applications. The Greeks and Hebrews made perfume out of this herb, while the Romans used it to sweeten the breath and in most sauces. Pliny recommended it for improving the mind and keeping vermin at bay. This last association is one that pennyroyal especially continues to bear. A few drops of pennyroyal will stay mosquitoes from children and fleas from pets. For health, mint in tea form aids upset stomachs, flu, and can even ease hiccups. Inhalations of the leaves in boiling water is recommended for head colds and asthma.

MISTLETOE

G/P/E: Masculine, Jupiter or Sun, Air.
Magical attributes: Luck, protection, the hunt, fertility, dreams, protection from faeries.
History/Uses: A ancient plant, sacred to Europeans as a symbol of immortality, the Druids called mistletoe the "plant that heals all ills." The priests would gather it ritually with a golden sickle, and use it as a talisman to protect from evil. In Austria, branches are placed in bedroom doorways to protect from nightmares. Today mistletoe may be used in the treatment of high blood pressure, migraines, and dizziness by an infusion of the leaves in water or wine.

MYRRH

G/P/E: Feminine, Jupiter or Moon, Water.
Magical attributes: Bless objects, lift energy, spiritual growth, focus.
History/Uses: Magically paired to frankincense, myrrh has long been used in religious rites, specifically in the Egyptian temples to Ra. This rosin was known 2000 years before the birth of Christ, and it was considered to have been born from the Goddess Myrrha's tears. Priests in the time of Moses anointed themselves with myrrh before serving in the temple. Today, myrrh oil can act as a mosquito repellent, and in tincture form myrrh is a good treatment for gums.

NETTLE

G/P/E: Masculine, Mars, Fire.
Magical attributes: To avert danger; protection, healing.
History/Uses: During the Bronze Age, nettles were used to create a sturdy fabric. To the Anglo-Saxon herbalist, they were believed to be an effective counter-poison. Today we know the nettle to be high in vitamin C, and when made into a tea can ease asthma.

OAK

G/P/E: Masculine, Sun or Jupiter, Fire.
Magical attributes: Power, luck, health, long life; the acorns if used as spell components—money.
History/Uses: The Greeks and Romans used the sound of wind through oak leaves as oracles, and the Druids took their name from the Celtic word *deru,* or oak. Thus, it was a sacred tree to these peoples. Bark collected and prepared in a decoction may be used as a gargle or douche. Leaves prepared in infusion are recommended for dysentery, and the acorns when roasted may be used as a non-caffinated coffee.

OLIVE

G/P/E: Masculine, Sun, Fire.
Magical attributes: Wisdom, peace, luck, to end arguments.
History/Uses: To the Greeks the olive was a symbol of wisdom, to the Romans an icon of peace. The carrying of an olive branch, like a white flag, is recognized as a message that hostilities are ceased. Ancient peoples made use of olive oil in food, care of the body, for warmth, and for medicine. For constipation, a tablespoon of olive oil taken in the morning or with soup will ease the problem. This is also believed to ease colic. Externally, when mixed with egg white the oil makes a good treatment for burns or bites. Chopped olive leaves in tincture form have been shown to help control diabetes and hypertension.

ORRIS

G/P/E: Feminine, Venus, Water.
Magical attributes: To divine by pendulum, protection.
History/Uses: This herb found its first popularity in the Middle Ages when its violet-like fragrance was used in perfume. Made from the root of the florentine iris, powdered orris makes an excellent body powder and fixative for incense. As a paste or tincture it also helps clean the skin and fight acne.

PARSLEY

G/P/E: Masculine, Mercury, Air.
Magical attributes: Victory, desires, protection, to break habits.
History/Uses: The Greeks featured parsley in funerals and formed it into crowns for the victors at games. Romans thought it caused sterility, and in the Middle Ages to pull up parsley while speaking a name would bring death to that person. To some relief, these beliefs did not keep parsley out of the medical or culinary arena. It is rich in iron, calcium, and vitamins, which make it a very healthy food for chopping into salads and soups. Fresh parsley leaves in tea form are a treatment for cramps, while the dried root in decoctions eases urinary infections and arthritis. Externally, crushed leaves relieve insect bites, and may be applied in poultice form to sprains.

PINE

G/P/E: Masculine, Mars, Air.
Magical attributes: Attunement to nature, centering, cleansing, healing, productivity, purification against illness.
History/Uses: Hippocrates prescribed pine in the treatment of pneumonia, and it has long been known for its disinfectant qualities. Pine buds prepared by decoction act as an expectorant and antiseptic. This same mixture can be used for inhalation for head colds, although it is easier to simply toss some needles in hot water. Green cones and needles can be added to bath water to ease muscle pains and swelling. For magic, pine is best suited for its aromatic qualities of bringing one back into balance, and enhancing connection with the natural world.

POMEGRANATE

G/P/E: Masculine, Mars, Fire.
Magical attributes: Wishes, divination, health, creativity.
History/Uses: The Egyptians used pomegranates in their barter system, and the Greeks sometimes picture Zeus holding this fruit. For magical writing, pomegranate juice makes a good ink. For health, it can be used to moderate fevers and as a mild astringent.

ROSE

G/P/E: Feminine, Venus, Water.
Magical attributes: Love, friendship, luck, protection.
History/Uses: The history of the rose, the queen of the flowers, is closely tied with our own. It has associations with everything from sacred Indian

rites and Roman warriors to political events such as the War of the Roses in fifteenth century England. The culinary uses medieval peoples, especially in China, found for this flower are astounding. Jams, cakes, seasonings, and wines sat comfortably alongside powders, sachets, oils, and creams. Conserves of roses or rose petals in honey are often recommended for nausea and sore throats. Roses are high in vitamin C.

ROSEMARY

G/P/E: Masculine, Sun, Fire.
Magical attributes: Improve memory, sleep, purification, youth.
History/Uses: The Romans considered this an herb which would bring peace after death and joy during life, therefore it appeared in almost every ceremony in between! Besides its more popular use in meats and sauces, rosemary promotes healing of wounds, acts as an antiseptic, and can be a mild stimulant. Because of this it is a good ingredient for teas treating flu, stress, and headaches. When leaves are soaked in wine for two weeks, small glasses may be taken as a digestive aid. Oil of rosemary is excellent in hair conditioners, and the flowers of this herb may be added to lotion recipes to improve the complexion.

SAGE

G/P/E: Masculine, Jupiter or Venus, Air.
Magical attributes: Fertility, longevity, wishes, wisdom.
History/Uses: Romans gathered sage for ceremonial use to protect themselves and grant longer life. In Egypt it was given as a remedy to fight the plague. To the peoples of the Middle Ages, sage was a necessary herb to any home, the feeling being that it had so many virtues that it was a universal cure-all. Sage is a pleasant aromatic which can be used in an infusion to aid digestion, or as part of a honey wine to fight colds and fever. When applied in compresses it can ease many skin discomforts, including dandruff. If made into cream it is good for muscular pain, and if dried and smoked sometimes gives relief to asthma.

SAINT JOHN'S WORT

G/P/E: Masculine, Sun, Fire.
Magical attributes: Love, divination, protection against ghosts, joy.
History/Uses: Take care not to step on this faerie weed, lest you be carried off for a day by the wee folk! For magic, St. John's Wort is best cultivated during midsummer celebrations. In this form it may be hung over any altar to bring fertility to your projects. It has little benefit

medicinally today due to negative side effects; however, the tops may be used for an excellent red/yellow dye.

THYME

G/P/E: Feminine, Venus, Water.
Magical attributes: Sleep, psychic energy, courage, healing.
History/Uses: Believed to have been born from the tears of Helen, thyme has been used since Egyptian times, most commonly for embalming the dead. It was frequently placed on altars as an offering, to beautify the skin, and of course, appeared in many ancient culinary texts. We now know that thyme is a strong antiseptic which when prepared by infusion is useful for poor digestion, exhaustion, colds, and infections, and with honey is an effective treatment for sore throats.

VALERIAN

G/P/E: Feminine, Mercury or Venus, Water.
Magical attributes: Love, calming, sleep.
History/Uses: An herb which smells a bit like old socks, valerian has long been used as a tranquilizer. Before bed, take one teaspoon of herb to one pint of water and simmer. There is some evidence that the Pied Piper of Hamlin may have used this plant to bring cats with him to drive away the mice of the village, and it does act as a good substitute for catnip.

WILLOW

G/P/E: Feminine, Moon or Neptune, Water.
Magical attributes: Making wands, bringing spirits, broom handles, divination, protection, love.
History/Uses: Willow bark is considered nature's aspirin and is perfectly safe to use in tea for treating chills, headaches, and fever. In bath or lotion form it can help ease aches and pains caused by arthritis.

WITCH HAZEL

G/P/E: Masculine, Saturn or Sun, Fire.
Magical attributes: Protection, chastity, healing the heart.
History/Uses: Witch hazel derives its name from an Old English word for "pliant," mainly because of its flexibility and use in archery bows. In tincture form it is good as a mouth rinse and to ease hemorrhoids. As a compress, witch hazel can be applied to insect bites and other skin irritations.

YARROW

G/P/E: Feminine, Venus, Water.
Magical attributes: Courage, love, psychic abilities, divination.
History/Uses: History indicates that this herb may have been known to humanity as much as 60,000 years ago. In China, use of yarrow stalks for divination slowly developed into the I-Ching. In poultice form, yarrow is useful against infections and swelling. In magic, there is evidence that yarrow was often used as a component in incantations.

HERBAL RECIPES

With a foundation of knowledge about herbs and their uses, we can then begin to look for recipes to try ourselves. It is important when reviewing guides, especially from older sources, to check all ingredients against more recent materials. Many of the earlier herbals included the use of items we now know to be dangerous, or cite them in too large a dosage. The best rule of thumb for remedial herbalism is if you're not sure, don't use it.

Magical herbalism can be looked at from two viewpoints. The first is the use of herbs as spell components, altar decorations, for making ritual cakes and wines, etc., because of their long-associated effect. For example, while amethyst is not considered an "herb," it is often included in herbal books as a protection against drunkenness. In this case, an amethyst might be adhered to your drinking cup. Or a crystal might be soaked in water, then that water taken before going to a party. While I think that abstaining is just as effective, this use of amethyst is an old belief which can be employed from the magical herbal perspective.

The second approach for the magical herbalist is to take recipes like those below, adding to them an extra dimension by stirring in a spell, visualization, or other magical technique while they work so that the final product is not only physically useful, but spiritually blessed! In this case, while preparing your lineament you might want to envision red light (a warm color) pouring into it, while repeating words such as "the pain I feel, now soothe and heal." The speaking and imagery work helps to focus your mind on the purpose of your magic.

ACID INDIGESTION

Warm a full cup of milk and steep four or five eucalyptus leaves in it. Drink this to ease discomfort.

AQUA VITAE

Considered an excellent elixir of health for hundreds of years, this liqueur may be prepared and taken once a day, like a vitamin. To a liter of brandy add five or six bay leaves, a teaspoon of cardamom seed, a teaspoon of clove, two teaspoons each of angelica, camomile, lemon rind, fennel seed, licorice, nutmeg, cinnamon, several slices of ginger root (to your taste), and a handful of juniper berries along with sugar or honey to sweeten. This may be warmed to incorporate the herbs, or left in a sunny window, then strained after about a month.

ATHLETE'S FOOT

Besides keeping your feet dry and powdered with orris root, try a vinegar rinse (one cup water, one teaspoon cider vinegar) to which one tablespoon thyme and red clover have been added. Soak for fifteen minutes.

BEE/WASP STINGS

A drop each of tincture of myrrh or onion juice will help draw out the poison.

BOILS

Paint the sore with a tincture of iodine, caster oil, cohosh root, and sassafras root mixed with one half pint of whiskey.

BRUISES

Take one pound of almond oil with one cup each arnica flowers, Balm of Gilead, and St. John's Wort, all of which should be bruised, and warm over a low flame. When the oil has taken all the color out of the buds, cool and strain the liquid, applying as needed to the bruised area.

BURNS

A poultice made from wheat flour, molasses, and baking soda will relieve a burn and often hasten the healing process.

CHANCRE SORE

Sorrel soaked in warm water until soft, then strained as a tea should help clear them up more quickly.

CHAPPED SKIN

To one ounce wax add four ounces of glycerine and four to five drops of oil of roses (or other scent you like). Warm until well mixed and apply as needed.

COUGHS

In three pints of boiling water place peppermint leaves, one cup of rum, one half cup lemon juice, one ounce cinnamon bark, and one ounce comfrey root. After these are well blended, strain and add a half pound of sugar and two ounces of honey, bringing the entire mixture to a rolling boil. Cool and store in an air-tight container for use as a cough syrup.

DANDRUFF

An excellent after shampoo rinse for dandruff can be made by taking one cup each violet leaves, peppermint, nettle, red clover, witch hazel, and rosemary, and mixing them together. Before shampooing, warm a quarter cup of the dried herbs in two cups water for your rinse.

EARACHE

Use ten drops of anise oil, sweet almond oil, onion juice, and a pinch of pepper tied into a small cloth and placed in the ear (carefully). Then wrap your head with a warm towel for fifteen or twenty minutes as you lay on the opposite side of your body.

EYE RINSE

In a half pint of water warm one ounce of elder flowers and a half teaspoon of salt. Strain and use as needed to refresh eyes or relieve itching.

FEVER

Warm one quart of whisky with the peels of two oranges and one lemon. Take two teaspoons after each meal.

HEART BURN

To four ounces of water add two teaspoons each cinnamon, lavender flower, baking soda, peppermint leaves, and one half teaspoon ground ginger and allow to steep like a tea. Strain and drink warm in half-cup quantities after meals.

INFECTIONS

To ten ounces petroleum jelly add two sliced onions and two ounces each beeswax, honey, and elder leaves. Warm over a low flame for about thirty minutes. Strain and apply to the wound with a clean dressing.

ITCHING

Blood root pulverized and steeped in apple vinegar until well incorporated will ease the itch. Lotions made from aloe, lanolin, coconut oil, and/or cocoa butter also help greatly. Another alternative is a poultice made from two tablespoons each tansy, catnip, horehound, and hops mixed with vinegar.

LINEAMENT

To one pint of cider vinegar add one ounce of aconite root, and a teaspoon each tincture of myrrh, oil of cedar, peppermint, clove, wormwood, and thyme. If you do not have the herbs in oil form, the whole herb may be warmed in the cider, then strained for use.

For a lineament which will be warm to the skin, add two teaspoons camphor, one teaspoon bayberry, and one teaspoon cayenne pepper to increase circulation.

NOSE BLEED

It is said that if you make chewing motions with your mouth while your fingers are in your ears, this will stop the bleeding.

POISON IVY

Tincture of one pint black alder bark to one quart water and one cup olive oil. Wash frequently. A viable and easier alternative is to make a poultice of clay mud.

SLEEPLESSNESS

Two raw onions eaten before bed with a healthy portion of bread and butter is said to aid sleep. However, due to the sensitive nature of many stomachs, I would recommend valerian, catnip, and peppermint tea as a good substitute.

SORE THROAT

A gargle made from black tea with a teaspoon of lavender flowers, a quarter teaspoon salt, and a quarter teaspoon vinegar will help reduce pain. An alternative to this is sage tea mixed with honey and lemon.

STOMACHACHE

A tea of mint, strawberry leaf, catnip, and blackberry with one table-spoon of brandy should ease the stomach.

An alternative is brown rice which is pulverized and allowed to stand in warm water for fifteen minutes. To this a dash of sugar, nutmeg, and an equal quantity of boiled milk is added then drunk.

An elixir said to ease sour stomachs is made from two pints of brandy, a half teaspoon of clove, two teaspoons cinnamon, and a pound of blackcurrant. Soak all together for two weeks and add sugar to taste. Take by the teaspoon after meals.

STY

A used tea bag which is still warm, applied to the sty overnight will help greatly.

TOOTHACHE

Oils of peppermint and clove mixed with a bit of rum and applied directly to the tooth should ease the pain until you can get to a dentist.

WARTS

A wild turnip or sliced potato rubbed on the wart for three days and then buried is supposed to be a sure cure. While I can not say if this actually works, there are many reports to indicate it does!

GARDENING WITH HERBS

Herbs can serve a number of purposes in your yard, other than the obvious ones of curative and culinary harvesting. For a scenic appearance, plants such as lavender and rosemary can set off a path with a flair, and give their perfume to anyone walking by. Smaller herbs such as thyme can spread between stones and bricks to form colorful ground cover. In shady sites, try placing a little violet, lemon balm, and goldenseal for hue, and in your damp ground plant mint and marshmallow so the land can be reclaimed.

In terms of landscaping, herbs can be added to border other plants, especially sage, foxglove, and yarrow. In the vegetable garden, sections of dill, anise, basil, and savory not only add variety but also ward off insects. Whatever you choose, however, remember that designing and maintaining gardens is hard work. Consider before you start which items you need and how to best use your space.

Sometimes it is easier to plant thematic gardens, such as the mandala garden spoken of in Chapter Five. Other possibilities along these lines include:

○ *Seasonal gardens,* each section of which will bloom during a different part of the year. This particular garden is especially nice if you can make it a focus for your seasonal celebrations.

○ *Gardens which form patterns* (knots are popular) as they grow. Good herbs for this type of effort include lavender, hyssop, lemon thyme, sage, and wormwood intermingled with colored stones. The nice part about this type of garden is that you can fashion magical symbols out of it, such as a rune of protection for your land, if you choose!

○ *Medicinal gardens.* To go along with your recipes, growing your own medicinal herbs can be very rewarding, especially if it is done without chemicals. Good items to plant include valerian, mullein, aconite, foxglove, arnica, and camomile.

○ *Dye gardens.* For people who want to make non-chemical dyes for their magical robes, marigolds (yellow, orange, rust), madder (green-yellow), saffron (bright yellow), safflour (red), woad (indigo and blue), dock (black), broom (green), and zinnia (grey-green) are a good selection. I have included some basics on natural herb dyes in *Victorian Grimoire,* should you desire specific techniques.

○   *Scent gardens.* For people who want herbs which can be used in anointing oils, potpourri and/or aromatherapy,[4] this type of garden is terrific. Violets, lavender, lemon balm, geranium, rosemary, and numbers of other flowers/herbs valued for their bouquet can be grown for this purpose.

○   *Magical gardens.* These are pretty personal in nature. Consider what herbs you prefer to use most in your magical preparations, then look to see which items will grow in your climate. Within this examination, you can also think about small thematic gardens instead of one large one. For instance, you could have marigold, yarrow, and thyme growing together for use in any spell or ritual dealing with psychic abilities, or aloe, basil, and clove for money-related matters. From there, all that remains is to clear the soil, dedicate the land (see also Chapter Five), plant your seed, and tend it with loving care. Once your herbs are grown, you may harvest them during different times of the day[5] or various moon phases to improve their potency, and to set aside for specific magics. In this situation, if you were harvesting some thyme to improve your ability to commune with spirits,[6] you might wish to gather it at midnight when the line between day and night is thin. It is, after all, the witching hour![7]

URBAN HERBALISM

The city-based herbalist faces some unique problems, most of which revolve around the amount of room they have to dedicate to their work. If they want to grow their own herbs, some indoor gardening can be done with good-sized window boxes or plant pots which are located appropriately for adequate light. Such boxes, generally speaking, usually shouldn't contain more than three or four herbs, or they will strangle each other out. In purchasing, be certain they also allow for proper drainage in the bottom (small stones work well to help this process).

The initial key to successful urban herbalism is to grow or buy only those items that you need. The medieval herbalists would not have had anything in their collection which couldn't be used for at least three preparations because of the costly nature of their art. For us, this translates into having less clutter to cope with in already small spaces, while still having adequate supplies on hand to make a reasonable variety of goods.

The next tip for the city herbalist is to consider the best uses for the space available. A partially empty wall is the perfect place for rows of shelves to be assembled to store your jars and bags. Please make sure all your items are properly labeled to alleviate any chance of accidentally grabbing the wrong green leafy thing and ending up quite ill in the process. Be certain that your storage containers have been thoroughly cleaned and dried before use (glass and stoneware being preferable to plastic) and that any toxic items are kept well out of the reach of pets and children.

Ceilings in dry, well-ventilated rooms, and especially those which have any hooks or panels, are the perfect spot to dry herbs and keep them out of the way. Barks should be gathered in vertical strips during late fall or early spring. Hang them from one end of the room to the other with clothespins on a line. Roots like comfrey are best when you pull the entire plant from the ground late in the fall. Wash them carefully, breaking them up into small pieces. Next, hang a piece of cheesecloth from two hooks in the ceiling, hammock-style, spreading out the roots and turning them once or twice a week to ensure even drying.

Seeds such as caraway, dill, and fennel are best picked when ripe and fragrant before they fall to the ground. Cut the plant while still green, tying no more than eight stems together, and placing them upside down in a paper bag to dry, again from the clothesline strung across the ceiling. This method is very effective, but be sure to label all of your bags.

Herbs should be picked halfway down the stalk to dry. Thanks to the wonders of modern conveniences, herbs can be dried quickly in a microwave oven by placing them between a layer of paper towels for three minutes. Stop every thirty seconds to turn them and be certain they don't burn, then store in air-tight containers immediately.

Flowers are best picked first thing in the morning before the sun gets hot. You can then lay them on the cheesecloth, as you would with roots, until they are dry. The extra advantage to this method is the wonderful aroma your space will have as breezes move through!

A third consideration for the urban herbalist is preparation space and tools. You really should store the pans employed for herbal endeavors, especially those for non-food items like skin creams, separate from your cooking utensils. If you have one small cupboard, a shelf, space under a table or platform bed, or other similar niche, keep all your tools together there. Cardboard boxes or milk crates function very well for this type of storage. I personally use containers fashioned from old wine boxes with latches and hinges (parts cost $7) and a second-hand sewing machine chest that I think cost all of $3, both of which are light and very durable.

Additional items you may wish to set aside specifically for herbal work include wooden spoons, good measuring cups and spoons, a mortar and pestle, sharp knife, cutting board, sieve or screen, an old blender for grinding and mixing, labels for your jars, storage bags, funnel, tea ball for steeping herbs, eye dropper, and recipe file (3 x 5 cards work very well). Most of these tools can be inexpensively obtained through junk shops, are small enough to be portable, and can easily be stored together in one package when they are not in use.

Finally, no matter the state of your home on a daily basis, it is important for any herbalist to take extra care in keeping tools and herbs clean, especially if you work in the remedial realms on a frequent basis. Dust, dirt, old bits of herbs which have not been taken properly from pans, etc., can really ruin your creations, not to mention endangering your health. So before you start to work, take that little extra time to wash everything down with hot, soapy water. While you go, add a visualization or spell to properly prepare your space. Then create and enjoy!

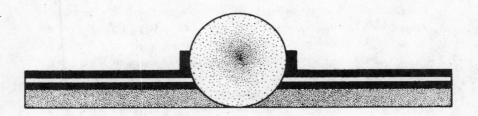

NOTES TO CHAPTER 6

1. *The White Hart* is a great stag of Celtic legend whose life is connected closely to the life and health of the land. The symbolism implied is a rejuvenation of the Earth through magical word and deed.

2. Oral tradition was how family and tribal histories were maintained before the advent of the written word. Certain people in each family or village, often bards, were given charge over remembering the lineage and important stories for their people. They would then pass these on to children, and so on.

3. There are certain general terms regarding preparations commonly referred to in this art that may not be understood by the novice herbalist. They are:

    Decoction: Place one ounce of herb in one pint of water. Make certain that roots are put in to boil before leaves. Once the water has come to a boil, simmer for about thirty minutes covered, then leave to cool completely. Strain and use as directed.

    Infusion: The original form of a potion, an infusion is not unlike a tea in quality. Pour boiling water over the herb in the proportions of one ounce herb to one pint water (although you may need much less for herbs that infuse quickly in water). Steep for fifteen to thirty minutes until a tea is formed. Use as directed.

    Macerate: To steep an herb in fat, such as is done with salve and ointments. Best oils to use are almond and sesame. Warm one cup of oil over a low flame and place one-half ounce herbs wrapped in cheesecloth to soak. Continue until the herbs have lost their color and the oil is rich with their scent.

Ointment: A fatty substance such as lard to which herbs are added. Choose herbs according to the effect you desire, or enchant them (or both). For healing ointments, choose according to physical ailment. Three teaspoons of herb to one cup of fat, steeped and heated several times should prove very nice. Vegetable shortening will work very well, especially almond and saffron. All ointments should be kept cool and in air-tight containers for best results. For magic, ointments work best when applied to pulse points or chakras.

Poultice: A portion of herbs placed in an equal amount of boiling water to steep. Once the herbs have been fully dampened, strain the water and place the herbs in gauze or cheesecloth applied directly to the affected area. This can be a little messy, so have a towel handy. It works fairly well, especially for rashes and other mild skin disorders.

Tincture: Four ounces of herb steeped in eight ounces of alcohol for about two weeks gives a reasonable tincture. The bottle should be sealed and left in a dark area, and the liquid strained when the tincture is ready.

Wash: A tea or infusion meant only for external use. A mild form of wash would be ¼ ounce herb to 1 pint of boiling water, steeped until lukewarm, then applied.

4. The idea behind aromatherapy is the fact that certain scents bring about specific responses in humans. For example, almost everyone who smells a rose will immediately think of romance, and often even sigh. The art of the aromatherapist is to find specific scents which can help people relax, improve general spiritual receptivity, aid natural healing processes, etc.

5. You may also harvest your plants at certain times of the day and use them instead of working during that hour. Say for example a spell you know of suggests working at 3 AM on a specific date, but you have to get up for work the next morning. In this case, you could substitute an herb picked at 3 AM the previous weekend to give the spell that particular vibration.

6. I do not recommend attempts at communing with spirits for fun or without good reason. This warning is not an attempt to "spook" the reader, but comes from years of seeing people get themselves into a real fix when the spirit they contacted wouldn't leave.

Usually this happens to the less experienced practitioner who has not properly prepared ritual space, or who is working without the aid of those more experienced to guide them. I also urge caution in accepting any information obtained from spirits as 100% accurate and true. Remember, these disembodied souls have to incarnate again, meaning they are likely to be subject to human error, personal prejudices, and selfish motivations no matter who they claim to be.

7. The term *witching hour* for midnight probably comes from the old idea that it was at midnight when Witches rode on brooms, and the dead were released to walk the ground. Because this hour lies for a moment when it is neither night or day, it is considered very magical.

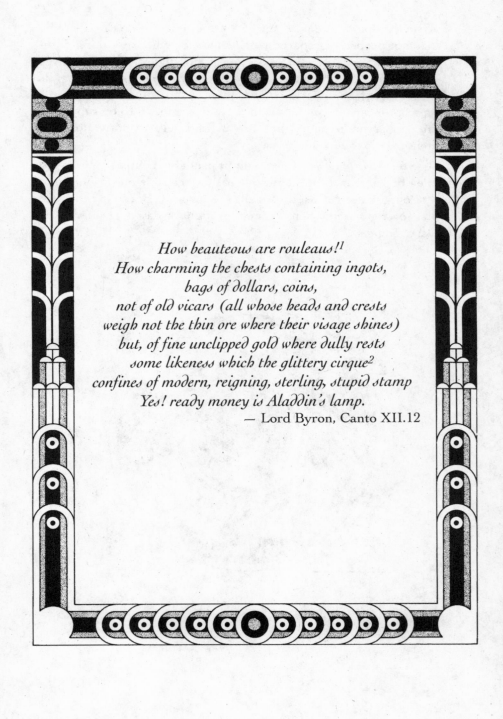

How beauteous are rouleaus![1]
How charming the chests containing ingots,
bags of dollars, coins,
not of old vicars (all whose heads and crests
weigh not the thin ore where their visage shines)
but, of fine unclipped gold where dully rests
some likeness which the glittery cirque[2]
confines of modern, reigning, sterling, stupid stamp
Yes! ready money is Aladdin's lamp.
— Lord Byron, Canto XII.12

Chapter

The Frugal Magician

Then leaf subsides to leaf, so Eden sank to grief,
So dawn goes down to day, nothing gold can stay . . .
— Robert Frost, *Nothing Gold Can Stay* (1923)

Up to this point in this book we have rebuilt our self-image, reworked our home and office environments to reflect our Paths, and even poured healing energy into the Earth. We have not, however, really discussed the technicalities of working magic, namely the tools commonly employed by Pagans and Wiccans today to help focus and direct energy.

Magic is not unique among religions in that it can quickly become an expensive pastime. Books, tapes, religious jewelry, and other forms of marketable paraphernalia have infiltrated almost all philosophical pursuits. Even in the Middle Ages, the Church found a way to market indulgences[3] which basically traded coin for the forgiveness of sin. The New Age has been no less bedazzled by hundreds of merchants hoping to make a living off the awakening desire in people to experience the supernatural.

In other words, the difficulties of trying to be an informed, aware consumer are not limited to the mundane realms. This is not to say that there aren't many reputable sales people out there . . . heck, I'm one of them, but we do have to be careful. Not everyone who purports to have "new age" knowledge, fantastic magical items, etc., is motivated by their good intentions.

173

NEW AGE CONSUMER HANDBOOK, OR HOW TO SUE YOUR SPIRIT GUIDE[4]

Finding quality goods and services for even the experienced magical practitioner is sometimes difficult. Like the supermarket, price does not always insure excellence. Also, there are not always shops available to people locally, so many are left to a somewhat unreliable mail-order system. Looking towards the future, even with an optimistic eye, it may be some years before magic can find its way comfortably into the yellow pages, so this situation will probably not change very rapidly.

With this in mind, I have tried to develop a system to help weed out some of the goods and services which may not be 100% "on the level." This approach is not only suitable for mail order, but applies to stores, merchants at festivals, and other goods or services which come your way.

As you review the prospective merchandise/service or talk to sales representatives, consider the following:

○ Do they make claims they can not possibly keep? For example, guarantees of love, health, etc., from a specific charm, prayer, or ritual. If so, a warning flag should go up. In most cases, purported magical potions and charms must, by law, carry a disclaimer stating that they are for entertainment only. Also, anyone who claims a 100% success rate in their magic wouldn't need to be selling their wares (and indeed, might not want to).

○ Are pictures of the products distorted? Do they seem a little blurry or out of proportion? This may be an indication that the photograph has been doctored somehow. The end result, by way of illustration, might be to make a crystal appear larger than it really is.

○ How are the prices in comparison to other sources you have done business with in the past? If they seem inordinately high, consider that unless they have something you really want or need immediately, you might be better off looking elsewhere. While the modern magical business person needs to make enough profit to feed their family and keep a business going, some type of balance needs to be exhibited. It might be worth reminding yourself that early practitioners of magic, herbalists, wise people, etc., rarely, if ever, accepted money for their assistance. It was viewed as a gift to be shared.

○ What kind of philosophies does the company seem to portray by their advertising? Do they make magic look like "hocus pocus"? Are they serious and down-to-earth? The best illustration I have for this comes from Earth Care Paper Products. Their catalogue is not just filled with products which are recycled, but has tons of useful information for the consumer on exactly how to begin recycling in their own homes and other valuable environmental information. They often provide this type of data free of charge. This, to me, reflects the correct ideology in their business practices, and inspires me to give them first consideration.

○ Does the company stand behind its merchandise? Do they offer any type of refund or exchange policy? Do they answer your questions or concerns within a reasonable amount of time? Anyone who offers goods and services for a fee needs to be accountable for the way customer service matters are handled.

○ How knowledgeable do the people you have contact with seem to be? Can they answer your questions without hesitation? Do you feel you get direct explanations instead of avoidance? If the sales people don't have a fairly strong background with the products or goods they are offering, you probably don't want to do business with them. This is especially true with herbalism, where inaccurate information can be dangerous to your health.

○ Are sliding scale fees offered with appropriate proof of need? Not all good companies allow for this option due to a very small margin of overhead profit, but it is worth looking into. Some of the most reputable service people will work for barter or trade. A prime example is the Association for Research and Enlightenment founded by Edgar Cayce nearly a century ago. This group offers scholarships or reduced rates to their various workshops for people who can show financial restriction. I have personally been able to benefit from this program once, and it works very well.[5] This exchange system in magic is an old tradition, dating back to the days when people commonly couldn't afford costly assistance, and the deep abiding belief that no one's spiritual needs should be hindered by the size of their pocket book.

○　Overall, how would you rate the presentation of the goods or service through their advertising? Is it assembled poorly? Copy quality? Organization? The way products are advertised will often be a direct indication of how much merit that business or individual really feels they have.

○　Did anyone that you know of locally do business with this individual or company in the past? If so, were they happy with the products and/or services?

○　Finally, does your own "little voice" within give you any good or bad feelings about this particular business? Sometimes we don't pay enough attention to our own instincts in these matters.

If after all your checking you go ahead with the purchase of any goods or service, and it proves to be inadequate or inferior in quality, you still have some recourse. First, return to the source and explain the problems you perceive. Most reasonable people will offer an exchange or refund if you are dissatisfied. If this attempt fails, write a detailed letter to them and keep a copy, sending a SASE (self-addressed stamped envelope) for their response. Sometimes getting a mediator who is familiar with that individual or company already to write as your representative is also helpful.

If no answer comes, or you are unhappy with the way the company/individual replies to your inquiry, you then have the option of contacting the Better Business Bureau in your area with a complaint. Send them as much information as possible, along with documentation and a copy of your receipt (retaining all originals in your own files). The BBB will investigate the matter for you and try to find a resolution equitable to all concerned.

With magic and the "new age" fast becoming a money-making industry, we have to begin doing our own house cleaning. Remember, even though you are dealing with the realms of spirit, the goods/services you buy represent businesses, which must conform to generally acceptable business practices if they are to retain a license. Anyone caught in fraudulent advertising, misrepresentation, etc., needs to either be approached privately for compensation, or exposed publicly to warn others who might come their way.

Do not be afraid to take legal action if you feel it is prudent and necessary. Most legal firms offer free consultations to tell you whether or not your case is worth pursuing in court. Ultimately as a consumer or merchant, it is our desire to promote an image for magic and the Craft which is honest and positive. Individuals who take advantage of lucrative atmospheres not only rob us of hard-earned money, but also often plunder the reputation of the magical community as a whole in the eyes of the public.

FINDING AND MAKING TOOLS WITHIN YOUR BUDGET

The time has come to slowly but surely collect the magical tools you choose to work with. For most people, this gathering takes a while, not only because of the cost factor, but because we are looking for just the "right" instrument for the job. In some instances, it is possible to make equipment at home so that you can be sure your tools will be personally and spiritually pleasing. For those people who don't feel quite as artistically inclined, alternative shopping methods and a little ingenuity often yield surprisingly magical results.

I have a dear friend who calls this second technique a "supplication to the Goodwill Goddess," which describes this system better than any clever phrase I can think of. It derives its name from the fact that one of the favored places to shop is Goodwill. Other second-hand stores such as Salvation Army, Catholic charities, many junk shops, flea markets, country antique and collectable stores, etc., also surrender some amazing items for pennies of what you would spend to buy them new.

The only difficulty with the Goodwill Goddess is that sometimes She is a hit-or-miss proposition. For that reason, I suggest taking time about once a month to quickly peruse your favorite store's inventory. You will not only discover some wonderful items for magic, but also often uncover inexpensive goods for your family and home.

If you do decide to attempt to create some of your own tools, I think you will find it a most rewarding experience. The final product will have more of your personal energy, and you will often learn a great deal in the process. Below, I have listed some of the more commonly desired items for the magical household. Wherever possible I have given basic recipes for you to try, alternative ideas, and suggestions on where to shop. Hopefully, by employing a wise combination of these methods, you will be able to make or find magical tools which not only fit your pocketbook but reflect your Path, and are agreeable to your higher senses.

ANOINTING OILS

Surprisingly enough, many health food stores have begun to stock essential oils because of their value to aromatherapy techniques. If you can not find them through these outlets or local cooperatives, try writing to:

> Lotus Light
> Box 2
> Wilmot, WI 53192
> 414-862-2395

Their selection of essential and scented oils is fairly good and the delivery time is excellent.

To make your own anointing oils, first consider the type of ritual(s) you wish to include them in. For example, both clove and camomile work very well as anointing oils because of their visionary and balancing properties, respectively. The key is to find scents that are personally significant and which don't make you sneeze in the middle of your rite.

As with any magical item, your preparation process is just as important as the final application. Use a good oil for a base such as almond, olive, or saffron. All of these are available at most supermarkets, and the almond can be found at health food stores readily.

The amount and type of herbs you place in the oil should reflect common sense. If the ingredients are expensive, make small quantities. If the herb is pungent or an aromatic such as clove whose flavor tends to hide the other components, use less. If it is known to be a skin irritant, don't use it at all; find a substitute. Magic doesn't require us itching all night to prove a point!

Almost all cooking herbs will incorporate themselves quickly into warm oil (within about two weeks). Rosins and woods such as frankincense, cedar, or myrrh, in contrast, often take as long as six months for the right strength of aroma to be reached.

Flowers and other plants admired for their bouquet are also very useful in making anointing oils, except you must take care to watch them closely. Each natural item will have a certain tolerance for heat and its own pace of decomposition. Flowers petals should be steeped (no green parts) until they lose their color and look almost translucent, but no longer than that or the oil will begin to take on the smell of old plants. The best teacher here, unfortunately, is trial and error. It has taken me as long as a year to perfect certain scents, but the time spent in experimentation is worth it!

If you wish to blend oils for specific magical effects, my advice is to make each base oil separately first, then blend them with an eye-dropper until you reach the desired scent. This alleviates a lot of trouble caused by persnickety plants that want to be treated differently from the rest. It also ensures a greater level of success.

BELTS

While not everyone might think of a belt as a magical tool immediately, I have found one to be very handy, especially when you have limited altar space. Belts allow you to have an immediate storage spot for your athame, wand, and herb pouches. Smudge sticks can be attached with a bit of yarn, matches or a lighter can be cleverly hidden in a draw-string compartment, and even hand-dipped candles can be hung over it, thus making yourself into quite a portable magic shop!

All kinds of belts can be found at inexpensive clothing stores and second-hand shops. If you would like to make your own belt, there are several methods you can try. One is to create a simple braid of three different colored cords (the kind used in curtains are available in fabric warehouses). The colors should somehow represent either the three-fold aspect of the God/dess or of your own nature. Often red, white, and black are used, but this is not a requirement. Each end of the braid can then be decorated with feathers, seashells, bells, or whatever suits your fancy.

Simpler still is taking several long segments of string and knotting the pieces together in equidistant intervals such as an inch. This type of belt is very lovely if you can use all the colors of the rainbow in it. If you like, you can add embellishments between each knot in the form of beads or anything which will slide over the strands. Items to represent the four elements are especially nice. The extra benefit to this belt is the fact that it not only holds your robe in place, but can be employed in knot magic (see Chapter Eight).

BREADS FOR RITUAL

Thanks to my husband and Morgana, a friend of ours, I have come to love the smell of different types of breads rising in my kitchen for various occasions, not the least of which is just for family snacking. I have suggested bread recipes in lieu of traditional ritual cakes for those people who do not want as much sugar in their diet.

Experimentation with flavors in breads is half the fun. Consider your season and associations, then think of the types of breads you might want to create. Apples and nuts or potatoes and oats for the harvest festivals, pumpkin and turnip breads for Samhain, fruitcake (to inspire the sun) come Yule, raisin or caraway to strengthen the light for Imbolc, egg breads for Eostre, spicy cheddar-dill on Beltane, and finally, hot herb bread for Midsummer with garlic, onion, and chili peppers for a real kick.

Most of these breads can be made with minor variations on a basic bread recipe. Mix one cup of warm water and one package of baking yeast in a four-quart mixing bowl. To this add one cup warm water, one tablespoon butter or oil, one teaspoon salt, and one tablespoon sugar (or honey), stirring until well blended. Add about three cups of flour and the other dry ingredients (spices, cheese, meats, etc.) and knead until the dough is smooth, elastic, and stiff. Please note that you may have to decrease your flour a little if you are including a fair amount of fillers. Continue kneading for ten minutes, dusting your hands and bread board with flour as needed. Place this ball into a well-greased bowl, also buttering the top of the bread, and cover with a towel for one to two hours until it doubles in size.

Take the dough from the bowl and punch it down. Divide this into two equal halves which can be formed into loaves. Place these in medium-sized (8" x 4" x 2") greased pans and allow them to rise again for 45 minutes before baking. Your oven should be preheated to 350 degrees. Bake for 40 to 45 minutes until golden brown. Should you so desire, you may glaze the bread with honey or butter just before removing from the oven.

If you don't have time to make bread for your ritual, call a couple of local bakeries to see what they have in stock, then make a tasty dip for a side dish. My personal favorite to inspire kinship is dill dip made from one cup sour cream, one cup salad dressing, two tablespoons dill, a dash of garlic, and one package Hidden Valley Ranch powdered dressing. Remember, magic is hungry work!

CAULDRONS

Many iron cauldrons are found in farm and country shops because they are widely used in rural living. If you can't travel that far, and don't mind a substitute without "feet" attached, consider going to a wholesale distributor for restaurant and kitchen equipment and finding a sturdy iron pot with handles to use. These pots can be set over fires on a tripod base, and function equally well on your stove for soups. The only caution here is to never use a cauldron which has held inedible herbs or plants for family cooking.

CRYSTALS

If you want to grow some special crystals of your own, there are now hobby shops and various science museums that carry crystal growing kits. These crystals will not be as fancy as those you could dig up or purchase at shows, but there is something fun and educational about giving it a try.

In purchasing crystals for use in magic, shop around. Prices vary greatly from one place to another. Some of your best buys may be at rock and mineral shows or from a local college's geology department. Another source may be lapidaries, some jewelers, gift shops, and obviously most new age stores.

CUPS

Need a durable ritual cup? Try a large seashell which has been boiled clean. A wide variety of usable coffee mugs, especially stoneware ones, can be procured from art festivals, second-hand stores, and pottery shops. Drinking horns, if desired, should probably be purchased at an antique shop in the interest of animal rights. Wooden and other decorative bowls also make for unique ritual cups and post-ritual feast gear!

I do not recommend buying crystal or glass goblets for the sake of durability. If you travel to festivals, camp, or enjoy any outdoor activity where you hope to take your ritual gear with you, glass is not a good choice. If you fall in love with one, however, you might wish to have another set aside which is not breakable for just such occasions.

GOD AND GODDESS IMAGES

See suggestions in Chapter Four for those that are easy to purchase. To make God/dess images to correspond with a particular season, I recently came up with a new approach. Basically this is a version of simple salt-dough for children, except that you can vary your ingredients to correspond with your observance. The basic salt-dough recipe is one cup salt, one cup flour, one cup water, kneading all for ten minutes.

In spring, add crushed wild flowers to your paste and a few drops of rain water to form your God/dess figure. During summer you may want spicy or headier scents; in fall, dry leaves and grains are appropriate. Come winter, wood shavings and rosins might mingle for the desired effect.

The nice thing about these figures is that they can be baked (325 degrees for one to two hours), glazed or painted and saved for next year, or given as gifts. They make an excellent holiday project for the children of your family or coven, and are sturdy enough to be decorated with bits of cloth, hats, miniature garlands, etc.

HERB PILLOW/MAGIC SACHETS

The use of cloth containers for herbs has long been employed by magical herbalists. In the Middle Ages, the thrifty housewife would use sachets and herb pillows to keep bugs away and cover the scent of people who didn't bathe frequently. Later this practice developed into the pomander, a little scent ball, which was believed to protect one from the plague.

The idea of using herb pillows and sachets for protection, cleansing, and even as an aid to sleep has continued in magical traditions. While you can purchase mugwort or balsam needle pillows at various gift shops during the holidays, it is much more economical to make your own, and takes very little effort.

For sachets, gather the herbs of your choice, mixing them until the scent is pleasant to you, and until you feel the energy of your magic has set into them (through visualization, chants, or whatever). If you were making a herb cache for your beau, for example, it might be filled with traditional flowers of romance such as rose, lily, lavender, and daisy. Next, cut a square cloth of an appropriate color; for love, red or pink would be best. Set your herbs in the center, tie up the bundle with a little ribbon or lace, and it is ready to share.

The herb pillows are a larger version of this, requiring some sewing. In this case you need two squares of cloth, a little cotton for stuffing, and your herbal sachet already prepared. Since they don't have to be overly large, the stitches can be made by hand to increase the magical energy and alleviate the need for a sewing machine.

Begin by sewing three sides of the pillow with right sides together. Turn the whole pillow inside out now (so the seams are inside) and stuff it with the cotton. For a healing pillow, ingredients such as angelica, camomile, fennel, lemon rind, mint, pine, and oak leaves are all good choices for the herb cache. This bundle should be placed in the center of the bunting so that the pillow isn't bumpy. Now turn under the last seam and stitch it shut. If you want to add lace or other decorations, do so! These are great gift items, especially if you enclose a card listing the ingredients, their meaning, and whatever spells you may have used during preparation.

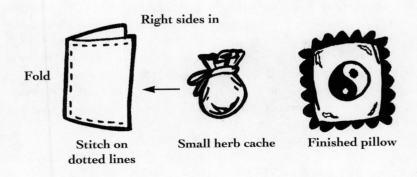

Right sides in

Fold

Stitch on dotted lines   **Small herb cache**   **Finished pillow**

Herb Pillow Construction

INCENSE AND BURNERS

I have found incense and items which can easily be made into burners in a number of unusual locations. For incense, any Oriental or import gift shop, some cooperatives and health food stores, and herbal suppliers will often have a good variety available to you. My personal favorite mail-order suppliers of quality incense are:

Mermade Magickal Arts
Box 33-402
Long Beach, CA 90801

Castle Rising
The Ethnic Market
P.O. Box 3127
Morgantown, WV 26505

Both of these places have good delivery time, reasonable prices, and marvelously creative selections.

For incense burners, you can create make-shift ones out of almost any stoneware dish combined with a little dirt or sand. In this scenario, you fill your dish three-quarters of the way up with the soil/sand and set your self-lighting charcoal to burn in the center (this type of charcoal may be purchased at Catholic supply stores). The sand/soil protects your container from too much heat, while holding the burning charcoal securely.

To purchase inexpensive burners, check almost any second-hand shop. Inevitably there will be at least two, if not more, for you to choose from.

The simplest forms of homemade incense come to us through aromatic spices, woods, and rosins. The basic recipe is to take a couple of pieces of self-lighting charcoal and crush them up. To this add an equal quantity of wood shavings (cedar and sandalwood are best). From here, what type and quantity of spices, dried herbs, and flowers or oils you add to your incense will vary drastically according to the purpose of the final product, not to mention personal taste. For example, with love and harmony spells you might use roses, cinnamon, and a hint of myrrh.

Whatever you do, remember to keep your magical goal firmly in mind as you create, and take care not to make the incense too strong for the space it will be used in. The best results I have achieved are usually with those recipes which do not exceed four other ingredients besides the base of wood and charcoal.

One of my favorite recipes for incense is what I call "sleepy time," specifically made to calm the nerves and aid relaxation. Take a quarter cup of lavender flowers and henna, to which a tablespoon of powdered myrrh and fresh honey are added.

Sprinkle in a bit of peppermint, orris root, and a hint of cinnamon. Mix until well consolidated. Next, spread this mixture on a wooden board where it can sit undisturbed until dry. Store in an air-tight container. Sprinkle a little on charcoal when meditating, before bed, or any time you wish to bring peace to your home.

PENTAGRAMS

Many people like to have some type of pentagram visible at their celebrations. One possibility is to have the children in your home or group draw one on a large piece of paper in colors appropriate to the season. Another idea which I personally like is to bind together fallen branches, sturdy rope pieces, old metal rods, popsicle sticks, grape vines, or other media in basically straight sections of equal length (see illustration). The nice part about this pentagram is that it can be decorated with fresh or dried flowers, ribbons, bows, or whatever suits your fancy, and can often be kept for future observances.

ROBES

Caftans, reworked prom gowns, a choir robe, and even fancy bathrobes can prove to be very effective ritual clothing. The concept behind having special apparel for magical work is the same as it was when you donned your "Sunday best." What you wear does effect your mental attitude. If you have certain special clothes set aside specifically for rit-

Popsicle Stick Pentagram

ual, as soon as you put them on you are putting on the proper magical perspectives at the same time.

With this in mind, your actual "robes" might be nothing more unique than a dress shirt, pieces of special jewelry, or even a different way of wearing your hair. It is not so much how you change your appearance as the way these alterations make you feel that is important. Along the same lines, you might have variations on the theme throughout the year to reflect the seasons. For example, perhaps you will choose a pastel shirt-robe to wear during your spring rites, bright orange for summer, golds and reds for fall, or brown for winter. Alternately you could use temporary dye in your hair to physically exhibit the changing of the wheel. Another idea would be to have different pieces of jewelry that depict natural items, that are only worn at certain celebrations.

In this way, your magical robes can be creative, fun, and not necessarily costly. If you decide you would like to make a more conventional robe, I frequently use a piece of my own clothing as a pattern (usually a dress or shirt), leaving plenty of space for seams, and sketching out the rest of the garment with chalk. You can also check your local fabric shop for costume patterns (a monk's robe is ideal) which can be altered to suit your taste and size.

RUNES

A very old system of divination,[6] runes are fun and easy to make in a variety of mediums. The first way is to gather beach stones or shells of similar size, shape, and color, and paint your symbols on them. Afterwards, you may wish to coat them with a protective art spray so the paint doesn't wear off quickly with handling. A second method is to get molding clay, shaping your runes to a comfortable size, carving in the symbols, then allowing them to dry. These runes will be fairly durable and may also be painted if you desire.

The third technique, which yields a very attractive set of runes, is to take a small fallen branch(about one inch in diameter) from your favorite type of tree. Get a small hand saw and cut off thick slices of the branch until you have 25 of them. Sand down any rough edges, then paint, woodburn, or carve your runes in the center of one side. These may be finished with art spray, but I like to condition wood runes with lemon oil periodically instead. For people who enjoy detail work, you can also carve smaller runes that are personally significant to you around the edges of each piece (see illustration).

Children's runes can be made from the salt dough recipe given earlier in this chapter.

Rune Coin

SMUDGE STICKS

If you are able to get fresh dried sage, lavender, cedar, or sweet grass, a blend of any of these items when tied together in a bundle makes an excellent smudge stick. Prepared smudge sticks are often available at cooperatives and Native American supply/gift shops. An alternative to this method is to burn powdered sage and cedar (or other herbs of cleansing/purification), employing a large feather to lightly propel the smoke to the desired locations.

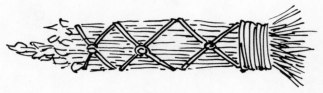

Smudge Stick

TAROT CARDS

Many stores which carry normal playing cards will also carry blank decks. Two of these can be used to make your own Tarot system. At first this may seem a little difficult, but you do not have to be terribly artistic to create a deck which will work for you. If need be, you could cut and paste pictures on to the cards, or use geometric designs instead of fancier drawings.

In fact, a normal set of cards will function fairly well for the Minor Arcana, numbers one through King (clubs = staves, hearts = cups, spades = swords, diamonds = coins), employing the blank cards for the addition of the Major Arcana and a Page or Knight (the Jack in the modern deck is a combination of these two). If you can't find the blank sets of cards, use cardboard cut into the correct size, or a good-caliber art paper.

In making your deck, try to keep a theme of some type in mind so that the cards are consistent in form and function. Do only one card at a time, meditating on the traditional figure from your favorite deck and what it means to you. Then allow those thoughts to be reflected in the way you finally present your version of the card. This is an excellent exercise for anyone who plans to use the Tarot for divination on a frequent basis as it familiarizes you with the cards in a much more personal manner. For more ideas along these lines see also Janina Renee's *Tarot Spells*.

TAROT DECK AND CRYSTAL RECEPTACLE

Most magical people like to have a special place to store things like their Tarot deck and crystals specifically so that visitors don't casually handle them, and to protect the tools from random energy. To these ends I suggest things like old cigar boxes lined with fabric, jewelry and gift boxes which are fairly inexpensive to obtain at Goodwill, certain import shops, and some Hallmark stores.

An alternative to buying little boxes is to make pouches for these items. The simplest form is that of a rectangular sack which can vary in size according to your needs. Made in similar fashion to the herb pillow to begin, the main difference is the way the open side is finished for a drawstring (see illustration). The color of the fabric should reflect personal taste and magical use. White or black are often colors of protection depending on your point of view.[7] The cloth, however, is best made of a natural material rather than polyester or another blend. This rule of thumb is good to follow with all your magical creations.

Stitch on dotted lines and add string

Finished holder with deck

Tarot Deck Holder

WANDS (STAVES)

Clay, wood, and metals such as copper all make good materials for wands and staves. The metals act as a good conductor of magical energy especially when combined with crystals. Clay and wood are nice, natural conveyors for the same purpose.

Clay wands can be fashioned in any manner personally pleasing. With wood, both wands and staves may be made from fallen branches. Go to your local park in the spring to find ones where the bark has been soaked off. If you can't find one where the bark is already loose, you may have to sand or whittle it down, then smooth the surface so you don't get splinters.

What I like best about wooden staves and wands is the fact that all the little nooks and crannies are perfect hiding spots for crystals. Powdered herbs can be added to tree sap or glue to secure them in place, making the items look as if they are growing right from the limb. Remember to treat your wooden tools periodically with lemon oil to keep them from drying and cracking.

Homemade Wand

Metal wands can be made from almost any piece of piping, depending on your personal tastes, but copper is probably the best.[8] A crystal or other decorative item can cap one end, while a small cloth or leather grip can be placed on the other. Fasten your grips in place with a thong, then tie it off with a few beads or feathers (see illustration).

Nice walking sticks can often be purchased at Renaissance fairs, through certain camping and hiking stores, and at antique shops.[9] Wands are not as easily found other than through local or mail-order magical outlets.[10]

WINES FOR RITUAL

I really never thought that I would be making wines at home, but have found it to be an enjoyable pastime which also acts as a tasty gift for most occasions, any time of the year. The items you need to make wines are not as complex as you might first think. I use one large soup pan, a wooden spoon, old screw-top wine bottles which have been boiled, packaged yeast, sugar or honey, fruit and juice, and that's all!

The basic technique for the wines is simple. Bring two to three pounds of sugar or honey to boil in one gallon water with a pound of fruit, one can of frozen fruit juice, spices to taste, a tea bag or one ounce bruised ginger root (for tannic acid), and one fresh orange or lemon (for citric acid). Once this mixture is blended, allow it to cool to body temperature and add your yeast.

The whole pot should now be covered with a hand towel and allowed to sit on your stove for about one week. Strain and pour into your screw-top bottle, leaving the top very loose for the next two weeks. After this time you may tighten down the cap more firmly, but continue to let the bottle air once a day by opening it enough to allow fermentation pressure to bleed off.

You will know your wine is progressing properly if you hear a satisfying "pssht" as the top is loosened. Usually within six weeks you will only need to do this once every few days. Within three months the wine is very palatable, and you should notice it starting to clarify to an almost translucent quality.

You can change your fruit and juice to match personal taste and the season. For example, an apple-honey blend is very nice for any fall festival, while you might choose strawberries or raspberries for summer. To have a non-alcoholic drink, simply decrease the sugar to taste, and eliminate the yeast. It will be very tasty when chilled.

Should you desire to use wine yeasts, which make a nicer-tasting brew, I suggest looking up brewing and/or hobby shops in your local yellow pages. Most major cities, especially those with colleges, have some type of brewing club you can contact for good ideas and advice.[11]

CREATIVE MAGICAL USES FOR MODERN ITEMS

This is what I call "techno-magic" — any rite which employs a common technological item as a symbol, component, tool, or aid to various metaphysical practices. The idea behind such customs is to take the best of what science offers us and use it creatively for positive, effective, and powerful magic. Doing so not only offers us a greater variety of items to draw from for daily magical living, but again, is far less costly than buying something new.

While I will be going into more detail regarding updated symbols for modern magic in Chapter Eight, this section is dedicated to more hands-on type work, giving examples of how specific items frequently found around the modern home or office can be applied practically within the realms of a spell or ritual.

BLENDER

To bring consistency, harmony, or coherence to any situation, make yourself a milk shake or other drink using fruits, vegetables, liquids and/or herbs appropriate to the situation. For example, if you are trying to renew accord in your marriage you might mix together two cups of milk with a banana for fruitfulness, a touch of anise for joy, and a teaspoon each of cinnamon and clove to bring love and dispel negativity. Drink this together to internalize the magic.

COFFEE POT

When you need perk, stamina, potency, or to increase the energy of any spell, the coffee pot is a perfect place to begin your working. Coffee itself is considered an active herb because of its invigorating effects on humans, but other items such as ginger and cinnamon may be added directly to the grounds to enhance the spiritual effects.

For people sensitive to caffeine, there are alternatives. Both ground dandelion root and toasted acorns make a tasty herbal coffee which promotes long life and health along with the increased energy you need for your magical work.

COMPUTER MAGIC

For someone like me, the relationship between my creativity and my computer are very closely tied. Yet until I began writing books I really didn't think of using my computer for magic. It can act as a good focal point for any spells dealing with organization, the mind, prediction, and the like. Even more effective, however, is using the way you file your documents as a magical aid.

While writing *Victorian Grimiore,* I saved each chapter under "victory" so that when I retrieved the data from the system I could also bring success into my life, specifically for that book. This time, I filed the chapters under "dance" so the energy and beauty of that movement would live within each page.

For saving parts of your personal Book of Shadows you might use words such as "growth," "wisdom," or any other term which describes the attribute you hope to bring to that writing, a situation, or yourself. As you recall the information from the system, your hands bring the magic into play, and that word reminds you of the power you have placed in your system. Since computers and magic are both somewhat electrical in their behavior, the two work together rather well.

For other items in your system, consider first what word you will remember when you are looking to retrieve the document, and second your magical intent, then find a good compromise. I also suggest you keep a list of your computer file names with a brief description, along with copies of everything on paper, just in case.

CUPS

Cups are fun for perspective work using the old saying regarding its fullness. Fill a cup or glass exactly halfway, then consider if you feel it is half full or half empty. The purpose of such an exercise is to help make you more aware of your personal outlooks, and give you the opportunity to look at a simple situation from more than one angle. Eventually, this type of activity will expand itself into the way you perceive and analyze more complicated situations.

A second activity, especially good for magical partners who wish to improve their psychic abilities, is to play a game of hide the penny (or other small item which fits securely under a cup). To begin, whoever is going to be the seeker should hold the object long enough to sense its energy.

Next, allow your companion to secure the object under one of several cups while your eyes are closed (no peeking!) and move the cups around. Try to remain focused on the energy you felt in your hand and look for it again by placing your palm over each cup. It will take time and practice to get really good at this, but as you improve you will notice that your ability to sense energy will show marked progression as well.

DRY ICE

I personally think the best application for dry ice in magic is to create a specific mood for a ritual. There is something quieting and mysterious about fog as it rolls across the ground or through a room. Because of this, I suggest considering applying dry ice for vision quests, augury, for ritual dramas, and especially on All Hallows. In combination with this, iridescent rocks in the colors of the four elements under blue lamps makes for a wonderful, visually rich magic circle!

LIGHT BULBS

Light bulbs are good for mental work, revealing secrets, and communication. If you prefer not to use a lamp, candles are an appropriate substitute. In any spell or ritual where you wish to employ either, make the lamp or candle the focus of your altar. Cast your circle without the aid of any other light source other than that from windows, and verbally disclose the intentions of your working.

On the candle or light bulb, place a drop of myrrh and clove oil. Visualize your goal, then light the lamp/candle to signify the working has begun (and quite literally shine a light in the darkness). Let the lamp/candle stay on as long as you feel appropriate, and each time you light it again it will continue to send out energy towards your aspiration.[12]

MICROWAVE

Not unusual to many homes, a microwave can be used to amplify the energy of any spell components, or to speed up movement which is perceived as being stalled. In either case, the components of the ritual or spell should be placed in the microwave (no metal objects, obviously) before you perform your working. You do not have to warm them very long (thirty seconds is more than enough time), but while you do, try to visualize the energy pouring into them from the machine. I usually see this as active atoms which continue to move within the components after I remove them. Thus, they have become "active" participants for your magic.[13]

MUSIC

The obvious uses for taped music are many, including meditation, guided visualizations, and just general background sound in ritual. Live music is likewise wonderful for any gathering, being able to respond immediately to the energy of the moment.

I have a fun way to apply popular and folk music to just about any magical situation. Pick a song, any song, then change the words to ones which reflect your magical goals. By taking a simple tune (Christmas songs work very well) easily remembered, and rewriting it for ritual use, you can create whole new musical accompaniments for your rites, not all of which have to be serious in nature.

The longest standing and perhaps lengthiest illustration of "filking" comes to us through the tune "Give me that old time religion." This song has seen more bawdy revisions over the years at Pagan gatherings than any other I know of. While the authorship for many of these verses seems lost in networking antiquity, I would still like to give you a couple of examples from my collection to spur ideas of your own.

To anyone who has taken part in writing any of these verses, I apologize in advance for not being able to share your names with readers. Then again, some people may wish to remain nameless!

Variety's life's spices
When Gods of old entice us
Just Ankh if you love Isis
She's good enough for me!

With your trusty old athame
You can cast a double whammy
Or slice and dice salami
That's good enough for me!

A more serious and beautiful illustration was given to me by a pen-pal, Janella (with my sincere thanks). It goes to the tune of "Tis a gift to be simple." This song is a perfect example of just how much variety can be found with a little creative rewriting on songs we have all heard for years. I encourage you to give it a try!

I will go to the Circle in the spring of the year
With my arms full of flowers and my heart full of cheer
I will go into the circle in the spring of the year
And sing our Lady's praises.

I will go to the Circle when the summer is nigh
I will dance in the grove while the full moon's in the sky
I will go to the Circle when the summer is nigh
And sing our Lady's praises.

I will go to the Circle when autumn leaves are brown
Joyful in the blessing of the harvest which abounds
I will go to the Circle when the autumn leaves are brown
And sing our Lady's praises.

I will go to the Circle when the winter snow is deep
Across the frozen mountains, dreaming in their sleep
I will go to the Circle when the winter snow is deep
And sing our Lady's praises.

PAINT ROLLER

The next time you need to apply a layer of fresh paint to your walls, you can add a few drops of homemade magical oil to the preparation to help protect your entire home. Choose your scent according to your environment's needs, and use the oil very sparingly so as to not disrupt the consistency of the paint. While you roll on the coats, visualize white shielding light pouring through the brush and on to the walls, empowering the oils you have already placed there!

PHOTOCOPIER

My favorite spell using photocopiers is one for improving financial outlooks. For this, make quite a few copies of paper money (on recycled paper, please). You can usually fit three or four bills on one sheet. Cut these up. Go home, light some green candles in your bathroom, and burn patchouli incense to help increase the energy for monetary needs.

Next, get in the tub and let your partner pour the copied money over you, quite literally bathing yourself with the answer to your requirement. As the money falls towards you, release your anxiety about the situation and try to focus on productive solutions to add to your im-magic (imagery + magic).

SPORTS BRAS

A local woman I know has a coven who puts these items to very practical use in their circles. Since many of the women there are heavily endowed, any time there is going to be energetic dancing, they put these specially decorated bras on!

For men, this could easily translate into jock straps and cups which they can likewise adorn for the celebration. While on the surface this type of activity may seem silly, taking care of ourselves to ensure personal safety and comfort is important to practical magic.

TEEKEE TORCHES

Excellent tools for any fire-related spells (often good for blessing, purification and protection work). They especially make a wonderful addition to outdoor circles when they are ignited just before sundown. For the urban practitioner without a large yard, consider employing your barbecue come Beltane (a traditional fire festival) or at any time during the summer months. After the ritual or spell, put the fire to good use for the family meal.

The fires of any of these items can be used for a form of divination. For this technique all you need is a flame and a little quiet time. Set yourself in front of the fire and relax, concentrating on a specific question or situation. Begin to watch the movement and color of the flames as you continue to ponder the circumstances. You may see actual shapes appear that have personal meaning by way of an answer. If not, you can use pyromancy interpretations from Tibet, first discovered in the 1300s. They used a butter lamp's flames, but any fire source will do.

If the flame is pale, there are problems being caused in your life by karma. If there is black smoke occurring, your vision is obscured and you may not be seeing the truth. If the flame is likened to a crescent moon, peace and tranquility will be yours, just be patient. If there is a pleasant smell to the smoke or the flames burn low, it is a sign of success and good fortune. Flames shaped like banners mean attainment of a goal, and dark red or black colors signify emotional conflicts in your situation right now.

Other examples of techno-magic include using a stapler as part of spells or rituals for bonding and security, swimming pools or hot tubs for any water-related enchantments, and the washing machine for cleansing and purification.

Please feel free to change, expand, and personalize any of these ideas to make them more useful to you. Write your own incantations, chants, or actions to go along with them. Don't be afraid to get inspired or excited, magical energy is very motivational! Most of all, allow your creativity to express itself so that the harvest of your workings is positive magic that truly reflects your inner light and Path.

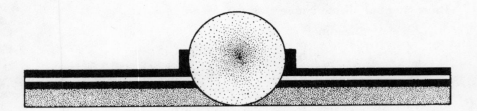

NOTES TO CHAPTER 7

1. Refers to round baubles or coins.

2. Edge of the circle, circumference.

3. *Indulgences* were basically small bits of parchment which insured the buyer that for a certain amount of money, all their wrongs would be forgiven by God. This was done with the priest acting as the intermediary between the individual and the divine judge.

4. This phrase came about due to a general hesitancy I have regarding excessive use of channeling. While I acknowledge it as a viable spiritual technique, I am leery of people who blame their errors on the spirit guides who speak through them. Being accountable and responsible in the Craft means that we are answerable for the way we use our gifts and the information we communicate as truth.

5. For more information on the A.R.E. write to:
    P.O. Box 595
    67th Street and Atlantic Avenue
    Virginia Beach, VA 23451

6. For informational purposes, the names and signs of traditional Norse runes are given below. For a complete explanation of the runes, a bit of their history, and some interesting uses for them, I recommend purchasing either *A Practical Guide to the Runes* by Lisa Peschel, Llewellyn Publications, or *The Book of Runes*, Ralph Blum, Oracle Books.

Rune Symbol	Rune Name	Basic Meaning
ᛗ	Mannaz	The Self
ᚷ	Gebo	Partnership, Gift
ᚨ	Ansuz	Messenger, Signals
ᛟ	Othila	Separation, Retreat
ᚢ	Uruz	Strength, Change
ᛈ	Perth	Initiation, Secrets
ᚾ	Nauthiz	Necessity, Constraint
ᛝ	Inguz	Fertility, Beginnings
ᛇ	Eihwaz	Defense, Foresight
ᛉ	Algiz	Protection, Emotions
ᚠ	Fehu	Possessions, Satisfaction
ᚹ	Wunjo	Joy, Light, Clarity
ᛃ	Jera	Harvest, Productivity
ᚲ	Kano	Opening, Clear intention
ᛏ	Teiwaz	Warrior energy, Awareness
ᛒ	Berkana	Growth, Rebirth
ᛖ	Ehwaz	Movement, Progress
ᛚ	Laguz	Flow, Emotional needs
ᚺ	Hagalaz	Disruption, Awakening
ᚱ	Raido	Journey, Communication
ᚦ	Thurisaz	Gateway, Non-action
ᛞ	Dagaz	Transformation, Day
ᛁ	Isa	Standstill, Ice
ᛊ	Sowelu	Wholeness, Life energy
	(Blank)	Unknowable, The Void

7. White is considered protective because it reflects all wavelengths of light away from itself, and thus away from magical items. Black, conversely, absorbs light, absorbing any negative energy before it can reach your tools.
8. Other metals which may be used to decorate wands, if you can afford them, are gold to increase masculine sun energy (good for mental work, strength, endurance etc.); silver for the feminine water aspects, including intuition and healing; lead for grounding and solid foundations; and tin for luck. You may also wish to research the traditional meanings of the crystals you choose for

your wands and staves. Good and readily available choices include agate for vision, amethyst for peace, bloodstone for wisdom, coral for fertility, malachite for healing, moonstone for psychic abilities, quartz for increased energy, and turquoise for protection.

9. My husband and I belong to a historical recreation society whose merchants also often have magical supplies including staves, herbs, books, crystals, etc. This organization is literally world-wide, but is split up into smaller associations designated by location. These regional representatives can often help you find merchandise and other materials through the mail, if there is not a group within driving distance or even in your own town. For information on the groups and events in your area send a SASE to:

> The Society for Creative Anachronism
> Office of the Registry
> Box 360743
> Milpitas, CA 95036-0743

10. Two mail-order outlets for wood products of all sizes and shapes, and other tools are:

> Bard's Lore Creations
> 3979 Ockler Avenue
> Hamburg, NY 14075

> Hammer and Shell Productions
> c/o J. Feavearyear
> 176 Virginia
> Rochester, NY 14619

11. I know two local people who are able to ship supplies for brewing without too much difficulty. If you order from them, however, please be considerate and send enough money to cover the extra costs of postage. Catalogues are sent via SASE. These people may also be able to give you contacts in your area.

> Brewers Emporium
> 249 River St.
> Depew, NY 14043

> Hennessy Homebrew
> 470 North Greenbush Road
> Route 4
> Rensselaer, NY 12144

12. Some candle burning rituals also suggest that carving your need/goal into the candle before burning it aids the process. You obviously don't have this option with the light bulb; however, you can trace a single word on the bulb with your oil before working for the same effect.

13. Please practice microwave magic carefully. If working with flammable components or non-food items, it might be best to have the item absorb energy in a purely symbolic manner by leaving the oven off.

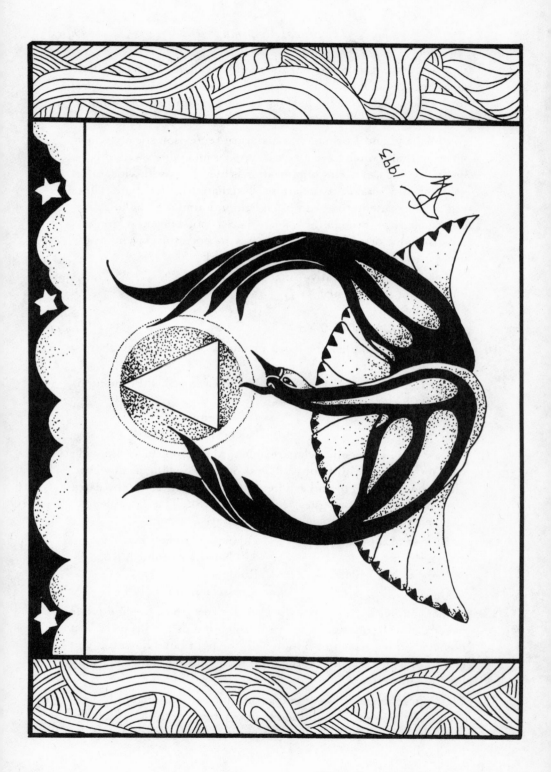

ONE STEP BEYOND

Exploring New Symbols and Artistic Expressions

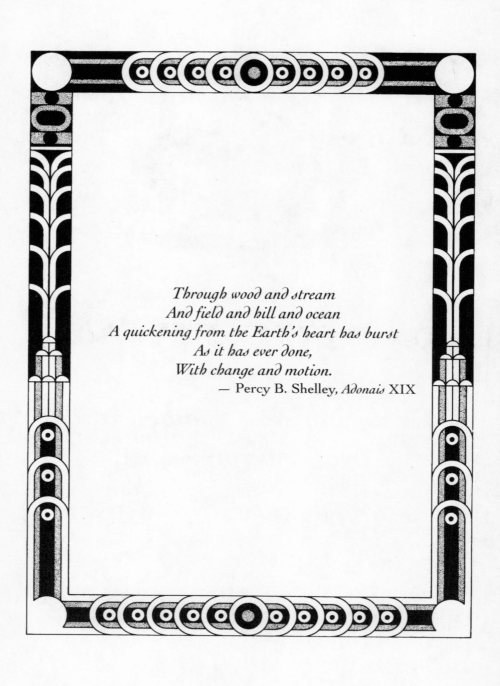

Through wood and stream
And field and hill and ocean
A quickening from the Earth's heart has burst
As it has ever done,
With change and motion.
— Percy B. Shelley, *Adonais* XIX

Chapter

New Symbols for a New Age

All that is visible must grow beyond itself, extend into the realm of the invisible. Thereby it receives its true consecration and clarity and takes firm root in the cosmic order.

— I Ching, Book One

Back in the 1960s, dream interpretation was very popular. Books were readily available on neighborhood shelves describing almost every imaginable item or circumstance to come up in our dreamtime, and a carved-in-stone explication of same. As the science of psychology grew, and humanity's understanding of mental processes grew with it, the realization that symbols are expressions of the self combined with the outer world became more apparent. Now we are left to reexamine our symbolism both as a species and as spiritual beings to discover what our symbols mean for here and now, with enough foresight to also make them applicable for our tomorrows.

Since magic should be something which grows and changes, expressing our own transformations, it would be rather naive to assume that all our hallmarks and standards would or could endure unchanged for countless generations. True, some icons such as the grail seem to remain consistent in their meaning; the only thing that really changes is the jargon we use to describe our interpretations. Yet other items are

touched dramatically by the shifting and growing awareness of humanity. For example, deer have often been considered the symbols of gen-
tleness and grace. Today, however, because there is so much
controversy over hunting and skins, the first thing that comes to my
mind with the deer is unfortunately the hunt. Indeed, this connection
has become so personally powerful that if a deer comes to me in a dream
or crosses my path, I might consider walking cautiously for a few days,
keeping alert to anything out of place and watching for "predators."

Likewise with so many new gadgets revolutionizing our lives, we
have a whole new set of symbols to work with that our ancestors could
not have even imagined. If we dream about computers, it may mean that
we've worked with them too much that day or it could bear a deeper
connotation; the need for input, organization, or focus.

Add to the factors of sociological and technical growth things such
as intense personal experiences, cultural flavor, preconceived notions,
"old sayings," etc., and you can quickly see how this adds up to a large
assortment of associations for any one item or circumstance. It should
be noted at this point that I do not believe symbols only come to us in
dreams. Awake, meditating, or asleep, if something or someone needs to
make itself known for your betterment, it will! The question is whether
you take notice or not.

In the interest of not over-spiritualizing the mundane, it is important to balance this idea with the realization that not every animal you
happen across or every odd sneeze is going to have metaphysical significance. To use a rather colorful contemporary phrase, "shit happens."
There are going to be moments in our lives when a stray piece of energy
wanders our way and we trip on the sidewalk or find a five-dollar bill.
There will also be moments when we can get close to a squirrel or other
animal. My point is that we have to live in tune with life enough to
know what is happenstance and what we should take to heart.

If you are not familiar with sympathetic magic, you might wonder
at this point what function symbols can have for your personal magical
work other than interpretive value. The applications can be almost as
varied as your imagination will allow. From dream interpretation and
meditative insight to visualization, representative magics are very powerful. The key to working with them well, though, is a strong personal
association with the symbol employed. For example, the next time you
need to improve your communications with someone, try using the
phone as the focus for your spell or visualization. For most people the

immediate relationship between telephones and personal discussions is enough for a solid, usable magical connection. Another example might be using an airplane in im-magic when you need movement in your life.

With this in mind, I have listed below several symbols and interpretations in alphabetical order. This is not a complete list, and ultimately what you perceive as being important in your experience is far more significant that anything I can share with you. This list should therefore act as a guide only. I have also included some ideas on spells and rituals to which your own personal chants, incantations, and creativity can be added to give that special personal flair and empowerment.

OBJECTS

Airplane	Movement, air element; to bring something into your life or move it away. Visualizations work well, but for a more specific focus, make a paper airplane and write the purpose of your spell on the side of it. Float the plane in the appropriate direction,[1] adding the significance of a particular prevalent wind to empower the spell.
Answering machine	Annoyance, not getting through to someone, missed connections, any communication spell. If you wish to reach someone, place their name underneath your machine and scribe a pentagram in the air three times above it. Focus your mental energy on bridging the gap between you and them. If your discourse has been dissenting with this individual, I suggest using a banishing pentagram to release negativity before you call them again.[2]
Arcade	Temptation, distraction. If you have been feeling inattentive to something you need to do, try placing a game token which you have blessed and charged for stamina on your altar, or better yet, on the project itself. This is a way of taking your focus away from "playing" to putting that energy to more positive uses.

Armor	Protection, slowed movement, pending battles. Best used for visualizations. Put a helmet of white light on when feeling mentally stressed or psychically attacked. A breast plate may be donned to shield your heart, and take up a sword when you need to cut through and find truth.
Arrow	Warning, messages, directions, the warrior spirit. An upward pointing arrow is usually a positive sign, while a downward one indicates final judgment falling.
Atom	Energy, strong bonds, change. Good for a visualization to increase creative flow, bringing power into yourself while still retaining balance. In this instance, see yourself as the nucleus of an atom. As the protons and neutrons swirl around you they increase your auric energy, which can then be directed towards your magical workings.
Back door	Sneakiness, beating around the bush, indirect meanings, caution.
Balloon	Hot air, inflated ego or ideas, need to ground yourself. As you blow up a balloon, allow excess vanity or flighty notions to pour into it. Take this out into the wind and pop it, allowing the winds to carry it to a landing spot. Take a little soil from this area and pot it with the balloon and a flowering plant to help keep one foot on the ground.
Baby	Innocence, new beginnings, possible financial burdens, the need for restraint.
Bank	Security, financial matters of any kind, savings. For aid with money flow, place a piece of silver in the bottom of your bank where it will be undisturbed. Leave the bank near a green candle which can be lit once a week for three hours, strongly visualizing your need, until it is met.
Bar	Social interaction, secrets, deception, relationships.

Barbecue grill	Change, family, gatherings. If you need to change something in your life, write it down on paper and burn it away with the charcoal. This will also act as a purifier, sending your desires to the wind with the smoke.
Basketball	Feeling jumpy, need to rise above seemingly impossible odds. For a spell, write your need on the side of a basketball. Concentrate on whatever you feel will solve that situation while shooting hoops. When you finally make a shot, stop, wipe off the basketball, and relax, allowing your athletic energy to work for you.
Beans	Hot air, half-truths, people being two-faced.
Bed	Rest, security, sensuality.
Black sheep	Guilt, feeling left out or uncomfortable.
Bomb	Destruction, drastic change which is frequently not positive, anger which needs control, lack of subtlety. For visualizations, bombs can be used to clear away barriers.
Book bag	Education, burdens, the mind. If feeling unusually encumbered by circumstances, envision the problems being packed neatly into a book bag, laying this down, then calmly walking away, leaving them behind you.
Boots	Indirectness, secrecy, difficult progress, protection from rough weather.
Bottles	Full bottles are always positive, especially in matters of relationships. If it is half full, check to see what is missing. If it is empty, there is nothing good for you in this situation. Float a small glass bottle with a wish in any moving water source, allowing the waves to carry it to the intended destination.
Brick walls	Overlooking the obvious, lack of attention, hidden matters, blocked progress (often from within). Excellent for visualizations for coping with fear, obstruction, or anything which you feel impedes your forward movement.

Bridge	Overcoming difficulties, positive change, life transformations, passages, endings and beginnings. When you want to leave something behind you, the visualization of "burning the bridge" is very effective.
Bubbles	Lightness, unburdening, possible warning of lack of thought. If you feel sad, pour those feelings into a soap bubble and let it float away!
Buddha	Meditation, contemplation, peacefulness, drawing towards Eastern mysticism. Legend tells us that if you rub the Buddha's belly, luck will come your way.
Cake	Prosperity, sometimes at someone else's expense; dualities, selfishness, celebrations. Bake a nutcake, naming the nuts after your personal needs. As the cake rises the magical energy is released, and when eaten you internalize that power.
Calculator	Financial matters, money under scrutiny, audits, the need to verify your sources.
California	The Sun's energy, free thinking, progress, need for stable foundations. Use a picture of California as part of any warm-weather ritual, drawing the picture closer to you via an attached string to help bring the sun around.
Camera	Surprise, sudden awareness, special occasions, possible entrapment, travel. Film will often capture pictures of spirits, faeries, and other "supernatural" creatures even without your notice. When you have a little film you want to use up, go to a favorite natural setting, and simply relax. Welcome any nature spirits to the location, then take a few pictures and see what develops!
Car	Movement, enjoyment, job; a car horn by contrast is often anger, noise, or blockage.
Chocolate	Magic involving the senses, cravings, dietary changes, pleasurable pursuits. Carob is an appropriate substitute.

Clock radio	Any spells involving time. With an alarm, it is trying to get you motivated or alert you to missed opportunity. If you are working a spell to help bring any project to fruition, set a wind-up alarm clock to go off at the end of the spell, sounding that message from your sacred space to the God/dess.
Clothes line	The element of air, any string or rope magics, spells or rituals for freshness and renewal. To bind gossip, hang the name of the instigator outside by clothes pins, binding them to the rope, and allowing the winds of truth to work for you.
Computer	Focus, memory, positive use of technology. A great place to keep your dream log or Book of Shadows. (See also Chapter Seven.)
Condominium	A modern-day castle. Watch your money flow, make sure you build on strong foundations.
Condoms	Protection, wise choices, sexuality, modern morality. Any time a couple chooses to invoke the Great Rite, prudence suggests proper birth control is also a good idea in any form. This may seem overly mundane, but it is responsible magical action.
Confetti	Celebration, a well-earned day off. Sometimes it is a good release to tear up some paper and scatter it merrily to the winds, allowing yourself to be refreshed by the air and joy of the activity.
Crockpot	The perfect tool for the kitchen Witch to slowly stir up culinary magics with. From sauces to pot roast, soup, and stew, visualize your magical energy moving clockwise 'round the pot until the meal is cooked, then enjoy!
Dagger (sharp knife)	Separation, cutting words, male energy. Great for scribing pentagrams for protection in the air,[3] opening, closing, and casting circles.
Dam	Blocked or stored creativity, water element. If you need to release imaginative energy in your

life, visualize it behind the dam wall, then break down the barrier and receive the fresh flow!

Doorbell

Guests, news. Ring it three times a day, each time envisioning your tidings coming closer. The usual span for this spell to take effect is in sets of three,[4] depending on what you are waiting to hear about. Most often three days or weeks, but some more difficult circumstances may require months for the magic to work. If you do not have a doorbell, any hand-held bell may substitute.

Doughnut

Distraction, attention in wrong place, fellowship. If you are missing a friend, set a place for them at the table, setting out tea and doughnuts, and lighting a candle in their memory. Usually not long thereafter you will hear from them.

Dryer

Air element, easing burdens, light, airy feelings, freshness. Toss your clothes in here on a cold winter day before putting them on to feel warm and relaxed. Add a few dry herbs for cleansing and protection, not to mention a lovely scent.

Drum

Warnings and announcements, any magic dealing with cycles or rhythms. Wonderful for dance, chanting, centering. Allow the energy of the beat to naturally grow and diminish with your working. Also makes an interesting alarm clock for Pagan festivals, if you can run fast enough!

Eclipse

Obscured vision, transitions, in between the worlds. One application of a visualization is for a group setting. Begin the circle by a guided meditation of the first part of an eclipse. Use the moon for feminine energy and the sun for masculine, depending on your needs or the celebration being performed. Once the leader has brought the group to the place where they visualize a full eclipse, the regular workings of the circle can begin (e.g., at this point the group is mentally attuned with the "out of place, out of time" ambiance of magical circles). Conversely, close the circle by finishing the visualization and grounding the energy.

Electrical outlet/lines	Power, connections. If you are very tired, try seeing yourself plugged into an outlet which pours radiant, refreshing light into your body.
False teeth	Insecurity, false first impressions, something hidden or misrepresented.
Fan	Air element, refreshing, cooling off, winds of change. An excellent substitute indoors for various directional winds when the weather outside is prohibitive.
Feathers	Laughter, a well-received gift, messages, honesty. If owl feathers come to you, you need to be more forthright with yourself. Feathers can carry your wishes on the wind, or they can be blessed and placed under a pillow to ensure restful sleep. If carried in your medicine pouch, they will help keep your mood light.
Fence	Protection, interrupted communications, privacy. Visualize fences of solid light around anything you wish to keep safe.
Filing cabinet	Need for organization, cleaning out of old matters, sorting out priorities. I have one in my house just to keep track of good magical information and sources filed by subject matter.
Fireworks	Inspiration, creativity, sensuality. When experiencing an artistic blockage, try visualizing small fireworks exploding from your pen, paint brush, or even from the palm of your hand. Feel the strength of the energy flowing from within you, then try to approach your project again.
Food processor	Change of form or state, making things conform to a particular size or image. An excellent tool for the modern herbalist.
Football	Pass on this situation or tackle it head on. Stop pussyfooting around. If you hope to make progress in a specific situation, use water-soluble

markers and write the information on an old football. Next, go to an open field and focus on your desire, allowing that energy to move down your arm. Finally, throw the ball as hard as you can, releasing your magical energy with it. You can go pick up the ball later.

Game shows The wheel of fortune in Tarot, forces of luck, and influence of the Fates figures highly now.

Garlic This has long been, and still is, a protective symbol. Grow some garlic and make a braid for your kitchen to protect your home and for use in cooking.

Glue gun Quick fixes, "stick-to-itive-ness," repairs needed. When you need a fast piece of ritual garb, you can use a glue gun instead of a sewing machine to affix the seams. You can always improve the design later.

Grain Prosperity, faith, sustenance. Keep some grain on your altar to share with any in need and you will never go hungry. Good for any ritual which calls for a token offering of first fruits, or during harvest season.

Greenhouse Protection against natural elements, warmth, and growth. When you desire spiritual progress, visualize yourself in the center of a greenhouse, rooted in rich, damp soil, with your arms reaching like branches to the sky. Feel the radiance of the sun as it moves down through you, nourishing the center of your being. Stay in this light until you feel refreshed, whole, and full of clean energy.

Gun Anger, lack of control or focus, bitterness, or the possible hold-up of an expected situation.

Hair net Constraint, restrictions, control, work. In the realms of a magic circle, hair nets can serve two functions. First, they can keep hair neatly away from open flames. Second, an old legend says that a witch's power is increased if they loose their hair during a spell. Hair nets are easy to remove to test the accuracy of this bit of lore!

Hair piece — Humor, partial honesty, attention to superficial.

Hamper — Pay attention to signals which warn of gossip or the need for cleansing. If you have a tense day, toss your anxiety into the hamper with your clothes and leave it there.

Handcuffs — Good in any visualization for binding spells. For example you may wish to have a poppet or other item which can be named after an individual who has done you harm. Place the handcuffs around this item to symbolically keep them from harming you again. This is not a manipulative spell, but an impeding one.

Hands — Healing work, sharing, companionship, assistance. If you do not have the time for a ritual bath, it is a nice gesture to rinse your hands in scented water before magical work as a symbol of cleansing and pure motives.

Hard hat — Protection, especially for the mind.

High heels — Change in perspective, outer appearances, festive occasions.

Hockey puck — You are getting the short end of the stick in a situation which may be close to violent in nature. Slippery ground slows footing.

Incense — Interest in spiritual realms, meditation, quiet time. Your choice of incense will vary according to the situation at hand. Look to Chapter Six for details on herbs to use, and Chapter Seven for specific recipes.

Jerusalem — Religious struggle, search for spirituality, holiness, history. Use the Star of David as a less noticeable alternative to the pentagram.

Keyhole — Snooping, gossip, embarrassing information, revealing secrets. Sometimes at junk shops you can find old decorative keyholes which can be held up to your eye and used for scrying.

Keys	Doors opening, new beginnings, movement, travel. Use keys as components in spells involving interviews, new homes, and other lifestyle changes. After your spell, carry the key with you to keep the doors in your life open.
Laboratory	Study, science, close examination of facts.
Lamps	If lit, new insights and understanding. If dark, the need for examination and rethinking your options. See also Chapter Seven for specific spells employing lamps.
Lawn mower	Cutting away old, outgrown ideas and ways. Name your lawn after habits you wish to get rid of, and allow the blades to cleanly swipe them away. You can then put that energy to good use by collecting the scraps for compost!
Laser	Accuracy, the cutting edge, clarity (especially visual).
Lock	Closed paths, places where you are not ready to go, fears. Good for imagery in binding spells/rituals.[5]
Lottery ticket	Temptation, luck, fate, money matters. While I don't recommend it, there are many people who use numerology and various psychic techniques to pick lottery numbers to improve their finances. Hard work is probably far more reliable, but once in a while it can't hurt to try as long as you keep things (like your family budget) in proper perspective.
Meteor	Flash of inspiration, warning against using too much energy, burning out. If you need drastic modifications, envision a meteor bearing transformation for your life in its tail. You may actually want to see it spelling out words as it moves your way. When it passes you, bring yourself into the visualization and let the light of the tail cleanse you and plant the seeds of change.
Microfilm	Attention to detail, nit-picking, also may indicate a personal gift of Sight[6] which needs to be developed.

Microscope | The feeling of being small or insignificant, a close examination of the self with respect to the world. May be a part of any spell or ritual where you wish to make problems "smaller." For money spells, however, a coin may be placed on the plate while you look through the eyepiece to "enlarge" your gains.

Moon | The significance of moon phases is fairly well known to magic. In the Tarot, the moon card represents something hidden. In a dream or meditative setting it could indicate the need to focus on the feminine, intuitive nature. The moon as a tool for visualization in any matters of healing or inspiration is excellent to employ.

Neon lights | Too much attention to self, being "starry-eyed."

Nuclear reactor | Intense energy to the point of being dangerous; consider the motives of your magic. A reminder to use power responsibly.

Nylons | Support, appearances. Old nylons may be cleaned and used to steep herbs for teas and tinctures. They also make good cleaners for brushes, stuffing for herb pillows, etc.

Olympic torch | Victory, the spirit of cooperation, energy of youth, the element of fire. Envision yourself carrying one to your desired goal's completion!

Parachute | A need to bail out of a situation gracefully, find an element of freedom, or as a focus for any air spells. In this scenario, if you can get a hold of old parachute cord or fabric you can tie the cord to a tree with knots of fabric for three wishes. When the wind naturally blows the knots free, it releases your wish to begin working.

Pizza | Slice of life, gatherings, sharing, the wheel of fortune. Makes a great post-ritual snack, with toppings that can be changed to suit your celebration. For example, you could add a little garlic and basil to the sauce, and top the pizza with olives for love, protection, and wisdom.

Planets	Cycles, dreams, outside influences. When you need perspective or are trying to develop a "one world" mindset, visualize yourself standing on another planet looking back on the earth. From here, you can also see yourself as part of the universe!
Pollution	Awareness, cleansing, need to reconnect with nature.
Rainforest	Ecology, healing Gaia, earth-related spells, water.
Red pens	Brooding over mistakes, self-correction, or harsh correction from another. A good tool to use as a focus or component to magic involving self-improvement and introspection.
Red tape	No positive progress, stalling, and run-arounds. Any magic which pertains to delays, restriction, or binding. To release yourself from obstructions, tie a red tape around yourself, then cut it off during your ritual as a sign of freedom.
Remote control	Power, possible manipulation, need for regulation or supervision, life on "pause." To me, one of the greatest uses for this device is to turn off the television for a while and read a good magical book instead!
Rocket	Exploration, rapid growth, movement. Paint the name of your greatest goal on the side of your imaginary rocket and watch it take off!
Rune	Specific to each country of origin, runes in general deal with the sensitive, psychic, and magical energy. Each rune may be used as spell components, amulets, talismans, etc., as appropriate to its interpretation. See more information on runes in Chapter Seven.
RV	Vacation, rest, a haven, possible travel.
Satellite dish	Sense of hearing. If pointed away it means you are not heeding good advice. Pointed towards you indicates receptivity to new ideas. Use it turned to an appropriate direction in visualizations to help guide your magical energy.

Scales	Balance, weight loss, considering your options. For the latter, even bathroom scales will work simply by placing a list of all your choices on the scale and allowing them to be weighed by the fates. Release this energy to the winds, then meditate on your decision to see what the breeze carries back to you for perspectives.
Scissors	Cut away anything, negative feelings, separation, change, creativity. When you wish to disengage something from yourself, attach a symbol of it to you by string, and cut it free with scissors during your ritual work. This icon can then be buried to signify the death of that connection.
Smoke	Signals, communication, health matters, cleansing. Allow the smoke of incense to float through your home to clean away negative energy and increase protection. Send smoke to the winds to carry a message to an old friend.
Space station	Adventures, new frontiers, possibly a new job or home.
Sports car	Life in the fast lane, a warning to slow down and watch more carefully. You are moving too quickly to notice important lessons and opportunities life is offering.
Stereo speakers	Too many opinions, need for focus and clarity. Take some time alone to listen to your own heart. During meditation, they can have a very positive effect by setting them up on each side of you with soft music playing. The underlying rhythm helps bring relaxation and attunement to your own physical cadences.
Synthesizer	Be like the chameleon and know how to blend with your surroundings. Any magic involving flexibility and change.
Tarot	Like the runes, specific to each card. The whole deck is a symbol of divination, intuition, and the focusing of psychic energy. For information

on using the Tarot for magic, see *Tarot Spells* by
Janina Renee, Llewellyn Publications, and
Chapter Seven.

Telescope   New horizons, new perspectives. A higher outlook for your personal and/or spiritual life. New
understanding of your place in the universe.
Time travel.

Television   The media, distraction, the family, enjoyment.
When turned off, the television screen makes a
good scrying surface.

Test tubes   Study, health, fertility, sterile atmosphere. For a
family desiring a child, place the wish in a test
tube on your altar with a stuffed bunny before
your rituals for conception or before your pregnancy tests.

Tissues   Sorrow, cleansing, possible sickness. In the
winter, colored tissues scented with essential oil
can be used to make paper flowers for your
altar and Yule tree, bringing a little springtime
to long, cold days.

Toothbrush   Hygiene, care of self, cleansing. For magic, an
old toothbrush functions well to clean silver
jewelry and tools, especially those which are
intricate in nature. It is soft, pliable, and can
reach the little spots a cloth can't.

Trash can   Waste, prudence, cleansing. Good place to
dump emotional garbage.

Typewriter   Repetitive motion, unbroken cycles, habits. If
you don't want to hand-write spells and rituals,
as you type them up allow magical energy to
flow through your fingertips into each key
through visualization. Then, anoint your paper
with a hint of essential oil, so that as it is read
the power under the words will be released to
the room.

Video player   Need to review a problem or situation with
close scrutiny. On fast forward, you are moving
too quickly without wisdom. On slow motion,

you are being overly cautious, allowing something to impede your forward movement or growth.

Wheel	Cycles, the World card in the Tarot, the Arthurian round table, and wheel of fortune. Any magic involving fate or luck. Coins are appropriate substitutes.
Whirlpool	Blending, movement, the element of water, relaxation and healing. Whirlpools are often used by individuals adept in rebirthings.[7] An excellent place to work any type of ritual for inspiration, renewed health, etc.
Windmill	Natural energy, return to basics, air magic.
Zodiac	The various signs can be employed in magic as a focus or component, but for interpretation it usually speaks to us of relationships which are not totally honest, a need to look to others for a little perspective.

ANIMALS/INSECTS

The use of animal symbolism (both real and mythical) is very old, based on the idea that the God/dess can be best understood through His/Her supreme creation — nature. In many cultures animal spirits are considered companions to the human soul to help it learn and grow. These spirits are often called power animals, or totems. Outside of the spiritual realm, many Witches have special pets, known as familiars, with whom they develop a unique empathic relationship.

In considering ways to employ animal symbolism in your rituals, some immediate applications come to mind. First, pictures or statues of animals can stand guard at the four major points of our Circles as representations of the directions and elements. Second, connecting with animal spirits through visualization and meditation is often very educational and enlightening. They offer us insights into our more carnal characteristics and the natural world which we might not normally acquire ourselves. Finally, when they appear to us in dreams or visions we can employ the interpretation of attributes to help clarify such experiences more definitively as they apply to our lives today.

Bee	Sweet things in life, pleasure, germination, caution against getting "stung." The bee was sacred to Venus (the Goddess of love and fertility) and is often considered a symbol of wisdom because of the queen bee's many followers.
Beetle	The scarab of Egypt has become the icon of new life, truth, regeneration, virility, courage, and the sun's energy.
Butterfly	Metamorphosis, the human soul, element of air. The butterfly has a body made of three parts, representing the three-fold nature of both humanity and the Divine. To help center yourself, try visualizing yourself as a larvae within a cocoon slowly being transformed into the butterfly, whose flight can free you from burdens.
Cat	Sacred to Bast, the Egyptian cat Goddess, the cat is symbolic of natural forces, eternity, balance, and divine motion.
Dog	Service to others, discipleship, faithfulness, transcendence, and the power of listening closely.
Dove	Oracles and prophets, redemption, peace and purity.
Dolphin	Ecology, element of water, joy, spirituality, rescue. The breath and rhythm of life itself.
Dragonfly	Dreams, luck, ancient memories and energy, the art of magic and the winds of change.
Eagle	Sun or Great Spirit in flight, healing, grace, tests, the time of initiation, hard work, and the ability to soar above the mundane. Fly with the eagle when you need refreshed perspective for a new endeavor.
Fish	Often associated with the world on a spiritual level, and various savior figures in history. Oannes was the fish man of Babylonia, the first incarnation of Vishnu was born of a fish, and the loaves and fishes of Christ speak of ethereal food. It is also the symbol of good fortune (bringing in full nets) and contentment.

Frog	Cleansing, water, fluidity. Refreshment and purification. In some Native American traditions, the shaman would pour water out of his mouth while visualizing the frog to prepare and cleans himself for ritual work.
Hawk	Vital breath. Ra, the Egyptian sun God, was often depicted with head of a hawk. Akin to Mercury because of speed, it is the creature of observations, signals, perspective, intuition, and especially attention to detail.
Hummingbird	Duality, flexibility, love charms (the feathers), joy and love of beauty, the nectar of life itself, bursts of energy.
Lion	Solar energy, spiritual life of humankind, vigilance, protection.
Lizard	Messengers of the gods, associated with Mercury. Review your dreams before bringing them into reality. Facing fears and hopes with balanced outlooks.
Owl	The ancient mysteries, wisdom, truth. The companion to Athena, also a sign of clairvoyance and insight into hidden matters.
Otter	Fun, energy of joy, play, elements of earth and water, healthy curiosity.
Phoenix	Before the phoenix was ready to die it would make a nest of incense and flames, and has thus become the symbol of new life, light, and resurrection.
Peacock	Beauty, aspiration, wisdom, immortality and sometimes false pride. The peacock was sacred to Thoth, a god of learning.
Scorpion	Among ancient Pagan traditions, some initiation ceremonies took place during the sign of Scorpio because it symbolized the fires of illumination. The Scorpion is believed to be the protector of the rising sun, so this would aptly symbolize new beginnings, especially of a spiritual nature.

Skunk	Respect, strength, self belief and assertion.
Snake	Sacred to the temples of Delphi[8] and the Druids, also appearing as part of Hermes' staff. Snakes offer self-knowledge for good or ill. It is the symbol of growth, change, creation, and sexuality. It is fire and earth energy, the power and responsibility of leadership and balance.
Spider	Networking, traps, the fates, wheel of life, the future, and the power of creativity.
Turtle	Longevity, the world, protection, slow but steady movement forward, Goddess energy, grounding. The world has been depicted as moving through space on the back of a turtle.
Unicorn	The horn of this mythic beast was right over the third eye as a sign of its insight. It is the icon of our inner nature, purity, defense, and innocence.
Whale	Age, ancient wisdom, the crone, other-worldness, connection with water and air. Clairaudience, telepathy, universal mind, and languages. To develop this universal outlook, be like Jonah and go into the center of the whale and let it become your teacher.

TREES

When we look at a tree, we think immediately of foundations, roots, and grounding. The long life of these beautiful plants is a standing reminder to us of strength, perseverance, and durability. For urban magic, I suggest applying trees in several ways. First, you can go and sit or stand under them during meditation (if there is one nearby). If not, perhaps you can acquire an indoor tree or bush such as the Japanese bonsai.

Second, you can imagine certain types of trees during visualization to help connect with their specific energies and draw some life-giving "sap" into your own life. Third, you can consider collecting the leaves or

fallen branches of various trees to keep for decorations at different seasonal observations, as appropriate. These same leaves and woods can
function very well as components in incenses and oils, too. In this case,
it is always good to collect only parts of the tree which it has already
released to the Earth, with a thankful heart.

Apple	Healing, knowledge, home of the unicorn. When in full bloom, the apple tree is the symbol of success. Collect the buds for spring gatherings and any time you wish to bring fruitfulness to your magical workings.
Birch	The Lady of the Woods, this tree is the life of the land. It is very shamanistic, dealing with the spirit of Gaia, balance, and getting rid of old ideas no longer suitable to new realities.
Cedar	Inner potential, cleansing, auric work, and healing. One of the best woods to act as a base in incense, it purifies magical space very well.
Elm	A faerie tree, the elm has always stood for the ability to overcome our weaknesses and make them into strengths.
Fig	The Buddha found enlightenment under a fig tree, and you may do likewise. This tree seems to awaken the intuitive nature, release blockage, and gives birth to creative forces within.
Hazel	The branches of a hazel tree are often used to form dowsing rods and may also make excellent magical wands. It is a tree of peace, wisdom, and divination.
Maple	Balance, grounding of magical energy, aspirations. At the end of a ritual, try visualizing yourself underneath the boughs of a great maple tree and pouring your excess magical energy into its roots.
Redwood	Time, immortality, perspective, imagination, and soothing are all part of this wood's nature. Standing in front of one, you can not help but for a moment feel a part of eternity.

Rowan   The senses, protection, developing familiars, Goddess energy, the muse, vision, and elemental guides can be found in the branches of this tree. It has long been used by magicians and is an excellent place to perform almost any ritual. Rowan wood makes for good magical tools.

Walnut   A good tree to combine with the animal symbol of the butterfly. This is the spirit freed and the cycles of our lives. If the tree itself is not available, the fruit is perfectly appropriate.

FLOWERS

For this section of the book, I have confined the list of flowers to those which are interesting, functional for modern magical practices, and have not already been covered in Chapter Six.

Plants lend a number of dimensions to magical work, from being able to utilize them as ingredients for incense, anointing oil, and potion preparations, to employing their fragrance for aromatherapy and decorating our sacred space with their natural beauty. In meditation you can don the scents of various flowers to help improve your concentration according to your goals. In visualizations try seeing yourself in the center of a particular bloom, drawing the spiritual nectar they embody into yourself.

Buttercup   A flower of joy and youth, the buttercup speaks to us of refreshed vision, new directions, self-worth, and understanding.

Clover   Luck, love, fidelity; a good flower for protecting pets and to use in consecrating ritual tools. This particular plant represents the mischievous spirit of the Faerie folk.

Daisy   Awareness, nature spirits, often associated with the Dryads, creativity, and love. Also somewhat related to love divination from the old tradition of plucking petals.

Foxglove   This plant was cultivated in 1000 BC as a medicinal flower; however, for modern magicians it is best employed if you want to have the vision to see the world of the fey.

Gardenia	Action, purpose, protection, and well-being. The fragrance can improve empathic abilities and draw good spirits into a ritual space.
Heather	An excellent flower for any herbalist to keep in the house to help them connect with that energy. It is good for grounding, beauty, and spiritual transformation.
Iris	The Goddess of the Rainbow, the iris is a flower of great potency for creative endeavors. It is the flower of inspiration and rebirth.
Lilac	Clarity, productivity, and spiritual balance. Lilac is an excellent scent to use for any past-life work.
Lotus	Creativity, spiritual energy; often used to symbolize the chakras. Growth, endeavor, the plane of the Masters, visionary states, harmony, and serenity.
Morning glory	The dawn of a new day, new beginnings, and a flower of spontaneity. Greet your mornings like the blossom of this plant, opening wide to the warmth of the sun to be renewed.
Periwinkle	The flower of healers and the wise, a good blossom to add to charms for protection, rebirth, love, and healing.
Snapdragon	The ancient power of dragonkind is in this flower. Good for guidance, strength, expression, and protection.
Tulip	Success, trust, discernment, and grounding.
Violet	A blossom of simplicity, peace, and stillness, the violet is sacred to the faeries. Because of this its scent is very good when employed to increase psychic awareness.
Zinnia	The power of youth, joy, and the simple pleasures often overlooked. Endurance through humor and a positive attitude.

COLORS

There are many symbols which we can use to tap portions of our mind not commonly reached by daily activity. With colors, we can quickly implement their ascribed characteristics to our magical space through candles, altar cloths, robes, and even the pigments of incense used. On a different level, colors can easily be applied in visualizations to aid and focus our awareness. One such example might be found with blue. As the color of tranquility, in your mind's eye you might like to see waves of blue light rolling over you in soft, rocking pulses to help bring relaxation.

As with any other symbol, please remember that the personal meaning is most important to how you finally employ one or any combination of colors for a specific magical effect. To determine this for yourself, just consider what first comes to mind when you think of that particular shade. This initial response, if noted, will be helpful in your creative use of sympathetic magics.

Black
Black represents the presence of all light. To some people its absorbent qualities make it a color of protection with regard to magical items. However, when black spots or clouds can be seen in a person's auric energy it is often an indication of sickness, tension, or other difficulty. Because of this dichotomy, when the color black appears in your dreams or visions you may have to consider your own feelings about it. Black is the color of night and dreams, the shadows of our own being, mourning, and endings which may or may not be for the better.

Blue
The throat chakra and sign of Capricorn, blue is the color of water. It a lazy, quiet, peaceful tone for meditation. If you want to know if a person is telling the truth, watch for blue in their aura. A good color for inspiration, healing, and refreshment.

Green
Associated with the heart chakra and sign of Cancer, green is an earth and water color. It is cool, energetic, and an indicator of growth and fruitful labors. A good pigment for money-

related magic and getting in touch with nature.

Orange

The golden orange of Leo, located near the stomach chakra. Attuned to warmth, friendship, plenty, the season of autumn, and fire. Good to use in magic which deals with kinship or prosperity.

Purple

The color of the psychic realms, purple is aligned to the crown chakra or third eye. It corresponds to the signs of Virgo, Sagittarius, and Gemini. This is a soft, sweet color which raises energy and power in any room. Good for invocations, supplication, and meditation.

Red

Most often associated with blood, red is the color of life, fire, love, anger, danger, and strength. It is considered aligned with the base chakra in the pelvic region, and is often near our center of gravity. Red is a good color for magic pertaining to vitality, courage, cleansing, and drastic change, and is related to the signs of Aries and Scorpio.

Yellow

Just below the heart chakra in the chest, yellow works well with the signs of Libra and Taurus, being a summery hue full of light, charm, and exhilaration. It is also a color which can indicate sickness or jealousy. In magic, yellow is best used for empowering talismans, increasing energy, and inspiration. A pale yellow is a good color for meditation to help bring restful sleep.

White

Known to indicate peace and surrender, white is used almost universally as the color of protection and positive magic. White light visualizations are used for everything from casting a circle to auric healing work. Magical items are often wrapped in white cloth to shield them from unwanted energies.

CRYSTALS

Crystals have been used for talismans and amulets in many ancient civilizations. The most notable example is the scarab of Egypt, but this tradition continues to evidence itself today in the form of birthstones, crystals as healing aids, in meditation, and much more.

For your own purposes, crystals are nice to just have around the house because of their natural, simple beauty. They may be charged with protection or any type of desired magical energy, soaked in water to make "gem elixirs" (the soaking is believed to draw the attribute of the stone into the water, which is then consumed to internalize that energy), placed on the third eye to aid meditative states, etc.

If you can not find or afford crystals, consider getting a candle of a similar color (some magical shops sell candles with ground crystals in them) to substitute. Other appropriate surrogates for crystals can include, but are certainly not limited to, flowers, pieces of tinted cloth, paints, colored glass, and ribbons. The stones noted here are ones which are fairly inexpensive and easy to obtain.

Amber	Often used as medicinal amulets, these stones are sometimes thought to house spirits. In ancient lore, the amber was formed from the liquid tears of a setting sun, and is frequently carved in the forms of animals to bring increased energy to the final product.
Amethyst	This stone has long been associated with our more rowdy nature in that it is supposed to help control evil thoughts and prevent drunkenness. If carried by a leader, its energies improve the ability to make shrewd decisions and will give increased protection for victorious outcomes in any situation.
Beryl	A stone of friendship, strength, and a quick mind, beryl is best used to reawaken lost love in marriage. For this, the stone might be best given as a gift, and worn close to the heart.
Carnelian	Luck, protection, dignity, and hope. The carnelian, when made into a gem elixir, should be drunk before speeches to bring courage and boldness to your words. The prophet

Mohammed was believed to have worn this stone on his small finger. If placed in the wall of a home or into a door frame, it should protect all who dwell within.

Chrysolite

For best results in magic this stone should be set in gold, especially to dispel nightmares and beings which dwell in shadow-times. Chrysolite is good for banishing undesired enchantments and restoring personal energy.

Coral

This gift of the sea may be used to settle the mind, increase vigor, and help draw wisdom into your life. If used in a talisman, the coral must remain unbroken to retain its power. If it breaks, return the pieces to the sea with thanksgiving and look for another piece to use instead.

Gypsum

Known in Egypt to be carved in the form of eggs, this is a stone of protection, purity, and good fortune. It is very soft, and may be scratched off easily for use in candles, oils, and incense preparations with just a fingernail!

Hematite

Before you face a difficult struggle, rub your body with hematite to bring success. It is an excellent stone to carry any time you have legal matters on the horizon.

Jade

In China, this is a popular stone for young couples and is believed to promote health, love, and fertility. It has even been carved into chimes for use in court and religious ceremonies. In magic, these traits may apply, along with protection for children and as a gift in a coming of age rite. For the latter, it is believed that handling the stone frequently will insure longevity.

Lodestone

Virtue, true love, power. Lodestone, because of its magnetic ability, has been believed to protect against malignant spirits and draw only positive things into one's life.

Moonstone	The sacred stone of India, a crystal of luck — especially for lovers. When the moon is full, put a clear moonstone in your mouth while meditating to help bring spiritual insight and knowledge.
Turquoise	Protection from falling, keeping yourself on time. If you see your face in the surface of turquoise during a full moon, it is a sign of good luck. This stone is good for healers, and has often been fashioned to please guardian spirits of animals.

Stone oracles may be made by collecting one stone of each type desired, preferably those which are close to the same size and shape, and keeping them in a pouch as you might a set of runes. When you have a question, focus on it and draw one stone from your bag. Look up the significance of that crystal on this list or in alternative books for your reading. This basic technique can be expanded to almost any layout which is done with runes. For some reason readings of one, three, and five stones seem to yield the best results for me.

With the other symbols mentioned in this chapter, an alternative exists. For this, take equal sized pieces of strong paper or cardboard and place pictures of the items listed above on it (or better yet, create your own list to work from). When finished, shuffle these as you might a Tarot deck, focusing on your question, then pull a card and read your interpretation. Any traditional Tarot spread can be used for this method, with very interesting personalized outcomes because of the energy you have given to creating the oracle. For more ideas on developing your own rune sets and Tarot cards, see Chapter Seven.

SUMMARY

As you can see by glancing at this chapter, this list embodies only a brief glimpse of all the symbols we could use for modern magic. A study of this kind could fill volumes with as much variety as their are people on this planet! The idea behind sympathetic magic is to find among the thousands of items you could use those few which really provide a deep personal reaction, the energy of which can then be directed for your spells and celebrations.

If you are interested in exploring symbolism further, just stop and look at the world around you. You do not need hundreds of books to see what is right before your eyes; there is potential for creative, timeless magic every day.

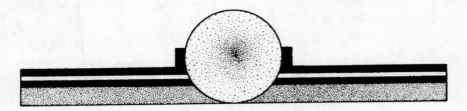

NOTES TO CHAPTER 8

1. In magic, each of the four directions has a specific significance which can be used during spells and rituals to help amplify the energy. The same principle holds true for the winds which come from those directions, although air is not the most dependable element to work with.

    ○ The East is the direction of the rising sun, the element of air, and the season of spring. It represents the mental nature and all types of learning. It is a good bearing to work with for new endeavors, especially those of changing modes of thought.

    ○ The South is where fire is born. It is the noonday sun in summertime which brings new energy to the earth. This is the direction of life-forces, determination, conviction, and purification. The fires of the South can also mean healing, but are often drastic in nature, destroying to rebuild.

○ West is traditionally the direction of water, on whose blue-grey waves move the twilight and the season of autumn. Here we find our feelings, intuition, fertility, and healing. Humanity was born of water, and because of this the West is a source of inspiration and comfort.

○ Finally, the North usually represents the Earth, winter, and midnight. This is the direction of growth, financial situations, grounding, and sustenance. I say usually because there are some instances in which the urban magician may wish to change these slightly to better suit the reality of their situation. For example, if you happen to live in an area such as the South Pole, it makes more sense that North might be "fire." Or if you live on the East Coast near the ocean, East might be considered your direction of water simply because of logistics. Do whatever makes the most sense to you.

2.　A banishing pentagram is traditionally drawn as shown below:

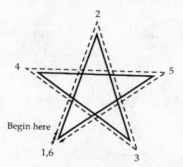

3.　A protective pentagram may be drawn as follows:

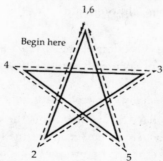

4.　Many numbers in magic are believed to have special significance. Frequently three, the number of our own triune nature and that of the Divine, was lucky. In many old folk spells the practitioner is instructed to repeat certain processes or phrases three times, or in multiples of three. The repetition is believed to strengthen the magic by adding the blessing of the numerical energy, and helping the practitioner to focus more strongly on the goal.

5. *Binding* is a means of magically impeding negative intentions and energy. It is similar in some ways to protective magic, except in this instance the security is placed very specifically around one person or group perceived as having malicious intent. This type of magic does not seek to harm the individual or group involved, but simply nullifies their efforts to harm, like a dampening field does with electrical current.

6. *The "Sight"* is a type of psychic gift which gives people enhanced visionary abilities. These talents can include, but are not limited to, a unique sensitivity to people, the ability to see into the future, and extraordinary perceptions in a wide variety of circumstances.

7. *Rebirthing* is a type of meditation and visualization technique believed to help relieve many adult stresses and misconceptions regarding the self. During this process, the participant is literally taken to the moment of their own birth. At this point the rebirther helps the participant cleanse and release any pain associated with the birth, believing this trauma can be a foundation for other emotional problems later in life.

8. Delphi is one of the oldest known oracle centers in Greece. Here, people came from near and far to seek the council of prophets who used a wide variety of methods to receive their insights. These methods included castings, lots, and scrying by water or fire.

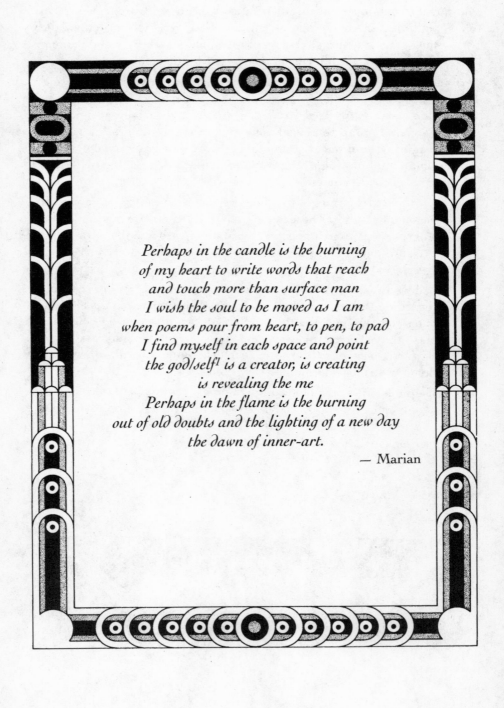

Perhaps in the candle is the burning
of my heart to write words that reach
and touch more than surface man
I wish the soul to be moved as I am
when poems pour from heart, to pen, to pad
I find myself in each space and point
the god/self[1] is a creator, is creating
is revealing the me
Perhaps in the flame is the burning
out of old doubts and the lighting of a new day
the dawn of inner-art.

— Marian

Craft Art and
the Art of Craft

The breath whose might I have invoked in song descends on me.
—Percy B. Shelley, *Adonais* LV

CRAFT ART

I truly believe that with magical knowledge and the number of practitioners growing rapidly, the importance of Craft-related art forms will also blossom. Not because it is a tool or a necessity, but because of the simple beauties and inspiration art forms bring to our lives.

Our ancestors respected and even venerated various art forms because they knew they somehow reflected something far deeper in humanity; part of the mysteries of our spiritual nature. Art has the capacity to reveal the truth when blatant facts are sometimes ignored. It can motivate, transform, communicate, and even tends to take on a life of its own.

Because of this vibrant nature to art, magical crafts can take on a whole new dimension which actually grants energy to that living spirit. By finding a medium through which we can express our Path, we have the marvelous opportunity to share magic with the world in a way that is far more commonly acceptable! Many art forms also have a longevity which allows this magical spirit to live on long after it is produced.

235

Since the well of inventiveness feeds both the expression of our magic in our Circles and our arts, the "art" and the "craft" become linked in this flow. Thereby the two can inspire one another, take root in each other, and become an essential element in a living, breathing faith which grows with not only ourselves, but our changing world.

Frequently our "art" can reveal lovely talents and personality traits we might not have been intimately aware of before. It is always most difficult to have a well-rounded perspective when it comes to the self. When given a chance for outward expression, we can suddenly step back and look at ourselves more objectively through that expression, often with surprising results. In this way, we are confronted with solid, immutable proof of the grail within,[2] given to us by our own hand!

One should be forewarned, though, that this deep internal search is not always beautiful. Revelation of our hidden natures can be quite ugly and shocking. We often try to deny the darker aspects of our soul, yet it is important to recognize these things in the light of day and cope with them honestly and constructively. Craft art affords us that opportunity; through magical art forms we can not only face ourselves, but also begin to transmute our own shadows into something positive.

As we work with magic, images and emblems become central to our thinking (see Chapter Eight). One can not study magic honestly without realizing that much of what we employ in terms of tools are really symbols for something much deeper, something which helps us connect with our spiritual fountain to release the flow of real magic for ritual and our daily living.

The more we meditate, visualize, and come to a deep abiding understanding of our Craft, the more this fountain pours out, and we discover it holds far more than just spiritual nourishment. The inner well flows with creative, intuitive energy which can be represented in many ways. The artist suddenly finds hundreds of faces epitomizing strong divine images, new histories never recorded in any book, legends and mythic beasts, and a myriad of other people and objects which lend themselves so wonderfully and uniquely to illustration. Our faith, thus, gives us the foundations to draw from, our individual traditions add flavor, and our life experience grants texture until the final artistic expression itself becomes a three-dimensional, living thing that outwardly reflects the divine spark within you!

In many ways the creation process is not unlike giving birth. For the true magical artist, a little bit of life energy goes into every stroke until the finished piece is like a child who you have tended carefully and must now release. But where to begin? How do we step back and allow the energy of the universe to communicate itself through us?

The first step is what I call "finding your voice," for lack of a better term. This voice is the manner in which you best express yourself; the medium through which people see the best aspects of your spirit. This is not an easy process. I did not find my voice until I was twenty-seven. It is funny, because as it turns out it was something I had always loved to do; write poetry. Yet, for some reason the obvious conclusion did not occur to me; that it was through this same love that I could really express my vision and share about the things I deemed important to help others.

Poetry is one of the more obvious mediums which lends itself to relating magical principles, but there are many more. The way to depict your creativity in terms of your Path are as limitless as your imagination. Painting, drawing, communication, sculpture, prose, musical instruments, song, dance, mime, jewelry making, and wood carving are all good examples, but I am sure you can think of more. More subtle types of arts include using sewing skills to make dream pillows, magical robes, or mandala quilts, or pottery to fashion ritual cups and rune sets.

An Eastern philosophy tells us that an item's use is determined not only by its shape but what it holds. In other words, by examining both perspectives we can find a balance which allows us to express magical ideals in daily living as well as our circles. For example, on the surface you may not consider herbalism an art form, yet by adding a personal touch, guided by research, you can make hundreds of magical items which will be enjoyed and treasured (see also Chapter Six). An illustration might be creating soaps with herbs of cleansing for use in ritual baths. The special energy you put into such items will not go unnoticed, and give that creation the life-essence basic to all arts!

So, look to your life. What do you enjoy doing the most? What are your hobbies? What types of things do you enjoy sharing with or teaching to others? Somewhere among this list will be a key which can help you unlock your vision of faith and share it with your world in a beautiful, gentle way.

EXERCISE 1: CREATIVITY VISUALIZATION

Lie in a comfortable position and begin breathing in an easy, connected manner. As you exhale, release all your tensions, all the problems of that day, and let them move away from you like the wind. Continue to do this until you feel peaceful and relaxed.

Next, picture yourself in some area which reflects serenity to you, perhaps a place where you played as a child or where you go when you need to retreat from the world. When you can see this area clearly in your mind's eye, allow the image to become three-dimensional. Smell the air, feel the earth beneath you, let this private inner-realm take you totally away from the mundane world to a place where you are safe and whole.

Once you feel yourself truly a part of the scene, turn and look to your left and you will see a beautiful wishing well, almost as if it appeared out of a faerie tale. It is strong, like a keep, built of stone and mortar, with a chain of silvery steel and a bucket of bent wood. This is your own creative well, the fountain which lies within each of us.

Move towards the well and let the bucket down into the clearest, crispest, coolest water you have ever seen. It is lightly blue and seems to shimmer in the light. When you have retrieved the bucket, take a little of the liquid in your hand and let it run through your fingers. Sense how soft and gentle it is, how cleansing, how powerful. Cup some of it and drink your fill. Feel how refreshing it is as it moves within to permeate each muscle and cell. This water is your strength, your magical power, your art, filling you to overflowing.

Now spill a little of the water on the ground to symbolize your own artistic ability pouring out to the world. Frequently, a flower will bloom where the water has spilled in your visualization as a signpost that your working has been successful.

Finally, whenever you are ready, replace the bucket and slowly bring yourself back to normal levels of awareness. Take some notes on your impressions, if you can; more than likely you will want to go work on your art form immediately. Because of this, you might like to have whatever tools you need completely prepared before you do the visualization, that way there is no delay in carrying the flow of creativity right from the meditative state to your chosen medium.

There is nothing wrong with repeating this meditation any time you are working on imaginative endeavors. My only word of caution is that if you go to the well and find it running low, it means you are pouring too much personal energy into your art to the point of being harmful to your health and well being. The dry well is a sign to take a break and refresh yourself, then return to your work with wholeness and restored vitality.

EXERCISE 2: PHYSICAL ARTS

When angry or upset, certain physical artistic outlets such as archery, martial arts, wood carving, and many sports can be very helpful to constructively channel those emotions. The energy created also helps the end product if handled properly. For example, the trained martial artist would never consider entering into competition with someone when they are angry, because that colors their perspective too much. Instead, they might choose to go practice their kata[3] to help work off a little tension and bring themselves back into a centered, balanced state.

Anyone who has had the opportunity to observe kata knows that it is, indeed, an exquisite art. Likewise, the wood carver can use the physical power of emotions to help mold the timber into something beautiful, thus transmuting the negativity into loveliness. Now that's real magic!

So as different situations arise in your life that leave you feeling completely out of sorts, try turning to your art to find perspective. This does not necessarily have to be a physical art to be productive; paint wildly, sing to the trees, do free-flow writing or whatever seems to release pent-up tension. Bodily exertion does seem to help tremendously, but sometimes just having the opportunity to liberate ourselves through any medium is a relief. Interestingly enough, the final product created at these times does not necessarily reflect the underlying emotions of the artist. Instead, frequently the energy is transformed through that medium into life-affirming images which stand as a testimony to the power of art.

EXERCISE 3: BLIND WORK

This is a good exercise for any medium which does not employ physically dangerous tools such as carving knives. We know from experiments in sensory deprivation that people who are blind or deaf often acquire enhanced abilities in other areas of their life. For this exercise, you will be trying to produce your art as a blind person might.

To begin, either shut your eyes or place a thick cloth over them so you can not see. Take a deep, calming breath and familiarize yourself with your surroundings, where all your tools are, etc. Once you feel you have your bearings, visualize in your mind what you want to draw, mold, paint, etc. Hold that image firmly so that you can see it from above, below, and all sides.

Next, get your tools and begin to create. Stop whenever you need to refresh your inner vision of the final project. Continue in this manner until you think the picture (or whatever) is done. Then open your eyes and see what developed! The first few times you attempt this exercise you will probably be a little disappointed by the outcome. Developing a strong artistic inner vision takes time; with practice you will improve. After a while, you will be able to use this visual sense (eyes open) to see your art in finished form while you're bringing it to life!

For writers, I suggest a slight variation on this technique. In this case, try to envision a blank page in your mind, and a pen. As words appear on that mental sheet of paper, copy them onto the one before you. If possible, keep your eyes closed so you don't interrupt the flow. Sometimes having a ruler guide for lines will help this portion of the exercise. Usually the words and phrases that appear are those central to your thought process, and ones which will spur other ideas to help inspire fluidic writing.

HINTS FOR WRITERS AND ARTISTS

We are blessed to have many talented writers and artists in the "new age" community as a whole. Their proficiency, however, is often found in the newsletter realm. Taking the writer/artist from one who works in small publications to one who can produce an exhibit or book with timeless quality is a difficult process for both the interested publisher or gallery and the artist themselves.

From experience I can tell you that the traditional methods of approaching the artistic community for public exposure and acceptance doesn't always work with magic. Magical businesses are a little different from those in the public domain. They are serving a very definite, and often very picky market, so their reaction to your work will reflect this. These people are also, for the most part, intuitive and are not afraid to rely on gut instincts from time to time.

So, before you sit down to your medium, first realize that creating a magical art form for other people to enjoy is no picnic. From my own experience in writing, I can tell you that it will take many hours of time, research, dedication, introspection, and a healthy portion of fortitude to get a completed product. For some people, the process can take several years. If you are willing to make that kind of commitment, and stick to it, then you are in the right field.

Your next step is to contact several established individuals in your field and ask for their advice. For example, if you see someone's work consistently in a journal you enjoy, try sending them a letter via that newsletter, with a SASE. Most of the time they will be happy to share with you their insights and suggestions for getting your work out to the public. After this, you can review various businesses to see what their guidelines and suggested topics are. Much of this information can be obtained through an inquiry letter which should be brief, professional, and to the point (again enclose a SASE). These are busy people who will appreciate the courtesy.

Once their guidelines have come back to you through the mail, read them carefully. Decide which of the businesses best suits your intended topic, and get to work. As you create, consider the market that business serves, and whether you are producing an appropriate item.

Through your medium, choose timely topics that will not become quickly passe, yet ones which inspire you to do your best. In other words, let your final product be one which sings of your personal vision and portrays a certain authority on your subject; one which educates and inspires, and one which will meet the needs of the business you hope to sell it to.

Finally, when you submit your work make sure it includes all information requested in the guidelines. For example, with manuscripts the pages should be numbered, word count given, spelling and grammar should be checked, and major typos corrected. Share with the company a little of your background and reasons for that particular piece of art. This way, they should have all the insight and tools needed to judge your art in the best possible light. Direct your creation to the correct individual or department and give them ample time to review it (usually three to six months, depending on the company) before getting discouraged.

Don't be surprised if you are turned down the first time, or asked to make drastic revisions. Remember, this is a learning process and the company is trying to teach you what they want and need to market your idea. If revisions are suggested, try not to get overly sensitive about them. Read them once — rant, rave, and cry privately, then reapproach your work with their eyes. This is hard for any artist, but well worth the effort.

Your agent or purchaser can be your best friend and guide to an amazing final product, if you allow it. This doesn't mean giving up your "voice," or following their advice word for word. It does, however, mean heeding their input with careful consideration, knowing they have been in the business longer than you. Many times they will give you new, exciting perspectives you never even considered before!

If your work is accepted, you need to reflect a little on how this changes your life. In some ways a magical art form will open your broom closet drastically. The creative process is also personally trans-formational. You may discover yourself a much different or more aware person at the end of the journey.

With all this going on, you will also have to consider if you want to continue to create in this medium. Usually if the company is happy with your work, they will want to establish a relationship with you and dis-cuss your ideas for future projects.

If you do decide to keep producing magical art, I highly suggest at this point you find a way to actually meet the people at your supporting company. Become more than just a name or voice on the phone to them. Share your ideas face-to-face, and get feedback. This can be a very rewarding and motivational experience. It will also help your future communications with these people to be more personal in nature.

If, on the other hand, you simply can't come to a mutual agreement with that particular firm, try another one if you feel the product has real merit, or ask the rejecting company where the problems exist. Again, take advantage of the wealth of knowledge they can share with you.

Remember, not everyone is meant to write a book, be a painter, or whatever. Not everyone who writes a book or carves a wand is called to be a "writer" or "woodworker." These examples are only some of the art forms where we have the opportunity to share our magical path and ideas with others and hopefully help them on their way. Newsletters are just as viable in their teaching, and your writing or art is certainly appreciated there. So, if you find in the long run that book or gallery formats don't work for you, please don't stop sharing your vision if you love it! Believe me, your local new age editor appreciates the input.

ART OF CRAFT

Originally Wicca was called the Craft of the Wise because it employed any number of country talents, from herbalism and animal handling to more psychically associated abilities such as foreknowledge and divina-tion. The people of magic were not all high priests/esses dancing around fires and espousing theology. They were a simple folk who used the best of their inherited knowledge and energies to heal the sick, help farmers with crops, keep villagers safe, and improve the overall quality of living as they could.

Because many of the early practitioners were not wealthy by any means, Wicca became a Craft of hearth and home for them. It had to be creative, using whatever herbs and tools were available. If the Druid of a lower caste in medieval times needed her knife in the kitchen, she used it. Good knives were valuable and far too costly to leave sitting idle between holy days.[4] Likewise with their herbs. Many remedies employed were based on readily available plants, native to the area. Items such as pepper and other exotic imported herbs were very expensive and hard to come by for the average person. So, they were left to their wiles to get by, learning to be imaginative "kitchen Witches," and using what some consider simple magics as a way to better their life spiritually and practically.

Bringing this type of mindset into a modern setting and looking towards a new century, I can see where these "simple" magics are becoming very important from many perspectives. First, the creative approach allows us a wider variety in our rites so that they can truly reflect personal vision. Second, this mindset is one very much in keeping with the ecological awareness and preservation so desperately needed for our future.

Third, the inspired, spontaneous magics release us from many time constraints we all face, substituting short, meaningful activities whose results can be just as powerful, if not more so, than full-blown ritual. They offer us a little bit of simplicity amidst the chaos, and help us to relax and flow with whatever tradition we work in.

This is not to say that there is not a place in Craft for traditionalists and High Magic which are complex in nature. Tradition offers us a rich heritage which should be respected. The knowledge and wisdom offered by these paths is wide and varied. Indeed, tradition itself is an art form when expressed by those who understand it on an intimate level. Even as the Latin mass of the Catholic Church can be inspiring if handled by a priest of deep conviction, so too can High Magics (or any form) be beautiful, motivational, and powerful when produced by loving hands.

The idea behind the "art of craft" is using our own abilities and vision to help make our traditions more alive, less static, and more meaningful to all who participate. We should not be afraid to let inspiration have its own way sometimes. Certain situations in the modern world call us to break away from the norm (needs do not always recognize propriety in their timing). I sincerely believe that our future will be filled with even more of these occurrences. We should not be so stagnant or inflexible with our magic as to set these moments indifferently aside until a traditionally "appropriate" moon phase, zodiac sign, or celebration date appears on our calendar.

To me, rituals, spells, invocations, etc., with no personal meaning are really wasted energy. Magic is the direct result of our ability to move energy by using specific focals. If these focals have no connection in our conscious or subconscious mind with the ends desired, then it makes them basically ineffective. The key here is in using a little common sense. Read over the basic material you plan to use for a spell or ritual, and ask yourself the following questions:

- ○ Does the material make sense, considering the circumstances? If not, you may need to rework it to be more suitable or find another source for your ritual or spell.

- ○ Do you understand all the terminology used? If not, please take the extra time to look it up in a good magical dictionary. One such source is the *Woman's Dictionary of Symbols and Sacred Objects*, Barbara Walker, Harper & Row, 1988. This book and other occult reference texts are often available through your local library or inter-library loan systems. The reason it is important to understand your terms in magic is the same rational which is applied in cooking. If I think that "tsp." stands for tablespoons, my biscuits will have a lot more salt than they need. Preparation for magical work needs to be no less informed and aware.

- ○ Is there anything about the material that you are personally uncomfortable with, and why? If your answer to this question revolves around minor wording changes, by all means make them! Our rites are not, and need not be, carved on tablets of stone to have abiding meanings. It is better to use a language which is comfortable on your lips, and comes from your heart, than ones which, for all their loftiness, have no meaning to you.

- ○ Does this material ask you to do anything which you object to morally, spiritually, or emotionally? If so, *do not do it!* Part of creativity in magic is listening to that "inner bell" which can warn you against potentially dangerous or negative situations.[5]

- ○ Do you understand the reason for using this material and its desired effect completely? If not, wait until you do. Magic is much more productive if you have solid perspectives on the "whys," "whens," and "what-ifs." Too many people use magic without these understandings to less than positive ends. Be responsible.

○ Are you comfortable with the flow, set-up, components, etc., of the ritual/spell? If not, what would you like to change, and why? More than likely your personal adaptations will make the working much more meaningful to you, and therefore more effective. The only time where I do not recommend this is with regard to certain rites of High Magic where the words and motions are set up in such a way as to be very specific, for good reasons. These types of magicians work with powerful elemental forces which need stricture to handle properly. As the old saying goes, if it isn't broken, don't fix it. Once you have examined your material thoroughly, are comfortable with its intentions, and have made any changes that your inner voice and art deem necessary, you are ready to begin!

EXERCISE 1: MAGICAL PRINCIPLES EXPRESSION

This exercise is meant to help you learn about any one aspect of magic by changing the way you perceive it. This is done by expressing that principle through three different mediums. For example, if you were interested in clairvoyance, do a little study on the subject, then write a poem about it, paint a picture, and mold some clay into a object which represents that principle to you.

When we take a step to the right or left, whatever we have been examining takes on a slightly different outlook. Magic can be much the same way. Things which at first seem unreachable or incomprehensible can often become clear just by moving a little and gaining another viewpoint. Try this exercise with several different aspects of magic and make note of how your perceptions change in the process.

Please note that you are not expected to create fantastic art pieces for this activity. No one else ever has to see the outcomes of these efforts unless you want them to. It is more important that your feelings and focus are directed fully into the medium, without distraction, so that the final product encourages a harmonic response that allows for personal learning and growth.

EXERCISE 2: WRITE YOUR OWN SPELLS

In my own mind I define a spell almost as a mini-ritual, because it encompasses many of the same techniques and approaches as a full rite. Magic is essentially a means to bend and move energy towards a desired goal. With this in mind, a spell becomes one of the tools which can help make such movement possible. Creating your own spells allows you to meet the needs and problems of your rapidly changing life with magical energy born from your own living experiences.

For any spell to be effective, it must have certain basic parts. First is a way to focus your mind, your purpose, and your desire towards specific energy. This can be accomplished through chants and/or symbols. Next is a way of directing the energy which also may be achieved through symbolism, speech, and visualization. By this definition, certain prayers can be considered a spell, which in actuality is a deliberate process for achieving a goal except that the normal material procedure is replaced with metaphysical techniques.

So, for example, you wanted to work prosperity magic for yourself, and you were also interested in candle magic. You might use a candle for the focus of the spell, carving the word "prosperity" into the side of it. You then might anoint the candle with patchouli oil (which is frequently used in magic for money matters) to help direct your energy towards your goal. Then light the candle and visualize your needs being met in whatever form makes the most sense at that moment, such as being offered a position at a firm you recently interviewed with. Finally, blow out the candle and allow the smoke to carry your energy to its intended destination.

In creating spells for yourself it is good to work within natural law, never take anything for granted, and be very precise about your goals. Do not allow your work to manipulate or harm anyone, including yourself. Lastly, always consider your motivations at the moment. Try not to concentrate on spells when you are angry or upset. It is far too easy to unleash those emotions in the wrong way. If your heart and head are in accord, and your components meaningful, you can not help but be successful.

Just remember that magical work is not always answered in the way we think it should be. The universe has its own set of laws and a concept of what we really need. If you send out energy, you must trust in those laws to bring a response which will truly be best for you on all levels of being.

EXERCISE 3: WRITE YOUR OWN RITUAL

By definition, a ritual is anything where procedures or facets of an approach is followed regularly. To write your own ritual you first need to have a good understanding of the basic elements for any rite. For something to be considered a ritual all you need do is create a Sacred

Space, perform actions with a specific magical goal in that space, and close the Sacred Space. While this may seem too simple, really everything else is icing on the cake.

Rituals can be as formal or informal as you like. Since magic is a combination of will-power, imagination, and faith, the most important factor is that you believe in what you are doing. Generally speaking, rituals are held to commemorate the natural cycles and passages in life, unlike spells which are formulated for almost any circumstance. While Chapter Eleven will discuss an urban wheel of the year, observance dates should not keep you from holding a ritual any time you feel the need.

To begin, consider how you want to prepare your ritual space for magical work. You need somehow to set it apart from its normal usage, through words, actions, or personal attitude. Perhaps you will want to enter through a different door than usual, or burn some incense, but whatever you choose remember that once you are finished, the area is magically different and should be treated with appropriate respect.

Next, decide how you would like to cast your circle. People who are not comfortable with vocalization may simply light appropriately colored candles at the four basic directions. Other individuals may want to write their own invocations. Your decision on this should be based on what symbols are personally significant and what best inspires your magical attitudes.

The third item for consideration is what, if any, tools you want to use in your rite. Tools are not necessary to the effective working of magic, but for many people these instruments help them to focus their mind on something other than the normal world. Some of the common tools include music, incense, candles, cups, wands, an athame (ritual dagger), God/dess figures, representations of the elements (see also Chapter Four), and crystals.

Once your sacred space is prepared and everything you need is within, the type of magic you work here is totally up to you. Perhaps you want to celebrate your birthday, the full moon, or just say thank you to the universe for a particularly good week. Whatever your desire, make it known to the Great Spirit and powers present in a creative, heart-felt manner, and you can not help but be enriched by the experience.

The main reason for trying to write your own ritual at least once is really two-fold. First, I guarantee that, no matter how long you have been in the Craft, you will learn something new about magic and probably discover a few things about yourself each time you create an original rite. Second, this creativity allows you to meet the quickening pace of change in this world with diversity of your own well in hand.

EXERCISE 4: CREATING VISUALIZATIONS AND MEDITATIONS

Consider meditation and visualization like a daily workout for your spirit. Both help hone your ability to concentrate and focus, and are therefore effective aids for magic. In much the same manner as spells and rituals, the way you meditate or visualize can be personalized to better accommodate your reality and needs.

Considering the hectic world we live in, taking the time to bring ourselves back into balance and center our minds is perhaps one of the most important disciplines we can acquire for healthy daily living, not to mention our magical training. Meditation[6] is best defined as exercising the mind in contemplation, especially religious, or to work mentally. From this explanation, we can assume that each of us meditates in some form, even unknowingly. Visualization is a secondary technique of utilizing our imagination while in these deepened states of awareness to help bring increased perspective, and sometimes to achieve certain goals.

Techniques for meditation vary greatly depending on culture and tradition, but almost all employ a slow, rhythmic method of breathing, and focus on an object such as a candle for a starting point. Frequently your efforts can be aided by playing soft music which you find peaceful, and burning some favorite incense. These types of tools help to signal our minds that something different is taking place, something which needs our attention.

The exact goal of your meditation and visualization should be determined before you begin. Choose your external tools and internal images so they match this goal, and are meaningful to you (see Chapter Eight). For example, when I feel out of balance I sometimes place a picture of an old-fashioned scale on my table along with a candle as a starting point. Then, I breath deeply, keeping that image in my mind, except I am sitting in the center of the scale. Next I add to the visualization concentric circles centered on me. This meditation is unique because I am both participant and observer as I watch the scale slowly move back to balance. In this illustration, the picture and candle act as the basic external tools, while the circles in the visualization help guide my energy back into my gravity center, thus bringing equilibrium.

It is important to note at this point that creating meditations and visualizations for group settings can be more difficult since you are coping with a larger number of unique individuals. Individuals given charge over writing and/or directing such activities for a coven should be extremely aware of the people involved and sensitive to group energy so that the exercise is productive for all participants. I find that, in this case, it is a good idea to practice your original, guided meditation at home with various types of music until you find just the right combination of pace and melody to engender the desired results.

If you find it is difficult for you to enjoy such activities while leading them, or if you even have a hard time concentrating on meditation when you are alone, an alternative is to tape guided meditations for yourself or your group. For this, you will need a tape recorder and another source of music such as a radio or record player.[7]

Find the piece you want for background and start playing it, then turn on the tape recorder while you read the words of the meditation/visualization you have created. You may have to try it more than once to get a good mix, but I find this approach very handy because you can then re-use or share the meditation any time in the future. The other option to this is to have someone in your home or group record the presentation for you.

RITUAL THEATER[8]

One of the more interesting ways that Craft art and the art of Craft can merge is through ritual theater. This is not just your everyday Circle, but one which has been planned, practiced, and created to inform, entertain, and hopefully educate the audience about everything from legends and lore steeped in magical symbolism to a "fictional" story based on any of the beautiful traditions and techniques of the Craft.

Mystery plays have been known to humanity for a very long time. The early church often used them to help teach the less educated populace about simple religious themes; those of life, redemption, death, and resurrection. While at first some people might balk at the notion of making magic into a play, there is much to be gained for the audience and the actors in such a performance. And, while ritual theater is not something which you can really enjoy alone, it does present a marvelous occasion for self-expression.

As you work on the initial planning stages for the ritual theater, it forces you to consider our celebrations from the perspective of an observer. Each movement and line, each phrase is pondered for its impact; music is chosen with care, and decorations are even more obviously symbolic than usual all because there is an audience involved. This type of thought and preparation will ultimately serve to give greater meaning to the observance for the participants, on and off the stage!

The ritual theater offers an opportunity for magical individuals with a flair for the dramatic to enjoy their rites and share them with friends or family through a medium (e.g., the stage) which is a little easier to accept than the sometimes awkward confessions of faith. Sometimes all it takes for better understanding and acceptance is to take magic out of the metaphysical realm and make it more accessible to the average mind. Theater, and often many other art forms, extend this approachability.

If you would like to try devising a ritual theater presentation of your own, first you will need to find a place to perform. Check your local Universalist Church or fire halls to see about reasonable rental fees. If the weather is nice enough you can try performing at a park, but this can be very difficult when taking into consideration other factors such as any sets you have made and the chance of getting rained out.

Next, you should gather a group of people who would like to help. Together you can decide on your subject matter and assign various duties as you would for any play. You need someone to help with costumes, makeup, set design, writing, and advertising (if desired). You also need individuals who can effectively play the roles designed. The personalities and abilities of your actors should be carefully considered in the writing process.

As you create your play, remember to include all the basic elements of ritual that you feel are appropriate to your topic. Generally speaking, however, preparing the sacred space and calling the quarters can be done before the audience arrives if it is more prudent. In this case, be sure to leave an obvious walkway of some sort open where your viewers can enter and leave as needed. Remember these people may or may not be aware of the energies of a circle. This type of planning will help prevent most disruptions of same.

Once all the pieces are together and a script has been written, you can begin to focus on creating the right mood for the audience and getting them somehow involved. Perhaps you can ask for volunteers to perform different small activities during the rite. If you can get your audience involved with the ritual theater you have won half the battle. Everyone has a little bit of "ham" inside just waiting to come out. Let your audience have this opportunity so they can enjoy the presentation on a more intimate level.

It is also good to consider having a brief foreword for any explanations which you feel necessary to understanding the play. After this, you can have someone act as a narrator to lead the audience in a bit of imagining (e.g., a guided meditation and visualization). Through this time you can help the audience relax and transport them to whatever setting you have chosen (which you ingeniously prepare while they are being taken through the meditation). Now, when they open their eyes, the world around has been transfigured into the new, magical setting!

During the ritual theater, give the actors opportunities to weave themselves in and out of the viewers. This helps bring greater connections and maintain interest levels. Other movements such as dance are also effective, especially if you can get the whole assembly involved! There will probably be lots of laughter and some breaking of the continuity to the play at such a point (which is also a good time for intermission), but what you are actually doing is teaching your audience that magic and ritual are not only natural, but can be a lot of fun!

Another tool to the ritual theater is that of song and other music. We have often heard the phrase "music is the universal language," and as such it can help carry the feeling of your rite to the audience even when they may not understand all the gestures or words. Music, especially songs with refrains, can be very catchy, and your viewers will probably find themselves humming the strains long after the play is over. In this way, you are allowing them to carry that magic with them out of the theater and into daily living.

Finally, at the end of your production it is nice to offer coffee and snacks to members of the audience who would like to stay and ask questions or socialize. Make sure you have some good pamphlets or books available for those who might want more information on the Craft rather than sending your audience elsewhere for information. This time of sharing will give them the chance to clear up any confusions on what they have just seen and tell you their reactions. I think you will generally find them to be pretty positive.

Since I realize this concept may be new to many readers, below I have summarized some of the basic elements of the ritual theater along with suggestions on same. However, please remember this is an art form and should be met with all the creative, dramatic flair you can muster.

THEME

Any seasonal observance, cultural legends with underlying magical lessons, original stories centering around your own experiences in Craft, parables that tackle one specific aspect of magic such as the folklore of herbs and how they came into existence, Greek or other legends indigenous to a particular country, different magical traditions personified, animal lore and perspectives on humanity, and environmental issues are all possiblities.

SETTING

These can be simple or complex, depending on the talents of your group. You can construct scenery from painted wood and cardboard and borrow appropriate furniture from various member's homes. For simpler backdrops, just use flowers fitting for your theme or season in large urns, or a potted tree. A piece of dyed cloth hung across the stage area makes a good make-shift curtain.

PROPS

Candles and holders, ritual tools which you don't mind having handled by other people (and which are not breakable), and general decorations appropriate to your theme. If the rental hall will allow, a little incense burning can enhance the overall mood of the audience, but such should be used sparingly for those who may have allergies. Anything you can place around the room to distract from what may be a very mundane looking hall will help improve the ambiance for your viewers. Other props are best determined by each player as they pertain to the script.

COSTUMES

It is perfectly appropriate to wear your magical robes for ritual theater, if they match your subject matter. If not, quick costumes can often be fashioned by a creative seamstress out of old sheets, curtains, bits of fur, buttons, felt, feathers, yarn, etc. For any of these items, checking your local second-hand store should produce good fabric at reasonable prices. You might also find some handy props there.

In making your costumes, don't overlook some of the items which may be right under your nose. Old halloween garb which can be reworked, long sea shells which can be fashioned into horns for Pan, prom or wedding clothing that you never wear anymore, and glitter from an old holiday project can all add up to some spectacular clothing.

I should mention that your costumes don't have to be historically perfect. Sometimes the subtle touches are even more important than the obvious. What is most important is that the item worn helps make the actor feel more alive in his/her part, and brings an immediate recognition or response from the audience. The best person for this job in your group might be a mother or father who has taken the kids through several school plays, or a teenager involved in their high school drama club.

MAKEUP

Depending on where you hold the play, you may not need conventional "stage" makeup. In a regular theater setting, heavy makeup is used to offset the white-wash effect of the spotlights. Under normal lighting this is not necessary. In either case, the individuals involved can decide if they would like to employ unusual makeup to enhance their costume. For example, a person playing Pan might want to purchase a ruddy or dark tone liquid base for their face and hands to intensify the illusion of being a forest creature.

As a side note, you can change the tint of most liquid bases available at drugstores by adding a little food coloring. In this case, if you happen to be playing a forest Deva[9] you might want a slight green tint to your skin. Add a few drops of the food coloring and shake well, then test it on your skin until you get the desired shade. By way of alternative, check in ● our area to see if you have a costume shop or theatrical store to go to for a wider variety of makeup supplies.

DANCE

Dancing in ritual is as ancient as the dirt beneath our feet. The ancients probably believed, as we do, that somehow by mimicking the movements of animals, planets, or other natural objects through the earth and space, they could learn more about the secrets of the universe. Also, for some reason human nature responds naturally to the movements of such dances (how often have you found yourself tapping a foot or swaying while watching others?).

In choosing the type of dance(s) for your play, consider that some of your audience and actors will have two left feet. Try and keep the steps simple, yet illustrative. Take the time to give specific instructions for the viewers who get involved, being very patient with them. Remember, this isn't a Broadway play you're producing, it's supposed to be fun! If the dance is supposed to have special significance, explain the history and symbolism to all who partake so they can appreciate the movements more. The children in your audience (if any) will appreciate this dimension of the play the most.

Music

Where there's moving feet, there best be music to inspire, motivate, and bring everything to life. Background music during the play helps set a mood. These sounds should be soft and unintrusive except where they need to be louder for effect. I recommend timing and taping this in advance to make things simpler. The music for your dances should also be chosen with care. It needs to match not only the atmosphere you have already created, but the movements you are about to produce.

If you are fortunate to have Pagan musicians in your group, they will be able to help create or modify melodies so they speed up or slow down as you need, otherwise you will have to do some hunting at your tape player or new age music store to find the right combination. By the way, drums, dried gourds, harmonicas, and even kazoos make good musical accompaniment for ritual theater.

Advertising

At some point in your planning you will need to decide if you are going to open attendance for your play to the general public, keep it restricted to the magical citizenry, or narrower yet, allow entrance by invitation only. I mention this for the obvious reason that not everyone who might show up at your ritual theater from the local community will appreciate the subject matter.

You can alleviate some of this difficulty by advertising only in journals or stores where you know the individuals will, for the most part, have some type of drawing towards magic. Also, you can invite friends and family who you hope to share a new dimension of your life with. However, I don't readily suggest advertising in the local Sunday News unless your group is really prepared for some possible confrontation with any neighboring fundamentalist organizations. This may or may not actually occur, especially because you are presenting your ritual in the form of a "play," but a little bit of spiritual and mental fortification beforehand never hurts.

AUDIENCE PARTICIPATION

If you do decide to get your audience involved in the show and get volunteers at the start of the play, it is always nice to give them some kind of signs or tokens of their part which they can keep. If you designate an individual as the flower Deva, for example, you might give them a paper sunflower headdress, or a bouquet of spring flowers to denote their role. This prop is then kept by that person as a memoir of the day.

These keepsakes don't have to be costly or fancy to be very meaningful to your participants, especially children. These souvenirs become the emblem of an enjoyable event that can brighten their home for the coming week, and may even end up in a scrapbook somewhere to be shared with future generations.

SUMMARY

Since I am proficient at only a few arts, with knowledge in only a few others, I can't really give instructions on many other ways for Craft art and the Art of Craft to combine. That job will be left for your own creative insights to discover. However, I do encourage you to share these ideas with others whenever you can. Part of the Art of Craft comes from the wonders of networking our knowledge and experience with one another so we can all be enriched in the process. By reaching out with active, practical perspectives, you may well be helping someone else past a stumbling block they couldn't traverse themselves; you may also inspire a fresh gush from the well of inventiveness towards new creations that can radiate magical beauty for today, tomorrow, and many years to come.

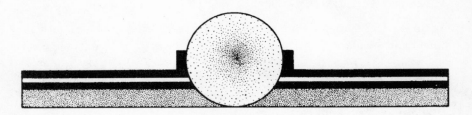

NOTES TO CHAPTER 9

1. The term *God/self* is a way of representing, with one word, the inner divine nature of the human soul.

2. The elusive Grail is not only the symbol of our connection to the land as portrayed in Arthurian Legend. In many cultures a cup, bowl, or horn has played key roles in mythology and often exemplified the inner wells of creativity and spirit inherent in humanity. In the same way, the magical ritual cup represents water, the feminine aspect, the imaginative and intuitive nature.

3. *Kata* is a repetitious exercise which eventually becomes second nature to the martial artist. At this point, the mind no longer has to focus on the pattern of movement, but instead is released so that instinct and intuition can take over.

4. Certain magical sects have very strict rules regarding how and when ritual daggers may be used. In some cases they may not be employed to cut meat, in other instances they are only brought out for use in the magical circle.

5. There are rules of magic regarding safety of self and others, most of which are based on a little common sense. Sometimes we get so caught up in desiring a spiritual experience that we forget to keep our wise discernment close at hand. Never sacrifice your personal principles to please others. Any reputable group or individual will always respect your choices, even if they may not agree with them.

6. Meditation is also sometimes considered a type of communing, as is done in prayer, because of the profound state of awareness it brings. Studies have shown that in some ways meditation mimics certain sleep patterns which help us to dream, which may explain why visionary experiences are more common when we have achieved deeper levels.

7.   For wonderful meditation music (on both CD and tape) by Loreena McKennitt, write to:

   Quinland Road Productions
   Box 933
   Stratford, Ontario N5A 7M3

8.   One group which I know works in the realms of participatory ritual theater around the country is The Rowan Tree Church. Rev. Paul Beyerl and his people have devised many beautiful, dramatic presentations specifically with regards to herbalism. If you would like to learn more about their efforts, please write to the address in Chapter Seven.

9.   *Deva* is a term generally ascribed to nature spirits with close ties to various natural sub-kingdoms. For example, it is believed that there are herb devas, flower devas, etc.

OUT OF SPACE, OUT OF TIME

Rituals for Urban Magical Living

Miniver loved the days of old
When swords were bright
And steeds were prancing
The vision of a warrior bold
Would set him quick to dancing.
— E. A. Robinson, *Miniver Cheevy*

All in a Magical Day

A little child, a limber elf, singing, dancing to itself.
— Coleridge, "Christabel" (1801)

The sun rises and sets as the Earth quietly turns on its axis, yet what happens between dusk and daybreak is rarely as calm as a picture from space might imply. From the moment we are born to this world until our spirits leave it, it seems we never stop moving except to sleep. And, as the years roll by, it appears that this hectic pace determinedly pulls us onward, leaving many feeling trapped by that rolling momentum and our daily responsibilities.

I know that when I wake up in the morning, feeling as if a whole army has traipsed merrily through my mouth, nothing appears more "spiritual" in nature than my first cup of coffee. This is almost a religious experience. Yet as I sit at my table, trying to get my achy bones moving for another day of work, I know that somehow there must be a better way to transform this living experience into something magical.

From such deliberation this chapter was born as an answer to my own heart's plea for a down-to-earth faith which could cope with daily situations creatively, again expressing the Art of Craft (see Chapter Nine). I hope that some of what I have discovered for daily urban rituals can likewise help you. Interestingly enough I found that not all of my answers were necessarily "mystical" in nature, but stem from old-fashioned good sense in the way I care for myself. This observation returns

to the idea I proposed in Chapter Three about the body being holy, and
our responsibility to it.

In considering everyone's daily routine, it is obvious that yours
will be different from mine. What I have tried to do is compile some
common everyday moments, experiences, and activities to which a little
bit of the magical attitude or practice can be added. By so doing, you
are moving your Path out of a passive role in your life to one which is
active, life affirming, and enriching every moment.

In the years ahead, I believe this creative ability will become a life-
line for magical people, allowing greater personal control over the
immense sociological changes we face. In this way our magic, our faith,
will grant positive alternative perspectives not just in our Circles, but as
we encounter each day.

DANCING, COME THE DAWN

Have you ever gone camping or just happened to be up very early in the
morning to catch a glimpse of those first few golden rays peeking across
the horizon? Almost anyone who has can tell you that it is not only
beautiful, but invigorating. My suggestion is this: once a month, or
every couple of months as you can, get up before dawn and go somewhere quiet. Settle your mind and heart, and listen closely to the world
around you. Watch in silence as the Earth is reborn.

As the orange-pink light of a new day meets you, allow it to saturate your being. Breath this into yourself as if it were air, filling each cell
and muscle with renewed strength and energy. As you feel this power
building within, stand and dance with the sunlight, reach your arms out,
and feel it embrace you! Thank the Goddess for a new day; a new
opportunity to learn and grow. Thank the Earth for her generous
bounty, and waltz with the morning air until you feel it is time to go. I
can't tell you how you will know this, but you will know.

When you leave this place, take a moment to reflect on the experience in your journal or share it with a friend. I can almost guarantee you

will depart with more joy in your heart and a better outlook than when you arrived. Carry this exhilaration tucked in your heart to help you through the coming weeks until you dance with the dawn once more.

RISING AND BREAKFAST

Even before you jump out of bed in the morning, take a moment to stretch and breathe. Stretching is one of the safest, healthiest exercises for your body. It helps get your blood circulating and carries sustaining oxygen to each cell. As you stretch and breathe, envision white light permeating you with energy for the day ahead. In much the same way you remember to fill up your automobile to keep it running, refresh your spirit before you start your morning. Thank the God/dess for another moment to experience His/Her creation.

For those of you who are not breakfast people, it is an important meal of the day. If you find you can't really eat, at least consider having a glass of fruit juice or milk. The word *breakfast* comes from combining two other words, "break" and "fast;" in other words, an end to a period of not eating. Figuring that most of us eat dinner around 6 PM, this means your body has been without sustenance for about 12-14 hours when you wake up. To really be at your best for the day, you need that extra bit of nourishment.

Before you eat or drink, there is nothing wrong with saying some type of "grace" to bless the food which goes into your body. The practice of grace has somewhat gone out of fashion in many Pagan homes, but I think it is well worth bringing back. Not everything manufactured today is good for us, and frequently has additives that our physical nature could do without. This little prayer is a way of entreating the Divine to let our bodies use what they need and discard the rest. You can also ask for a little blessing on yourself for that day at the same time!

BRUSHING YOUR TEETH/SHAVING

Anytime you are in front of a mirror is a good opportunity to remind yourself that you are a divine creation. Say out loud as you look at yourself things like, "I am beautiful/handsome within," "I love myself," "I am worthwhile," or "I am an important magical creation." Self affirmation first thing in the morning is a positive and transformational experience if practiced routinely.

These phrases are not egotistical, but instead a way of acknowledging to yourself and the universe your Divine purpose here; to grow, to learn, to become the best person you can.

Another exercise which can be done during shaving is to "cut away" old habits or views you wish to change. In this case, name your beard (or leg hairs) after the tendency you want to eliminate. As you shave, visualize reddish light pouring out from your razor to burn away that disposition as the hair is removed. Finally, you can wash this habit down the sink, or transmute it into something positive by putting the hair in your compost pile!

GETTING DRESSED

In some ways, getting dressed in the morning is like getting ready for a play. We all have roles in this life, some of which we don't always enjoy. Through meditation and visualization while getting dressed, you can help ease some of your discomfort in these functions.

Begin by laying out your clothes on the bed or a chair. Take a few deep, cleaning breaths. Name each piece of your clothing after a particular attribute your position calls for. If you happen to be a manager, you might name your pants authority; tie, respectability; shirt, organization; and so on. As you put that piece of clothing on, visualize yourself in whatever role you are going into, and performing it well. Continue in this manner until you have "put on" the visage and energy of everything you have to become for your character in this play called life.

Magical people who work in companies with less than scrupulous business practices might be an apt example. Very few of us are in positions where we can just quit a job because of our moral standards. Using this exercise in this type of situation could help the magical person with many difficult personal struggles.

On the other hand, I don't recommend this exercise for every facet of your existence. This is not a full-time persona, just one created out of necessity. There are people and situations with whom you should be totally yourself. This technique is created more for those situations where you feel you have to portray a certain image which you are uncomfortable with or ill-equipped to handle proficiently.

DRIVING OR BUSING TO WORK

This is the perfect time for breathing exercises, singing a Pagan tune or two, and sorting out your schedule for the day. Slow breathing in the car will help decrease your tension level and actually improve your awareness for defensive driving. Singing is a good release and can help bring the energy of joy to your day. If you happen to be riding the bus, however, you may wish to recite the songs silently in your mind instead.

With regard to schedules, I am a great advocate of basic organization. If you take the time to plan a little, frequently your whole morning will be less chaotic and you can find extra time for pleasurable breaks. Even if it is fifteen minutes with a good book, a brief walk outside for fresh air, or just to stand and stretch, these types of intermissions will make a world of difference in your overall attitude and tension level by the end of the day.

AFTERNOON

AT WORK

Whenever you have the opportunity, take a walk to the lavatory and do a little stretching and breathing. Stretch out your hands and head slowly, allowing the muscles to release stiffness. Just as with rising, this exercise is very healthy and aids in reducing tension. Spiritually, making activities like this part of your routine will generally help keep you in a more balanced, centered state where you can not be easily bowled over by a "crisis."

Stop for a moment and call a friend or loved one to hear a friendly voice, or give a smile to someone across the way, allowing the God/dess to beam from deep within you. Remember that you are a magical being who carries special energy wherever you go. Don't be afraid to let a little of it spill out, bringing fresh light and perspective to your work environment.

LUNCH BREAK

Get outside if you can, and away from the daily grind. If not, try to find an activity in your lunchroom which you can enjoy. In most cases, you have 30-60 minutes which are totally yours. Perhaps there is a ritual you have been meaning to write, a book you hoped to study, or a spell you wanted to weave — why not start now?

Many aspects of spell work are not overt and can be done without anyone around you even noticing. Visualization is one such example. Another illustration is writing your spell on a piece of paper and then securing this scrap in the soil of a nearby potted plant to allow the energy to grow. Each time you see that vegetation, you will think of your magic, thus giving it more potency! There are hundreds of variations to this short but effective bit of spell work, limited only by your imagination and work space.

DRIVING/WALKING OR BUSING HOME

On the way home is the best time to drop any excess emotional baggage which you didn't already avert. This way, you won't be gruff with roommates or family members for something which isn't their fault. This improved state of mind can be achieved a number of ways, several of which (such as slow, focused breathing) are already suggested for other activities in this chapter.

One visualization which seems to work for me is to imagine little balls of black light which symbolize frustrations forming in the palm of my hand. These I throw fiercely at the ground to bury that energy. Another alternative is to take some four part crackers named after your problems, break them apart (dispersing the negative energy), then eat them by way of signifying your victory.

The added advantage to the second option is the fact that no one will really think you odd for eating a cracker on the bus, however a bystander might wonder about your mental state if they see you throwing invisible items at the ground! In other words, use some common judgment in what type of activities are best in your circumstances. Using a little ingenuity, I am sure you can either adjust these or think of some other more appropriate ones.

CHANGING CLOTHES

When you arrive home at the end of the day, instead of puttering for a while, go and get changed. Allow your worries and tensions to fall off of you with your "costume." Ladies, get those heels and bra off; men, undo the heavy work boots or tie and breathe a little. Don't worry about the garments, you can always pick them up later (fussing with them immediately is symbolically like accepting back your anxiety). Stretch out again as you did in the morning. Slowly feel yourself returning to the real you. Look around the magical living space you have created and know you are safe within it.

Now put on something that you enjoy, which is also comfortable. What you wear will often make you feel better, or at least different, almost immediately. Unless you absolutely have to, try to take at least thirty minutes to readjust to being home. Remember, this space is your sanctuary in the storm. Don't allow it to be disrupted by the negativity you may carry in from the world outside. If need be, after you're relaxed, purge any unwanted energy from your home with a little of your favorite incense.

Get into the habit of doing this daily. Remember, life itself is ritualistic in nature, and routines are a part of that. The more you incorporate magic principles into that routine, the less awkward and more effective they will become.

EVENING

PHYSICAL EXERCISE

The modern world is rediscovering the value of exercise. A body which is unused deteriorates and becomes more vulnerable to dis-ease.[1] Workouts refresh, rejuvenate, aid circulation, calm, improve blood pressure and the metabolism, burn calories, and generally expedite a greater inner harmony for people who follow some type of daily routine.

I choose to exercise in the evening because, frankly, I just can't get that motivated first thing in the morning. There are many things at night which also lend themselves to simple exercises. Instead of just letting the dog out, I take him for a walk around several blocks. Or, if I need something from a nearby store, I will hike over. Walking is one of the most convenient and safe exercises for people of all ages to enjoy, and it helps decrease air pollution, besides!

While you are doing the dishes you can also do isometrics such as tummy tucks or contracting the muscles in your legs to improve their tone. Small repetitive movements like walking on your toes or heels from room to room help stretch and massage leg muscles, again allowing oxygen to move more freely.

The value of stretching and loosening your muscles can not be overemphasized. Before you start any vigorous workout routine, you should always prepare your body. If you exercise before your muscles are stretched you can accidentally pull something out of place. Remember, the purpose of exercise is to make yourself healthier.

Good warm-up activities include:

○ Reach up to the ceiling and embrace the sky with your arms, then extend towards the ground to reconnect with the earth. Repeat five times. A variation on this is to alternate reaching up with the left arm towards the right (right arm wrapped around the waist), and vice versa with the right arm, then bringing both towards your toes together.

O   Marching in place: stand in one spot with your back straight and arms at your side. Begin stepping as if marching, and if you like add some comfortable arm movement. Five minutes is good for this part of the warm-up. For those who have stairs at home, a couple of trips up and down also acts as an excellent means to get the blood circulating.

O   Cross-toe touches: besides the one mentioned above, begin with your legs spread apart about three feet and hands on hips. Now alternate touching your right hand to the left foot or left hand to right foot, ten times per side, each time returning to your beginning position.

O   Head and neck: touch your chin to your chest and move your head slowly around clockwise, then counterclockwise three times. After this, hold your head erect and tilt it to the left and right as if to touch your ear to your shoulder. When you feel a slight pull in the muscle, stop. This exercise is good for when you have a headache, too, especially if combined with massage afterwards.

O   Waist and hips: stand with your feet apart as above, and your hands on your hips. Now, turn first to your right, keeping your back straight, and moving as far in that direction as you can. Return to center and turn to the left. Repeat five times each side. Next, add some arm movement to this. Here, as you turn to your right, your right arm goes out straight to the right and your left moves in the same direction, out from your chest, at a 45 degree angle to your right arm (see illustration). Repeat this ten times each side.

At any time during warm-ups or actual exercise routines if you begin to feel winded or hurt, stop and walk for a few minutes. Your body knows its limits and needs to be listened to. A certain amount of persistence is needed to make an exercise program effective; however, there is a healthy difference between determination and carelessness for the sake of physical beauty. Please be careful. Also, as you advance you may increase the amount of time on each portion of your exercise routine and add in small amounts of free weights as you feel you are ready. Adding weights or boosting your time simply intensifies the physical effect.

The neat thing about exercise, besides its physical rewards, is the fact that you can often combine this time with breathing or positive

Exercise Positions

visualization for your spiritual well-being. One such method which I devised was to exercise through "the elements." This program begins with a few aerobics for the air element, breathing in and out through the nose. During this time, try to visualize birds in flight moving away with your tensions on their wings.

Next comes the earth element, breathing in through the mouth and out through the nose and jogging in place or lying on the floor for leg lifts. As you take in your breath, envision drawing nourishment from the earth like a tree might.

The third part is for fire, and done with more active "heated" exercise such as running, fast biking, weight work, etc. During this, breathe in and out through your mouth (if possible) and imagine the energy of the sun filling each cell.

Finally, after all this fill up a tub with warm water or go to a swimming pool. Allow the water to smooth and relax your muscles and refresh your skin. Breath in through your nose and out through your mouth, as you do with meditation. This is your rest after labor and a time to renew the energy you have just expended.

Other programs such as aerobics, stepping, jogging, traditional exercises (sit-ups, jumping jacks), yoga, and small amounts of weight lifting can be likewise beneficial. However, it is highly recommended that before you begin any exercise routine you consult your physician. Depending on your medical history and physical condition, your workout may have to be modified.

RELAXATION EXERCISES

Besides some of the visualization and breathing techniques discussed throughout this book, there are other easy ways to help get rid of some excess anxiety and help yourself relax. One is something my son's teacher came up with, called "shaking your sillies out." She devised this method to help calm the kids down when they were getting too rambunctious, but after watching Karl perform this activity, I realized it had marvelous potential for magical release, as well.

To try it yourself, stand up and begin to "shake out" each part of your body (like a wet dog, almost). You should start with your hands and feet, visualizing any negative energy being grounded[2] out as you flick it off. After you have done sections of your body, then try the whole thing at once. I know you will feel silly at first (I certainly did), but give it a chance. The movements actually loosen muscles and improve blood flow. After you are done, take three deep breaths, sip on a tall cool drink, and sit down. You should feel much better.

Other very relaxing activities include reading the paper or a good book, a leisurely shower or bath, playing solitaire, writing a letter to an old friend, etc. Whatever you do, try to find an opportunity to give this needed respite to yourself. The modern world all too often considers such repose as being lazy, but it really isn't. If you don't take care of yourself, the things you deem important will not get done well. If instead you can approach them with a healthy, invigorated body and mind, you can not help but be successful in all your endeavors.

FAMILY AND/OR PRIVATE TIME

Another thing which has been neglected in the ebb and flow of busy living is the aspect of family time and private time. I mention both here because, thanks to a very transient society, not everyone lives with their family, or even has them nearby. For people in this situation, this section might better be termed "social and private time."

On the surface you may not perceive either of these things as magical in essence; however, if you look at many of the symbols given to us in systems of divination such as the Tarot and runes, you will know that being among people and being alone play key roles to our spiritual learning experience.

The two of cups in Tarot and Gebo of runes (see Chapter Seven) are indications of partnership; our encounters with one other emotionally close person and how this relationship ultimately effects our lives. The Hermit and Othila speak of separations and times in the wilderness to sort things out and find our own way. These archetypes, which appear in many other magical emblems, tell us that we need to pay attention to the social issues confronting us daily.

Questions such as: *Are we getting enough input from others? Do we make opportunities to mingle with our friends? Are we listening to the people who care most about us? Are we giving our loved ones enough quality time and attention?* should be given consideration. Conversely, we also need to be aware of when we are giving too much of ourselves to others and not tending to our own needs, or moments when we are allowing the opinions of those around us to sway our convictions and sensibilities. These are the times when retreat is called for; quiet time for introspection and balance.

If we can find a way through magical perspectives not to neglect either need in the human temperament, we will find ourselves much happier people for the effort.

MOON BATHS

Out beneath the moonlight, in the shadow of a star, great magic can be born. Whether you are walking the dog, taking out the trash, going to a neighbor's house, or just stepping out for a breath of air, take a few extra minutes in the moonlight. This is especially effective if the moon is waxing to full (a time of fertility and prosperity).

As a balance to the male energy of the sun, look up to the moon, which is the representation of the Goddess and the aspects of imagination, intuition, healing . . . and allow the silvery light to fill you. Even as you danced with the dawn, frolic under a Harvest Moon[3] and enrich your existence with new productivity.

DREAMTIME (IN BED)

There are many ways to improve our sleep cycle, both common and magical. Generally you will find that exercising, or at least doing a little stretching before you retire, will improve your sleep and help to relieve a certain amount of stiffness. Meditation before bed has similar effects, adding the dimension of deeper sleep states and often improved dream memory. Visualization will sometimes allow you to actively "set up" your dreams by giving your conscious and subconscious mind something to focus on before sleep.

Other common methods employed by magical people to help insure restful nights include drinking herbal teas such as catnip, valerian, and camomile (see also Chapter Six), dream pillows (recipe variations in Chapter Seven), and finally, something called a dream catcher. This basically looks like a loop of wood or grapevine with delicate netting spider-webbed throughout the circumference. Frequently feathers, crystals, or other small objects dangle from the center. This dream catcher is placed over the bed, near the head of the sleeper to help direct pleasant or visionary dreams to them.

Besides their magical significance, dream catchers look lovely as a decorative item and can be found in many Native American shops, new age stores, and through Co-Op America (address given in Chapter Five).

OTHER COMMON OCCURRENCES/NEEDS

The entire realm of human experience cannot be covered in volumes, let alone one section of a book. However, there are other little circumstances which tend to come up frequently (but not necessarily daily) which I wanted to include in this chapter. These situations or aspirations are common to almost everyone at some point. They are placed here to serve as an example of how we can meet our ever-changing conditions, and often uncertain futures, with a little magical spunk.

Job Hunting

If you are either in a job you do not like or are unemployed, magic combined with persistence and professionalism can often help you achieve your career goals.

EXERCISE 1

Go through the newspaper and clip out all the ads you feel have potential for you. Please be fairly realistic considering your qualifications. Make a list of the jobs on a separate sheet of paper, which puts them in preferred order of interest. Next, place the newspaper clippings on your altar, lighting some incense of prosperity (basil, cinnamon, and elderflower make a good combination) and burn the clippings with it. Visualize the smoke moving out in all directions to the companies you will be contacting, like a path for you to follow. Next, make your calls, write letters, or apply in person as the ad specifies. Over the ensuing days or weeks, continue to burn your incense once a day before interviews, bless your resume, and use the time to mentally prepare yourself. Watch and see what doors open!

EXERCISE 2

Once your hunting is complete, come home and relax a little. Don't be surprised if you are tired; in some ways interviews are a lot like a sales position where you are your own promoter. Once you feel rested, try visualizing yourself at one of the offices you have visited, being offered a job, or the phone ringing with similar news. If it helps, before you begin try adding a burning green candle carved with the words "job offer" and a silver coin in the palm of your hand to help focus your energy.

On a normal level, remember to send a letter of continued interest and appreciation for time spent to the prospective employers you felt best about. This is important because it familiarizes them with your name, and presents a professional image. If the company has given you a date by which you will receive a response, try activating your visualization around this time frame, then calling for your answer.

Wishes/Desires

Every day we have moments where we think to ourselves, "I wish . . . " There is no lack in humanity of dreams and desires; nor should there be. This is part of what keeps us motivated and striving to become the best individuals we can. This energy can also be used for magic. In this case, take some spring water which has been charged by placing it in the light of a waxing moon for three nights.[4] Find something like a nice earthenware bowl or fish bowl to place this water in so that it fills it about halfway to the top.

To this water you may wish to add a sprinkling of pine needles for productive energy, lavender flower for wish magic, and an elder leaf for luck. Set this in a sunny window, and each morning drop in a penny named after your needs or desires. The added benefit of the wish-bowl is that as the sun warms the water, the herbal scents will be released to your room and actually help to fill your home with that magical energy. Once the bowl is filled, the pennies should be given to charity by way of reciprocity and thankfulness for everything you have already been blessed with.

Increased Energy for Goals

In Chapter Two I talked about making goal lists and then using them for spells. For this bit of magic, you take your list and put it in a cauldron (or other fire-proof burner) which is filled with herbs. I like a combination of cinnamon for power, ginger for success, sage for fruitfulness, thyme for courage, and a few oak leaves for luck. Start this whole mixture burning over charcoal, and then get comfortable nearby.

Begin to breathe slowly as you would for any meditation and start to bring your goal strongly into mind. Feel the energy of the herbs around you and inhale, allowing the power to fill your vision and your body to help engender your goals. Continue until you feel so full and prepared to step out towards attaining your dream that you can no longer sit still.

Go and do whatever you feel most motivated towards at that moment, allowing the incense to naturally burn out. You may repeat this exercise any time you feel the need. My only caution is that people with respiratory ailments or allergies would be better off simply carrying the herbs listed as a sachet instead of burning them. This will allow you to still savor their scents without any physical discomfort.

Changing Habits

Take a small, flammable object which, to you, is an emblem of your habit or negative thought form. Place this on charcoal with herbs of change and growth (cinnamon, clove, and myrrh are good choices), and burn them. As you do, visualize yourself in the center of the fire as a phoenix, who rises from the ashes more beautiful and stronger than ever before. Inhale the scents of the herbs along with the air to help transport that magical energy to each cell of your being. Continue until you feel more positive and strengthened to face the challenge ahead. You may repeat this whenever you feel the need.

One word of caution: as with any change in personality, honest effort on your part is always required for the magic to work effectively. The magic is an aid, but without actions to match your intent, the energy gets blocked.

Finding Lost Items

There is nothing more frustrating than misplacing items, especially those of deep sentimental value. Magic gives us various means to help bring lost effects back to us through many ways which can be as unique as you are. I have a couple that I personally find helpful, the first of which I call "drawing" magic. If you would like to try this yourself, begin with a hand-drawn picture of the item lost. As you recreate the piece, your art work is not half as important as a strong mental image of the item. While you sketch, you may wish to softly whisper to the likeness, "return to me." Next, attach this piece of paper to a rubber band somehow, be it by tying it on, with tape, or whatever. Finally, sit or stand in the last place you remember having that item. Find a tree or solid object to adhere one end of the picture to somewhat loosely (a little piece of bubble gum works), while you hold the other end of the rubber band in your hand.

Clear your mind and again bring that image clearly into your mental range. Begin to open yourself to white light energy (like sunlight from above) and channel that warm, powerful image into your arm and down the length of the semi-taut rubber band. When you feel as if the light has penetrated your picture at the other end, pull stiffly on it so that your drawn image springs back into your hand. What happens at this point can be significant. If the rubber band breaks, chances are you may not be able to retrieve your possession. If the picture stays on the tree and takes several tugs to free it, your search will be difficult, but successful. In this case the number of tugs can be indicative of days or weeks before attainment. If, on the other hand, the image frees itself easily and returns to your keeping in the spell, frequently you will find the lost item within the next few days.[5]

Another approach, less mystical in nature, is to simply get yourself into a meditative frame of mind and begin going over the activities of the last few hours or days since you last saw the possession. You may actually have to mimic your trips or other personal actions to trigger specific bits of memory for clues. As you trace your steps, ask those who were with you if they remember anything unusual happening, etc. This may not be the most magical technique on the surface, but you can always begin in your home with a short ritual that includes a picture of you with the lost item, a burning candle to light your way, and a slice of ginger root in your pocket to help bring success!

Traffic Lights

Magic is somewhat electrical in nature, at least in the way it moves on energy waves. Sometimes when we are particularly attuned to objects we can sense those waves and get impressions. In reverse, we also believe it is possible to give various items a storehouse of energy by pouring this magical power into them. So what does all this have to do with sitting at a traffic light when you really need to be elsewhere? Quite a bit, actually.

Some people will scoff at this proposal, but the best way to find out if it works is to try it a few times. When you are at an intersection and feel it is important to be on your way, keep your eyes open, but visualize a green beam of light moving from your eyes or fingertip to the bottom light on the traffic signal. This is a little difficult at first because you have to actually try and "sense" the frequency of green, and the energy of the signal before you. Take a deep breath and let it out, also envisioning the same green light moving out towards the light. With time, concentration, and practice, you should see some success with this exercise. Like the objects which you charge with magical energy, you are instead trying to alter the flow of energy in one specific object; namely the traffic light.

I should warn that this exercise is not an excuse to be reckless in traffic or to break vehicular laws. It is only a way of helping improve your transport time from one place to another when you feel it is essential. As with all things, don't waste your precious magical energy on whims, but save it for when you have a pertinent necessity.

Quieting Irritating People

I know that my work place is probably no different from yours in that there are certain people who have the uncanny ability to get under our skins no matter how hard we try to remain calm and understanding. In all reasonableness, just because we practice magic doesn't necessarily mean we're ready for sainthood. So how do we cope magically with these moments? First, you can try breathing through them, doing a traditional count backwards (silently) in your mind as you go. Second, try to focus your attention on something else which is positive about that individual (even if it's only the color of their socks). If neither of these approaches works, try this little visualization.

Whatever it is about the person which seems to irritate you, block it out somehow in your mental imagery. For example, if they talk incessantly, either see them with tape over their mouths, or see yourself with earmuffs! Pour white light into your protective object in the vision (e.g., the tape or the muffs) so that your magic is not harmful, only thwarting. The result of this visualization, with practice, is to eventually be able to tune out that irritating habit, or gain enough patience so those prolonged encounters don't leave you off-center.

Healing Sickness

While the American Medical Association[6] might not always want to put a seal of approval on "mystical" healing approaches, the fact remains that they can be very helpful to the recipient, if from no other vantage point than improving the emotional state. In Europe and Asia there are more professional medical approaches which employ techniques often considered radical to the American mind (touch therapy, acupuncture, osteopathies, herbalism, etc.). Slowly, however, we are seeing a growing desire in the public for less medicine and more healthy ways of living to help prevent sickness altogether. For the urban magician this represents marvelous options opening up to take their faith into new realms, even for the common cold!

We now have bio-feedback, aquagenesis, simple hot-tubs to ease pain, and many other physically productive healing methods which can be combined with the spiritual for increased effects (herbs for health are discussed in Chapter Six). The path you take for personal healing or that of another person really depends on vision and personality. I should warn that no matter your approach, do not consider your techniques as "medical" in nature or use them as a substitute for professional care. Simply employ them as additional aids to the healing process.

Here are some basic hints which should help:

○ In working with any type of healing rituals, both practical and symbolic, you should always employ words which have deep personal meaning for you or the recipient. If the actions and words don't make sense to you, especially on an emotional level, chances are the rite will be ineffectual.

○ In your personal life, you should set up a routine of cleansing and healing (see Exercise 1). Let's face it, almost every day there are tensions and problems which can lodge themselves into our minds. When these are not released, they sometimes later evidence themselves as dis-ease (note hyphen). This dis-ease may be as simple as muscle tension, depending on where that anger, bitterness, etc., snags itself. To balance this, let me say I do not believe all sickness is self-inflicted, but there have been many documented cases where a person has been cured physically when a specific emotional turmoil was resolved. That's why I encourage everyone to use their emotional reactions constructively, not wearing them like a badge of honor. When you release problems, you also free yourself to do much more functional magic.

○ Along the same lines we need to think in magical terms about our bodies. We have a gift, a physical vehicle for learning, and how we treat this temple is often very reflective of how we really view ourselves and our spiritual state. For example, if we abuse our body with cigarettes, it says we don't care about living to our fullest potential. It also is a negative statement about how we regard the planet, since tobacco takes seven years to decompose. This is an example which illustrates reality. In all fairness, I know many wonderful magical people who smoke and it is a very difficult habit to break; even so, it is not allowed in my home. That is my sanctuary and place for healing.

○   Remember that you are the only person who can take care of you 100% of the time. If there are things in your life that you really care about doing, realize they can not be done well or properly if you are sick. When you are ill, rest so that you can return to your projects with renewed health. Eat well, exercise, and take care of little things before they get big. On the spiritual level, this means not putting yourself in situations which are obviously abrasive to your Path. Watch the people you bring close to yourself with care. What kind of music do they create with you (see Exercise 3)? Are their words and actions harmonic or discordant? Do they ask with interest, or demand? Do they liberate you, or dispense bondage? The answers to these kinds of questions will tell you quickly those people or situations which should be put in the ten-foot pole department.

Exercise 1: Routine Personal Cleansing/Healing Ritual

Every day we are bombarded with frustrations, tension, pollutants in the air, crowding, and hundreds of other things that are not really healthy for us on any level. Even when our ecological awareness advances, we will still have regular anxieties to cope with. That is why a routine of personal cleansing and healing is probably more important to the urban magician of today than it has been in years past.

Basic relaxation techniques are pretty easy for anyone to learn. Most easily done while lying down, you can begin by breathing more slowly and taking close notice of your breath. As you feel yourself getting slightly sleepy, change your attention to the rest of your body and allow it to become so heavy you can't move. All your tension, anger, and sickness becomes weighty and pours out of the back of your body into the ground below.

From above you, a white-gold light pours down, flowing over your whole being with warmth and refreshed energy. Like a healing salve, it holds you in this place between worlds. Do not rush. Don't worry if you fall asleep. Just rest here until you feel whole again.

For some people, a nightly ritual of meditation serves to bring relaxation and more restful sleep. Others only feel the need weekly. Whatever schedule you establish for yourself, stick to it. By releasing these pressures on a regular basis, you are helping your body's natural healing processes to work better.

Besides this day-to-day discipline, I recommend performing self-cleansing and healing on special days, such as your birthday. In this way you are giving yourself a wonderful gift; energy towards another healthy, magical year.

EXERCISE 2: AURIC CLEANSING AND BALANCING FOR OTHERS

I have often been asked how auric cleansing and balancing works. For a moment you need to view the human body not as a physical thing, but a machine which employs tremendous amounts of energy to keep working. This energy has been photographed for us through a process known as Kirlian photography. Here, an actual visual representation of what magical traditions call the aura can be seen by anyone.

Kirlian photography has also shown there is a difference in the energy levels when someone prays, meditates, is angry or peaceful. So, we can base some of our auric work on this knowledge. If you know someone who does auric balancing already, have them do one for you. Experience is a great teacher. I learned the process from two people who helped me through periods of great physical pain after an automobile accident.

If you are not fortunate to have someone nearby to act as a guide you can learn to work with auras yourself, but it may take a little longer. If you can find a willing magical partner it will help because they will give you honest feedback on the results of your attempts.

While the process may vary for each person, the basic technique seems to be similar in all people with "healing" talents I have observed. Usually the subject is placed in a comfortable position on the floor or other large, flat surface. I add candlelight, music, and herbal oils to help bring a more relaxed state for both myself and the individual.

Once the proper state of mind is reached where the physical energy of the subject can be sensed in some manner, the actual work begins. Some healers actually feel auric energy like a texture or level of heat. Others can see it as color/light, and still other people smell or taste it. Which way the signals come to you depends greatly on which one of your senses you respond most strongly to.

Whatever indications you get, you want to look for consistency in the energy flow around the body. During the day, this flow is constantly pulled out of shape by random energy around us, our personal reactions to the day, etc. Frequently this imbalanced state evidences itself as feeling out of sorts, having a headache, and/or other minor malady like a crick in the neck. The job of a good healer is to first put the energy back in order so that the physical being can function properly.

You may want to start with a little massage on the more tense areas of the body to help bring your subject into a relaxed state. This will also help get you in touch with their personal energy, thus putting everyone at ease. Remember, healing is a gentle art which should not feel like a rude intruder at their door, but instead a quiet, warm wave.

Next, move your hands to about a foot above their body. This seems to be the most common place awareness of the aura begins. Move your hands slowly over the entire body at this level, making a mental note of where the fabric of their energy seems frayed, tangled, thin or too thick. These are the areas you are going to have to focus on.

Usually you will need to pull in some "clean" energy from outside to get these areas back in balance. The easiest way for me to describe this process is through visualizing yourself sprinkling silvery glitter into their aura. This is actually little nodules of white light energy added to help smooth out the overall texture. As you scatter them, you will notice that they move naturally to distribute themselves evenly. You can now begin the process of what I call combing.

Just like you brush your hair to smooth and shape it, you use your hands like an auric brush, gently shaping the energy into a smooth, consistent level all around the body. This needs to be done from both sides, so somewhere in the middle of your work have your subject turn over from their center of gravity (usually near the pelvic region) slowly. To move quickly will undo all the work thus far.

When you are finished, instruct them to lie quietly for as long as they wish. When they do get up, they should move carefully. Some people experience a slight giddiness after this experience and could literally pass out if they jump right up off the floor.

In the beginning an individual will often need frequent auric work just to get them used to being in balance. After a while you can tell them to visualize what you are doing so they can learn to help themselves.

EXERCISE 3: HEALING SPELLS

Throughout history, some of the most popular folk remedies have been based on sympathetic magic. Here, symbolism and its effect on the mind of an individual plays an intricate role in the effectiveness of the magic. One of my favorite examples comes from an old rope cure. Here the country physician would go to the patient and tie a piece of rope loosely around their waist or wrist. Then, as knots were tied in the two ends they would say something like, "I do not bind Joseph, but this sickness." They would then describe the malady in detail, while continuing to tie knots (usually in multiples of three). The rope was then removed from the patient and either buried or burned to symbolize the death of the sickness. This particular approach still has certain validity today.

Another popular technique for healing has been the use of a poppet. Here a little doll stuffed with healing and protective herbs such as camomile, rosemary, sage, and cedar was made and named after the individual in need. Often it was sewn while charms were whispered such as "Mary, Mary, you're not wealthy, but you'll soon be very healthy." The chanting of the words helps to focus the maker's attention on the target of their magic. It could then be given as a gift, or placed in a safe place. There is no reason why the urban magician can not perform a similar spell with permission of the other person. If they are not magically inclined, you may need to take care with how the poppet is made so the energy does not manipulate, but is sent out like a gift for acceptance.

A third healing spell uses water and rock as components. Write the sickness on the stone with food coloring or nontoxic water-soluble markers and toss it in a clear, running stream. Turn away from it knowing that as water moves over the rock, it will also wash away the infirmity.

Much of the usefulness of spells comes from the fact that they allow us to become an active participant in the betterment of our health and that of those around us. Do not perform such magic if you do not intend to really make an effort afterwards to reclaim your well being. This means resting, eating right, and perhaps even seeing a doctor. You have already released healing energy to help the process along, but you now have the responsibility for using that energy wisely.

SUMMARY

Please do not be afraid to be inventive and original in the way you handle the various situations of your life. After all, it is your life. No teacher or book can be with you 24 hours a day to dictate your coping mechanisms; that job must be left to your own, capable hands.

There is a modern aphorism which says, "When life hands you lemons, make lemonade." This expresses exactly how you should consider each moment of your existence. When you wake up, when you cook for your family, while you're with friends, playing with the dog, or driving in the car . . . consider how you can bring magic to those moments. How can you begin to live in a reality where that wonderful energy fills each space and point of your life?

This chapter was designed to give you a strong foundation of ideas from which your own creative magic can be born to meet daily necessities as they arise. But instead of this being the end-all and be-all for your personal daily magic, my prayer is that it is only the first glimpse of a new beginning.

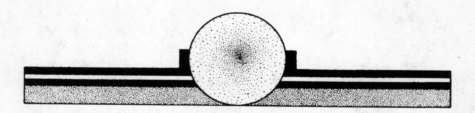

NOTES FOR CHAPTER 10

1. *Dis-ease.* I hyphenate the word here to show that sickness is not always caused by simply the physical realities. Our emotional state can and does play an important role in our overall well being. When we are upset, we are dis-eased because we are no longer in balance. Exercise offers a way to release much of our negative energies, increase blood flow, and generally make us healthier in body and spirit.

2. Mother Earth has always known how to handle dirt. When you visualize negative energy being grounded, it is sometimes easiest to see it as a brown-black wave moving from your hands and being disbursed in the soil. This will not harm the land as the soil acts in much the same capacity as sand does for hot objects, simply distributing the negativity until it disappears.

3. A *Harvest Moon* usually appears in fall. It is a full moon near the horizon which is almost golden orange in coloration. This is a beautiful phenomena brought about by light being filtered through our atmosphere, and has marvelous potential for bringing fruitfulness to any magical efforts.

4. Charging objects by waxing or full moon is well known to magic. I chose the symbolism of a waxing moon here because you are still working on something, it is not finished just yet. The waxing moon energies help draw you towards your goal.

5. Divination is not an exact art. While many people get amazing results from divination, it is not always 100% correct in its interpretations. Remember to use your own insights and intuition for any explication of a divinatory system as a final judge and guide.

6. The AMA is not very encouraging of alternative healing approaches, so if you do choose to work in herbal realms, take care not to purport yourself as a physician. This can cause you no end of trouble. Also, with regard to herbalism, take great pains to check your measurements, and cross-reference sources. Some herbs have a thin line between healing capabilities and harmful side effects.

Thou trade, thou king of modern day
Change thy ways, change thy ways
Let the sweaty laborers file
A little while, a little while
Where art and nature sing, and smile.
— Sidney Lanier, *The Symphony* (1875)

The Urban Wheel of Time

I took the road less traveled by
And that has made all the difference.
— Robert Frost, "The Road Less Traveled" (1915)

From working magic into our daily routine, the next logical step is to look at various celebrations throughout the year as opportunities to honor the Earth and the God/dess in all their aspects. Yet for the urban magician this commemoration is sometimes very difficult. Besides your own apartment or home, where can you go in the city to observe your rites, especially if you don't have a vehicle? Even within the home environment ritual can often be troublesome considering the added obstacles of non-Pagan/Wiccan family members, children, ringing telephones, barking dogs, honking horns, and any number of other distractions. So where can you find a little bit of mystical energy in the city?

Believe it or not, it can be done. City environments offer wonderful cultural centers like the planetarium, science museum, art galleries, theaters, parks, and playgrounds that are perfect for magical activities, especially meditation. The planetarium allows you to reconnect with universal movements. The science museum gives you a feeling for the history of the human race, looking back through time and forward towards our future. Art and theater provide a peek at the human soul (see Chapter Nine). Parks allow you to play near/with other adults and children without expectations, and enjoy a little nature amidst the concrete. The only caution on any of these public sites is that you need to check your area's laws to be certain your designated activities are allowable.

In our region we have the extra benefit of having one of the great wonders of the world, Niagara Falls, to visit. I can't even begin to describe the immense cleansing power of this experience. I am sure you might have similar places nearby, even if they're not so famous. What about considering a dam, water treatment plant, a particularly engaging old tree, an antique lamp post, a small pond, greenhouses, floral and theme gardens at a park, arboretums, and even certain ingeniously designed shopping malls or statues as locations for prospective magical work? Examples of this type of city-centered magic come from my own experience. Go to a large parking lot late in the evening to get a little peace and quiet for meditation. Or if you are feeling exuberant, play a little hopscotch and dance merrily around a lamp post instead of a bonfire. Another urban exercise which anyone can do is to watch where the sun is at a specific time every day. Observe its movement over housetops and trees, until slowly you can learn to predict where it will be the next day!

I happen to live very close to downtown Buffalo, and while I can't say I always enjoy the lack of greenery, there are some moments when nothing seems more magical than the towering buildings which appear to touch the sky and beyond. Some day, when it is close to dusk, go to a hill adjacent to a nearby city and watch as it comes to life. A little at a time, beams of light will shine forth filling your sight like a mirror of the stars above.

Reach your hands out towards those lights and colors and sense the amazing power in them. Just below you hundreds of people are laughing, dancing, going hither and yon, and putting out raw energy as they go. You can draw that energy to yourself through visualization, like breathing light into your being, then direct it towards the goal of a ritual or spell as you exhale! Remember that magic is essentially the bending of energy toward specific ends. Conversely, it can be just as rewarding to watch the same city between the hours of 5 and 7 AM when everything is just waking up, not just people but also insects, animals, and birds. When the sun touches the first building, listen carefully for the sounds of this reawakening.

Another activity I find very spiritually enriching in the city is walking certain "safer" streets by night. I watch the people, the way they interact with each other, feel the wind on my face, and bring myself back into focus for the reality around me. This verity is not always beautiful, but it is inspirational. When I see all the joys and sorrows, the isolation and socialization, the dark, the light, and the shadows which a city environment holds, it reminds me of how much work magical people have yet to do. We are the ones who can look beyond the surface and see potential for change, then take that possibility and turn it into magical reality. Those of us who live or work in the city can share this transformational energy wherever we go, like a healing salve which is desperately needed amidst the shiny steel and pavement.

As we learn to cope with urban complications for magic, and even make competent use of them, we will slowly discover that our rites likewise reflect a new peacefulness with their environment. Instead of seeing the noise around us as an intrusion, it becomes almost a companion and has a heartbeat all its own. The comings and goings transform into a patterned flow. With a little ingenuity, all these things can come together in the center of the city to spark magical energy which can enhance any of your commemorations.

CELEBRATING THE SEASONS

Learning the natural cycles that often pass us by unnoticed (except in the way we dress) is very important to living in harmony with the Earth. No matter where you live, the first step towards returning to more earth-centered perspectives is to be more observant daily. The awareness of these rhythms and their symbolism for profound lessons of a spiritual nature is not only significant but essential to our magical training and growth.

In creating a calendar for the urban magician, I decided that something completely unique was called for which could inspire a wide range of individuals and help to meet the needs of modern reality. While the dates of common Wiccan and Pagan celebrations will be included as applicable, there are many other holidays which should also catch our eye for their magical potential. Since we are living in a modern world where much of the history and meaning of many holidays have been replaced with consumerism, we have to find ways to work creatively and effectively within that realm.

To these ends, and to help motivate a one-world perspective, I have combined ancient and modern festivals from around the globe, including many which appear on your everyday calendar. Along with these you will find a seasonal review with ideas for home and altar decorations, the origins of the holidays and historically associated activities, and then finally suggestions on how to tie in the personal, magical element.

In reviewing these, remember that the exact dates for any holiday can change slightly from year to year, so be sure to check both your regular and magical calendars to note these variations. If a particular holiday changes according to moon phases or other cultural specifications, it is noted for your reference. In these instances you will probably need a lunar calendar to determine the exact date.

Some of these suggestions may have to change because of your climate. Please do not hesitate to make revisions accordingly. Likewise, I do not expect you to incorporate every holiday given to your magical observance schedule. I simply share them with you as ideas which can hopefully help enrich your annual observances and magical experiences.

With this in mind, you may wish to consider adding or substituting other more personalized celebrations, honoring things such as a birthday, anniversary, coming of age, croning,[1] death, or any other passages which mark drastic changes in lifestyle, expectations, and/or perspectives to your Book of Days. These types of rites need to be created with the individual being recognized in mind, and can then be moved into your regular timetable of festivals.

Spring (February – April)

This is the dawn of a resurrected Earth, when trees stretch to meet the sun and everything on the land rejoices with restored vitality. For magic, this is the season of the Maiden[2] when our positive visions and perspectives for the future can truly make a difference in the whole year to come. Spells and rituals which deal with inspiration, creativity, outsets of new projects, etc., are all effective now, especially when combined with a waxing crescent moon (first quarter).

Throughout this season it is appropriate to decorate your home or altars with fresh mown grass, wild flowers, the first buds of a nearby tree, eggs to represent fertility, and seedlings. Spring rain gathered from the windowsill can fill your ritual cup or may alternatively be used to asperge the circle. Any pastel cloths can adorn your magical space to sway with the fresh winds of change and rebirth. A broom from your hearth (or kitchen) can be used to sweep the circumference of the sacred space and move the old energies out; welcoming the new.

FEBRUARY 1–2

Holiday: Candlemas (Wiccan), Bridget's Day, Groundhog Day.
Origins: According to folklore, Bridget was an Irish faerie who lived beneath an oak in Kildare. She devoted herself to the care and love of baby animals and all woodland creatures, spending her life in service to the same. In Scotland she is known as *Brüd*. On the Isle of Man women go to their thresholds with rushes to welcome her to their hearth. The tradition of Groundhog Day probably had its roots in Germany where, on this day, they watch for bears, badgers, or other hibernating creatures to come out and view the sun. If the animal returned to slumber, it meant forty more days of winter.
Magical Elements: This is the beginning of the first signs of spring. The earth is just starting to crack open its eyes towards the sun, and the powers of darkness are soon to flee. A good time for spells or rituals which deal with luck, prosperity, or the health and well-being of animals. The traditional Candlemas altar is fairly plain, adorned with as many candles as will fit to bring strength to the sun and help it on its journey into the warmer months.

EARLY FEBRUARY

Holiday: Chinese New Year.
Origins: The date of this festival varies according to the first day of the full moon. It is traditionally a fire festival where fire jumping and firecrackers help frighten away negative spirits and bring protection. Offerings of flowers are laid out for both the Heavens and the Earth to enjoy, while a feast for the family is prepared including place settings to commemorate those who have died. Frequently the meals and offerings incorporate items in numbers of ten (considered a perfect number), including oranges for luck, chopsticks for family unity, and juniper for longevity. The following day is quiet, with the traditional greeting on the street being "may you prosper."

Magical Elements: Light some candles to banish any negativity in your home or life, and leave a small offering of fruit, grain or wine to thank the Powers of Earth and Sky for their continued providence. Consider magics which pertain to prosperity and the strengthening of your family unit, and perhaps find a pair of chopsticks, an orange, and a juniper branch to adorn your altar.

FEBRUARY 8

Holiday: Mass for Broken Needles (Japan).
Origins: In this country, needlework is considered such a fine and valuable art that the seamstress or tailor is incredibly respected for their skills. On one day of the year, all sewing stops to give the needle a merited rest. Special prayers are said and bent needles are mourned for the loss they represent.
Magical Elements: Today might be a good day to venerate your arts or crafts. Lay your creative tools on your altar, and bless them with spring water or incense.[3]

FEBRUARY 14

Holiday: Valentine's Day.
Origins: Valentine's Day grew out of the Roman festival Lupercalia when hundreds of young Romans would draw from various types of lots to determine the name of their lover-to-be. There is a long standing belief that birds and animals choose their mates on this day.
Magical Elements: On this day, a holiday for incurable romantics, try pinning five bay leaves to your pillow to dream of a future lover. Give trinkets of all kinds to those you care about, and venerate the spirit of *amour.* An excellent day for tributes to Venus or spells pertaining to lasting affection, renewing marriage vows, and just generally showing greater appreciation to the people you love.

FEBRUARY 15

Holiday: Birthday of the Pearly Emperor (China).
Origins: This god, according to Taoist belief, presides in heaven over success and failure. Since the Taoists abhor force and revere the spirit of contemplation and reason, offerings to this Emperor are made on his birthday to help ensure success and rewards on earth. The presentations to him include dry tea leaves, mandarin oranges for luck, dates representing a wish for future children, and vermicelli to symbolize long life.
Magical Elements: If you have a special project or dream, today might be the perfect time to perform rituals and spells toward those goals.

Prepare your altar space with oranges, tea, and perhaps long spaghetti noodles for appropriate icons, bring your project into the sacred space, and allow the Great Spirit to bless that endeavor.

THIRD MONDAY IN FEBRUARY

Holiday: Presidents' Day (United States).
Origins: Washington's Birthday was first observed in 1790 on an East Indian ship anchored offshore in New York City. In later years this was combined with that of Lincoln to commemorate all U.S. leaders who have served the country.
Magical Elements: Instead of a ritual, spell, or prayer for only U.S. leaders, now might be the fitting time to remember all the worlds' leaders in your magic, sending energy which will grant insight and wisdom for a long, peaceful future.

FEBRUARY 23

Holiday: Terminalia (Ancient Rome).
Origins: An early Roman King by the name of Numa determined that all landowners were required to properly mark their boundaries. Once a year after this declaration, the property holders would go forth to their boundaries and decorate them with garlands, leaving offerings for the god Terminus, who presides over all perimeters. This action was believed to keep the land safe and unviolated for the coming year.
Magical Element: If you don't have land, you can place an offering of flowers in each corner of your home/apartment and ask for protection and blessing on that space. More permanent markers can be set up and enchanted with magical energy, such as potted plants and crystals indoors, or rose bushes, trees, and other plants outdoors.

MARCH 5

Holiday: Kite Festival (Japan).
Origins: Today, everyone who can brings out an ornate kite made of paper and bamboo. The most popular kites are those portraying dragons and carp in the belief that these symbols bring strength, perseverance, and longevity with the winds. This festival is also commonly observed in China.
Magical Applications: Why not take a kite outdoors and loose the child within you? Name your kite after your problems and burdens and let them be lifted by the fresh spring winds.

MARCH 10

Holiday: Siamese New Year.
Origins: In Siam, the new year is always named like a child just born. At this time the people wear rings of unspun cord over their shoulders for protection, bless their animals, and show allegiance to the King in the royal Buddhist temple by drinking blessed water as a show of faith.
Magical Elements: Place some unspun cord near the boundaries of your home or on your altar for added sanctity, give your pets or familiars a special treat for their companionship, and consider renewing your magical affirmations of Path and goals.

LATE MARCH

Holiday: Earth Day.
Origins: Earth Day was first celebrated in 1970 as a reminder to people to conserve, recycle, and to protect our natural resources. In some respects it is the modern version of Arbor Day when seedlings are often planted (March 26).
Magical Elements: Rituals, meditations and spells for earth healing are perfectly appropriate today. However, even more useful would be to put out a little physical energy and clean up a park, help with a neighborhood recycling effort, and educate about how everyone can help reclaim the well-being of our planet. Begin to make Earth Day every day!

MARCH 27

Holiday: Smell the Breeze Day (Egypt).
Origins: Right around Easter, this holiday is observed by all sects and nationalities represented in Egypt. First thing in the morning people rise, break an onion, and smell it for good fortune. Then they dress in bright colors (pink being a favorite) and go on a picnic with their families, believing that the winds bring improved health this day.
Magical Elements: There is no reason why you can not follow this tradition yourself, enjoying a nice long walk to appreciate the fresh breeze that spring brings. Take special notice of the scents of new flowers and grass just appearing in the air. Excellent time for any magics pertaining to health, family, and any spells which you want to incorporate an air element into.

LATE MARCH

Holiday: Passover (Jewish).
Origins: This festival commemorates the safe deliverance of the Jewish people from the Angel of Death and the cruel hands of the Egyptian Pharaoh. *Matzoth* (unleavened bread) is eaten because they had to rush out of Egypt in such a hurry that bread was not given the chance to rise. A special meal known as the *Seder* is eaten, prayers are said, and stories of the holiday follow.
Magical Element: Consider the number of times you, too, have been delivered or liberated. Thank those that have helped you along the way, and give reverence to Divine powers who answered your calls for assistance. Give something to those in need as a way of reciprocating a little of your own blessings.

LATE MARCH/EARLY APRIL

Holiday: Easter, Purim (Jewish), Eostre (Wiccan).
Origins: The Easter Parade dates back to Constantine, who ordered the people to bedeck themselves in lavish colors and clothes to commemorate the resurrection. Hot cross buns come to us from the Anglo-Saxon tradition of Eostre, named after that fruitful goddess, and the symbol of the egg for fertility is almost universally a part of this festival.
Magical Elements: On the magical calendar today marks the first day of spring, when life returns to the planet giving an opportunity to begin anew. This is a joyous celebration which can include coloring eggs, lush candies, good meals, and time with family and friends to enjoy the warm weather. The sun has now broken free from winter's clutches and is preparing to shine brightly on all your efforts.

APRIL 1

Holiday: April Fool's Day.
Origins: When the calendar changed in the Middle Ages, moving New Year's Day to January 1, there were some people who refused to acknowledge the modifications. These people became the object of teasing, often receiving gag gifts on this day, their new year's. Slowly this developed into a day of prank playing and wild-goose chases of all kinds.
Magical Elements: A good day for unplanned fun and frolic, as well as considering the wisdom of "fools." Rituals involving changes you have wanted to make, but didn't have the personal fortitude to follow through on, are especially effective today.

SECOND WEEKEND IN APRIL

Holiday: National Folk Festival (St. Louis, United States).
Origins: This festival is held every year to commemorate folk traditions and share them with younger generations. Entertainment includes story-telling, fiddlers, square dancing, bell ringing, sword dances, miners and lumberjacks. The date of the festival changes each year.
Magical Elements: Modern society is quickly losing its knowledge of many wonderful, ancient arts because of technological advances. Today might be a good day to hold a ritual commemorating these types of crafts, or to go to the library and learn about one yourself. Spiritually awakened people have the opportunity to reclaim these skills and use them for positive magical ends (see the chapter on herbalism as an example).

Summer (May–July)

Summer is when the fire of vitality flows through the land. The sun is dancing high in the sky, and everything beneath is lively and active. This is the season for magical action and drastic transformations; a time when your focus on the spiritual matters is enhanced, and an excellent period to study your Craft under a shady tree. The Mother[4] aspect of the God/dess is exhibiting itself powerfully now through the full moon, illuminating the shadows in our minds with new knowledge and insight.

Your altar should find room for a few extra candles to celebrate the fire element and act as an aid for scrying. Take the time to do circle dances around an outdoor blaze, or if that's not possible put some candles on your dining room table and rejoice around that instead! Cauldrons or incense burners should be filled with kindling, prepared to burn brightly throughout celebrations in the summer months.

Other appropriate tools may include any fiery-colored plants or flowers for the sacred space and table settings, red or orange altar cloths, bright ritual robes, "fire" herbs in the incense (see Chapter Six), and a fire agate to carry, connecting you to that vigorous energy.

May 1

Holiday: May Day, Beltane.
Origins: May Day began with the Roman festival Floralia where the people gathered flowers dedicated to the Goddess Flora. Later versions of this festival included activities like the naming of a May Queen, May Pole dances, going a-maying, dancing, fire leaping for luck, and purification of cattle by passing them through the smoke of Beltane fires (Scotland). There is a long-standing belief that dew collected on this morning, when applied, will enhance beauty and take away freckles.
Magical Element: Beltane for Wiccans is a fire festival and one heavily laden with symbolism for cleansing, protection, and purification. Magics for healing, beauty, and fertility are enhanced by this energy. The May Pole is a standing reminder of the male aspect, with the ribbons being more feminine, thus suggesting a balance between the two. Consider the virtues you want to weave into or out of your life as you dance!

May 5

Holiday: Feast of Banners (Japan).
Origins: This day in Japan is dedicated to the masculine attributes of strength and courage. For each son, a special carp streamer of paper or cloth is hung outside because of the fish's believed bravery. Within the home there are dolls to commemorate knights, armor, swords, arrows and bows, again representing might and fortitude. Rice dumplings are a favored food, served alongside rice wine flavored with iris, a flower of resilience.
Magical Elements: This is a day to honor the God aspects, especially to give thanks to your patron God(s). Any type of ritual for the male mysteries can be performed today, perhaps most especially the coming of age for a boy in your family or coven.

May 11

Holiday: Ceremony for Rain (Guatemala).
Origins: *Chimares*, the local Indian priests, oversee an early morning sacrifice with the male villagers in attendance. Afterwards, they all gather in the village square and local church to pray, feeling that no aid (Christian or Pagan) should be overlooked. For the next four days the men split up and traverse the hillsides near the village, praying at each shrine before returning home. The fifth day the entire village gathers to serenade the Gods and Saints with maracas, which make a sound similar to rain sticks[5] in other cultures. They then return home and await the first showers.

Magical Element: A good day to work any type of weather magic, especially if it is directed towards drought areas. This may also be an appropriate time to perform rituals or spells for the fading rainforest lands, so important to the Earth's balanced ecology.

MAY 15

Holiday: Feast of Isidro (Philippine Islands).
Origins: Isidro is the patron saint of the harvest in the Philippines. After the rice is gathered, the streets of Manila fill with people carrying flowers, coconuts, sugarcane, yams, and other native fruits to display. In some ways this is a contest to see who can adorn the street most lavishly. After the exhibit, the local children run merrily through and carry off the wares like the candy in a pinata. In Columbia Isidro is a rain god, and in Spain he was simply a rather lazy plowman who trusted the angels to do his labors for him . . . and they did!
Magical Elements: This might be a good opportunity to bless your flower pots or land before you begin planting, calling on the spirit of Isidro to increase your yield, although I don't feel the harvest spoken of here is merely a physical one. The confidence displayed by the historical figure in the providence of good powers is a lesson we can learn from. Not that being lax will bring rewards, but that sometimes we need to rely on the Great Spirit, knowing our answers will come. In this case we reap faith.

ANY SUNDAY IN MAY

Holiday: Holy Wells (Britain).
Origins: Throughout Britain there are various wells dedicated to the saints. It is believed that on any Sunday in May you can travel to these sights to drink or bathe in the waters to cure sickness or receive guidance. Some wells needed an offering, often pennies, in order to work properly.
Magical Elements: You may want to start making your wish-bowl today (see Chapter Ten), or take a nice long healing bath with herbs such as camomile and lavender to relieve tension. Any magic pertaining to wisdom and insight, especially meditative work, could benefit from this timing.

EARLY JUNE

Holiday: Night of Observation (Moslem).
Origins: At the beginning of the new moon in the ninth Moslem month is when *Ramadan,* a time of fasting, begins. This marks the

remembrance of Adam's exile from Eden and the following forty day
fast. On this day, the leaders go to a nearby hill in Cairo to watch for the
new moon. When it arrives, messengers are sent to the streets to declare
the fast. During this entire month it is forbidden to eat between sunrise
and sunset, basically turning night into day. Those who can, sleep during the morning and handle all business affairs in the night.

Magical Elements: Introspection, the dark side of self, balance. We
often consider the light in magic, but the dark can often be just as
revealing. Facing our own limitations and negative aspects can be very
healthy, with proper perspective. Also, I think that fasting periodically
before rituals or when performing important magical functions has a lot
of potential. Foregoing certain foods and fasting can act as offerings in
your festivals (rather like Lent on the Christian calendar). Generally,
fasting eliminates many toxins from our body, thus becoming a cleansing instrument so that we can become more effective channels for
Divine energy. Should you decide to try a short-term fast, remember to
drink plenty of liquids, check with your doctor regarding health limitations, and do not fast for more than three days.

JUNE 16

Holiday: Night of the Drop (Egypt).

Origins: Once a year, the Nile drops to reveal rich soil which sustains
the economy of the whole region. This is the beginning of a joyous season full of celebration and oracular attempts. One favorite family rite is
to take a lump of dough for each member and place it outside for the
night. If one is cracked come morning, it foretells long life. Another
more practical ritual is the hanging of words from the Koran on each
wall of the home to drive out the insects.

Magical Elements: Any divination magics, water spells, and rituals/
spells for sustenance and prosperity to the home. Also an excellent time
to bless and dedicate any soil you plan to use for planting efforts
throughout the year. Bits of this soil could then be given to coven members to bring a rich harvest to their homes as well.

JUNE 20–23

Holiday: Solstice, Midsummer's Day.

Origins: This is a festival of both fire and water, when young people
often stay up to dance until they greet the sun the next morning. May
have been first celebrated by the Romans, who seemed to look for any
good excuse for a party, with many peculiar rites. Fires were lit across
the land to which wreaths were taken. The ashes of these wreaths were

believed to bring fertile fields, protect from lightning, and disperse negative energies. Common decorations for the home included fir boughs, birch, fennel, and lily. During this time it is believed that the faeries speak in mortal tongues.

Magical Elements: This is the best time to harvest your magical herbs, especially roses, rue, St. John's Wort, and vervain. Summer Solstice is the longest day of the year, and a good time to work magics involving strength, clarity of purpose, increased energy, and fertility.

JUNE 27

Holiday: Day of Seven Sleepers (Koran).
Origins: While the story is somewhat obscure in the Muslim Holy writings, the basic tale is that six people and a dog went into a cave as a test of their faith in God. The dog stretched himself across the mouth of the cave while the others fell asleep for 309 years! Because of this the Muslim is instructed never to say they will do something tomorrow, unless it is followed by "if God pleases." The dog is now believed to be in heaven caring for all matters of communication, especially letter writing.
Magical Elements: For people who have a tendency towards procrastination, this date is a good time to try and break free from that habit. Perhaps put a small statue of a dog on top of any project you keep putting off as a gentle reminder to do it today.

JULY 4

Holiday: Independence Day (United States).
Origins: In 1776, the Liberty Bell declared the thirteen colonies free of England. John Adams in a letter to his wife indicated a belief that from that day forward the event would be remembered with parades, sports, games, and illuminations. It seems his prediction was right.
Magical Elements: A day to pray for your country and her leaders. Also a good time to work magics pertaining to liberty, freeing yourself from bad habits, and just generally celebrating your own sense of independence.

JULY 10

Holiday: Panathenaea (Greece).
Origins: This is a special festival in honor of Athena, the patron Goddess of Athens and standing emblem of wisdom. For five days, races, regattas, and musical competitions were held. On the sixth day an image of Athena was presented with a new robe along with gifts of music, fruit, grain, and bread to ensure Her continued blessings on the city.

Magical Elements: For anyone who uses Athena as part of their personal pantheon, this day can be observed at home by making new ritual robes for yourself and presenting offerings to your Goddess image of thread, bread, and a little wine. An excellent day to work spells to bring wisdom to your life.

JULY 20

Holiday: Binding of the Wreaths (Lithuania).
Origins: On this day young lovers go into the forests to gather flowers for wreaths. They also search for twin birch trees. Once the wreaths are made and trees found, the branches of the birch are woven together to form an archway under which couples pass and kiss. These couples are then considered sweethearts for the remainder of summer and fall.
Magical Elements: July is a traditional month for weddings, and this type of observance could be quite beautiful for just such an occasion or a handfasting. If twin birch trees are not available, perhaps someone could weave an archway out of fallen branches or even decorate a commercially made one with fresh flowers and birch leaves for the couple to pass under after their vows are recited.

ABOUT JULY 27

Holiday: Departure of the Pilgrims (Moslem).
Origins: Every good Moslem must make a journey to Mecca once in their life to honor the birth place of Mohammed. On the twenty-third day of Shawwal each year, caravans leave Cairo to carry the pilgrims to their destination.
Magical Elements: Consider and study your magical path and what your goals are for same. Honor and pray for the country where your Patron God and Goddess[6] were traditionally worshipped.

Fall (August–October)

Fall is a season that sits with quiet grace between life and death. Practice magics which deal with endings, facing your personal shadows, and emotional healing during the waning moon for greatest effectiveness. This is a good time for introspection and careful consideration of our goals; a time to acquire wisdom from the Crone, who pours out from her caves bountiful waters of discernment for us to drink.

Decorations appropriate to this season include a moonstone or pearl for the water element, waxed fall leaves, late blooming flowers, braided corn husks, grain dollies, pumpkins, bowls of apples, and any other fruits of the harvest. Robes might turn towards darker hues such as burnt orange or pale browns. Your ritual cup could house apple cider, a traditional favorite for October, and the cauldron may hold spring water or other libations representative of labor's yield.

AUGUST 1

Holiday: Lammas.
Origins: One of the four major festivals in the Druidic year, Lammas is a harvest celebration. The name may be a derivative of the Saxon word *Hlaf-mass,* or loaf mass, because bread made from ripened grain was often part of the altar. Corn dollies were often made, being God/dess images, and given as gifts.
Magical Elements: Gather the fruits of your labors and begin thinking in terms of conservation. Bless some grain and leave a bit on your altar to ensure you will not want through the winter. Share the remainder with the wild animals and birds near your home in thanks to Mother Earth for Her bounty.

AUGUST 9

Holiday: Feast of the Milky Way (China).
Origins: On this day, it is said that a herdsmen who once married a weaver and was later banished is allowed to cross the Milky Way to see his lady love. The Spinning Maiden of the Sky oversees the areas of rain and rivers and is also the patron Goddess of all spinning arts. Burnt offerings of beautifully embroidered garments are often made today.
Magical Elements: Today you can think about bridging gaps in relationships and perhaps healing some old wounds related to them. Go to someone you haven't spoken to for a while and open the door for renewed communications. Also a good opportunity for sewing magical robes and pouches or studying any needle arts as they pertain to your magical work.

AUGUST 16

Holiday: Festival of the Minstrels (Medieval Europe).
Origins: This holiday dates back to the thirteenth century when bardic and oral traditions were very important to the history and enjoyment of

the gentle folk. It was a day and night of elaborate feasting, songs, and storytelling, until a King of the Minstrels was chosen for his ability to please the crowd and outdo his opponents.

Magical Elements: Perform a ritual or spell in thanks for the marvelous musicians we have today. Practice your own art, try writing some lyrics, or just listen to the sounds which have been created for us by talented hands.

AUGUST 25

Holiday: Feast of Green Corn (New York State).

Origins: In 1931, a man by the name of Tom Cook re-enacted a version of the Indian Thanksgiving celebration in Lake Champlain, New York. This performance was so well received that it has become an annual observance with pageantry to honor the Native Americans, their lore, and significant contributions to the culture of the United States.

Magical Elements: Give homage to the spirit of shamanism showing signs of rebirth throughout the world today. Spend some time in a natural setting, appreciating the wonders of nature. Learn a little about the Native American philosophies and how you might apply them for personal magic or daily practical living. Any elemental or environmental magics bode well today.

SEPTEMBER 7

Holiday: Festival of Durga (Bengal).

Origins: Durga is the Hindu Goddess of earth and power and wife of Shiva. This date marks the beginning of a five day celebration in Her honor, dedicated mostly to settling arguments and family reunions. On the final day of the festival, the image of Durga is thrown in the river to bury the disagreements and return the Goddess to the land.

Magical Elements: A date to consider spending time with family and friends, especially those who have been estranged for a while. Perhaps rituals or spells specifically to help heal these relationships (see also Chapter Two) can be done beforehand to assist in the restorative energies.

SEPTEMBER 15

Holiday: Birthday of the Moon (China).

Origins: To the Chinese, the Moon is the sky-bound representation of the Yin, or feminine aspects, including water, passion, and intuition. Today, according to legend, is the moon's birthday and it is venerated in many ways. The women often gather the fruits of the recent harvest and take them to their housetops to bath in the moonlight. Lanterns burn in

every home, and special treats known as moon cakes are baked for the children. In one story, the moon is believed to have given China the first seeds of the Cassia tree, which in their tradition represents immortality.
Magical Elements: If this date falls near a full moon, consider a ritual to honor the Goddess above and within. Focus on opening your mind to the more instinctive aspects. Spells relating to fertility, longevity, healing, and any water-related magics can be amplified in their performance.

SEPTEMBER 20–22

Holiday: Birthday of the Sun (Peru), Autumn Equinox.
Origins: Around the time when the Spanish arrived in Peru, they observed the celebration of the Incan Equinox. Three days before this, strict fasting is enforced and no fires are allowed in the homes. This is a period of repentance and cleansing after which the Sun God is invoked to balance human affairs. On this morning the arrival of the Sun is awaited and greeted with shouts, invocations, and song. Wine is given to the Earth and a small piece of cotton is ignited in the temple to rekindle all the fires of the nation.
Magical Elements: This is the time when night and day are in perfect balance. The winged disk of the Egyptians and the Wheel of Apollo to Romans, the sun is now moving towards winter, which on the magical calendar marks a time for rest after labors and thoughtful introspection. Autumn Equinox is also the second harvest, which is stored carefully to secure abundance for the long winter days ahead.

SEPTEMBER 22

Holiday: Festival of the Sea Goddess (Alaska).
Origins: In Alaska, the disposition of the sea can literally mean life or death. It is no wonder, then, that the Sea Goddess is venerated and feared. Known to some as Sedna, She controls winds, waves, fog, fish, seals, and whales. On this day, the Eskimos sing spirit songs as their shaman prepares for an astral journey to Sedna's home to appease Her. As he goes, the remaining people confess their violations of taboo to help the process. Finally, there is a tug of war, one side being winter and one side being summer. If winter wins, it means plenty of food for all.
Magical Elements: Astral work, water-related spells and rituals, honoring the Goddess of the Sea in your favorite tradition, and performing special magics for sea creatures are all possibilities for personal or group observances today.

SEPTEMBER 26

Holiday: Divali (India).
Origins: In India this marks the beginning of the business year along with the Feast of Lamps to honor the dead. The festival is dedicated to Lakshmi, the Goddess of prosperity. It is believed that moving to a new abode is very fortunate today. All bills are paid, family money is washed with milk and water, every lamp is lit, and then a huge feast begins. One sect in the area is even known to worship their account books by summoning a Brahman to mark them with lucky inscriptions and leave a coin inside. This way the prosperity is trapped where it is most needed throughout the year.
Magical Elements: All magics concerning finances, business, jobs, spiritual or monetary prosperity, and negotiations would be appropriate to this day, along with any special means of remembering loved ones who have passed over.

OCTOBER 3

Holiday: New Year's in Morocco.
Origins: This period is called *Asur.* Frequently straw is collected and burned on the roof tops to protect people from evil, then the ashes are made into amulets against disease. Most people get up and wash in the morning, keeping some of this water as a health aid for the remainder of the year and sprinkling the rest on their ancestors' graves. Herbs such as pennyroyal, thyme, and rosemary are hung around the home for safety, and burned later to rid the house of insects.
Magical Elements: One bit of lore says that a date rinsed with saffron water and roses, tied with one strand of your hair, then wrapped in cloth and buried or flung in a well will insure luxurious hair growth. The use of herbs for house cleansing is perfectly applicable almost any time of the year, and the tradition of the ritual bath is one that should be observed during any personally important magical activities.

MID-OCTOBER

Holiday: Yom Kippur (Jewish).
Origins: This is the most holy observance of the Jewish calendar, when no food is allowed from sundown to sundown. This is an observance of atonement in the belief that tears of repentance are the most precious of commodities to God.
Magical Elements: While magical traditions don't normally think in terms of "sin," none of us are perfect. This might be a good day to

contemplate your magical motivations through meditation and soul-searching. If there are areas you discover filled with clouds, purge them and allow the light to shine through.

OCTOBER 13

Holiday: Floating of the Lamps (Siam).
Origins: On or near this date is a special festival of lights to honor the Buddha, whose footprint was left by a sandy river bank. Flowers are offered to the image of the Buddha and little rafts with lights are put on the river so the Divine one can see them and be pleased. This is also the season when certain monks prepare to go into retreat and are often given provisions for their hermitage by anonymous donors.
Magical Elements: If someone you know has been feeling particularly alone, send them a little gift which you have blessed with magical energy to lift their spirits. Light candles to commemorate the power of illumination over shadows, and work magic so that your needs, and those of people you care about, are met.

MID-OCTOBER

Holiday: Kuan Yin Day (China).
Origins: Kuan Yin is the protector of wives and children in the Chinese tradition. On the nineteenth day of the ninth moon, which is believed to be the anniversary of her death, she is given honor for the gifts of gentility, beauty, and compassion she brings. Frequently parents will give their daughter a statue of Kuan Yin along with a censor and candles one month after her marriage to help keep harmony in the home.
Magical Elements: Definitely a day to honor the Mother aspect of the Goddess and give a little extra attention to the children in our lives. If there have been tensions in the home, call on Kuan Yin to help improve communications.

OCTOBER 31

Holiday: Halloween, Samhain.
Origins: According to lore, this is the night when spirits and faeries are free to roam the normal world, but if you happen to be afraid of such creatures simply wear red and you will scare them away. Many of the origins of Halloween have been lost in antiquity, but on the Celtic calendar it is the New Year and the time of the dead because the veil between worlds is thin.

Magical Elements: With the present, future, physical, and spiritual realms all coming close on this eve, the amount of energy which can be generated for magic is astounding. However, be forewarned that many other people are practicing too, so be sure to put up some type of protective energies. Samhain is a harvest festival, so items such as corn, apples, and even the traditional pumpkin are perfectly appropriate for your sacred space.

Winter (November–January)

Winter is the time of the dark moon; a fallow period and a time for rest. Here Earth sleeps and dreams, as should we. Within those night visions are great insights to discover, along with psychic powers hidden just beneath the snow.

The altar of winter should reflect this repose, covered with cloth of whites, browns, and blacks, and perhaps the occasional twig decorated with ribbons. Even if you live in a warmer climate, consider decorating your windows with paper snowflakes or other representations of the season. In each room of the house keep an acorn for the hope of spring to come. The cauldron can now stand empty, and the ritual cup can brim with winter rain or snow. Your robes and rites can also exhibit simplicity through plain white candles, incense consisting of singular ingredients, the lack of jewelry, etc.

NOVEMBER 11

Holiday: Feast of Dionysus (Greece).
Origins: A harvest feast where the animals were butchered for winter's meat, new wines were opened and tasted, rents paid, and a general time of good cheer. Dionysus and Bacchus are fairly interchangeable God figures connected strongly with the animal and plant kingdoms.
Magical Elements: If you want to try your hand at brewing ritual wines or meads, dedicate the day to Dionysus and get some fruit! Mead is probably more traditional, being that the Romans fermented honey.

NOVEMBER 13

Holiday: Festival of Jupiter (Rome).
Origins: This was a feast of the Roman senate where the figures of three gods, Jupiter, Juno, and Minerva, were brought to the feast anointed and adorned to enjoy the merrymaking. On this date, people often sealed friendships and commitments.
Magical Elements: Work a spell or ritual with/for a dear friend and take a look at your obligations to be sure they're being met. Magical couples can consider this an optional day for handfasting, and individuals new to the Craft might want to be initiated today.

LAST THURSDAY IN NOVEMBER

Holiday: Thanksgiving (United States).
Origins: In 1620, the Pilgrims landed at Plymouth Rock where the Indians taught them how to plant corn. One year later they celebrated the first harvest with games, feasting, and family. The first national observance of Thanksgiving was in 1863.
Magical Elements: This holiday can be celebrated in the magical household in much the same manner as others, except that it is a nice gesture to welcome your Patron God and Goddess to the feast. Leave a little of each item served on your altar, and later give it to the wild animals or birds outside.

DECEMBER 6

Holiday: St. Nicholas' Day.
Origins: St. Nicholas is the patron saint of maidens, pawn brokers, sailors, and children. He gave all his wealth to the poor, often dropping bags of gold down chimneys. This is the origin of our modern Santa Claus myths. His veneration began in Asia Minor, moved into Russia, and eventually spread throughout Europe.
Magical Elements: In the spirit of the Yule season, think about those less fortunate than yourself and give a little time, food, or money to aid their cause. Winter can be cold and lonely for many people; your sharing can bring some very down-to-earth magic into their lives in the form of love.

FIRST MONDAY IN DECEMBER

Holiday: Stray Sale Day (Texas).
Origins: On this day all the stray cattle and horses are taken to town squares in Texas and traded or sold in auction. Some people attend to find their lost cattle and bid, others just to exchange news.

Magical Elements: Anything you have been looking for, today is the day to try again. Work a little magic before you search, visualizing the item in your mind (see Chapter Ten), then go wherever your feet lead!

DECEMBER FULL MOON

Holiday: December Moon (Alaska).
Origins: In Alaska, the Eskimos believe that animals have souls and that these spirits must be appeased for the fishing and hunting seasons to be prosperous. So each year a special celebration is held at Point Hope specifically for the dead whales, where hymns are sung and the animals are thanked for their sustenance to these people.
Magical Elements: With the awakening atmosphere of ecological awareness, this might be a good day to forego meat to give life to one creature. Do a ritual for the whales and all animals of this planet that their numbers can be increased.

EIGHT DAYS BEFORE WINTER SOLSTICE

Holiday: Hopi Winter Ceremony.
Origins: On this day the Hopi begin a festival which bids farewell to fall and welcomes winter. They believe at this point the year is a very old man who looks forward to spring and being rejuvenated. Prayer feathers are made to bless the home and as a supplication that all might speak with gentle voices. The traditional place of worship for this festival is often underground where offerings are laid on the altar, sand paintings are created, and wishes for health and joy exchanged. Sprouting plants are given to all as a promise of life to come.
Magical Elements: This is a beautiful ritual which can be changed a little to suit your circumstances, but has all the elements necessary to the modern magician. Burn incense in your home which is moved about with a feather to bring blessing, consider the worth of your words, and plant some sprouting seeds that can keep your home green through the winter.

DECEMBER 19–21, 25

Holiday: Winter Solstice, Yule, Christmas, Hanukkah.
Origins: On the Hindu calendar, the nineteenth is sacred to the goddess Sankrant who wakes up after six months of sleep. On this day the oxen and cattle are blessed with water from flowers and sacred plants, and offerings of rice are made to the gods to ensure their continued providence. The ancient Druids picked mistletoe on the Solstice, and

according to Norse traditions, the Valkyrie looked for souls to bring to Valhalla. Hanukkah is the Jewish Festival of Lights in tribute to the Maccabean victory over Syria. In the United States, the first Christmas card was mailed in 1843.

Magical Elements: Ancient Pagans went to the forests during the full moon of December or on the Solstice to give offerings to the evergreen, a symbol of immortality. They believed that by so doing they ensured life through the rest of the harsh winter months. Thus, the first Yule trees were born. This is the longest night of the year, a season when the family unit and traditions should be honored, gifts of love exchanged, and candles lit to give the sun strength for its return to the sky.

JANUARY 1

Holiday: New Year's Day.

Origins: While the exact date of New Year's in various cultures has been drastically different throughout history (notably the Celtic New Year's being October 31), the basic celebration is similar. New Year's was most probably begun by the Romans as a festival day for revelry. In France, it was known as the Feast of Fools. In both instances gifts were presented to the gods to ensure a prosperous new year. Items such as pomanders,[7] gold, cakes, and wine appeared on many altars. It was also customary to give similar gifts and edible items to guests such as gloves, pins, sausages, and apples. In Portugal it is believed you should pay all your bills on this day to ensure they will be met for the entire year. The Pennsylvania Dutch believe if it is sunny today, they will have plenty of fish and fowl to sustain them. Finally, in Germany it is traditional to slice onions in half, hollow them out, and fill them with salt. These onions are placed in the attic of the home to predict the weather for the next twelve months. If the salt in the onion stays dry, it is an indication of an arid month.

Magical Elements: Open your windows on New Year's Day for a moment to let in a fresh perspective for the coming months. Sweep out any negativity with a favorite broom, and leave an offering on your altar to thank the Great Spirit for your health and blessings of the past year. Enjoy fellowship with family and friends, make some magical resolutions, and renew your energy for the months of winter still ahead.

JANUARY 6

Holiday: Twelfth Night.

Origins: This is the final night of the Yule season. In France, a special cake is baked with a bean hidden inside. Whoever finds the bean is named monarch over the feast, similar to the medieval custom of naming a Lord and Lady of Misrule who mock the royalty and generally have fun with the common folk. In England, twelve fires are lit, supposedly to represent the twelve apostles, but a more Pagan interpretation of the twelve houses of the zodiac or even simply the twelve months of the year can be found here. In Scotland, men are known to hang bits of cake on an apple tree and pour libations of cider on its roots in thanks for its fruitfulness. Many lands also observe a blessing of cattle, land, and pets in some form by water.

Magical Elements: Consider blessing some spring water and sprinkling it around your home or animals by way of cleansing and protecting for the year ahead. Whatever your favorite fruit drink, give a little back to the Earth to refresh the land during the cold months and as a symbol of harvests still to come. Take down your Yule tree and decorations, moving towards simpler wares for the observance of Candlemas in February.

LATE JANUARY

Holiday: Feast of the Kitchen God (China).
Origins: In China, there is a special picture above most stoves which represents the Kitchen God. This is his special abode, and no one in the house is allowed to spit, comb their hair, or speak in foul language near him. He is the keeper of the family's morality. Once a year the kitchen god must return to heaven to report on the family's behavior. The date, according to the Chinese calendar, falls on the twenty-third night of the twelfth month. At this time special offerings of candies or cakes are made (so that his report is sweet), incense is lit, and the picture of the kitchen god is burned to allow him to ascend to heaven with his observations.
Magical Elements: Depending on your perspective, you can approach this holiday in one of two ways. Go to your kitchen and leave a small offering for your hearth god or goddess, then eat out at a restaurant to give this being a well deserved rest. Alternatively, you could make a feast to celebrate the bounty and care of this God/dess, still leaving your offering in the kitchen while you and your family enjoy the edibles.

JANUARY 23

Holiday: New Year of the Trees (Palestine).
Origins: This holiday came about in connection with the agricultural rejuvenation of that land. Today, children go to the streets with flowered costumes, hoes, spades, and water, ready to plant trees. It is often the custom to do so as a memorial to a loved one recently deceased.

Magical Elements: Depending on your climate, you may not be able to plant a tree at this time of the year; however, you can take a moment to remember the living things of the earth, and perhaps do a little spell or ritual for same. Send some of this magical energy towards Palestine to encourage the work they are trying to do, and give tribute to your ancestors in story or prayer.

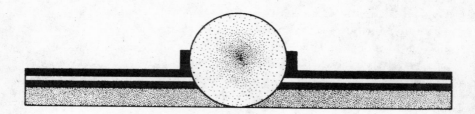

NOTES TO CHAPTER 11

1. *Croning* is usually done after a woman has reached the age of 65. It is a time when the Crone aspect of the goddess, the wise woman and seer, is recognized within her and called upon for continued guidance.

2. The Maiden aspect of the Goddess is the youthful woman, the crescent moon, fresh with energy and zeal, but not always tremendous amounts of wisdom. She is the blushing young lady, brimming with life and eagerness.

3. Incense blessings are very common in magic, some of the oldest examples of which come to us from the Celtic traditions.

4. The Mother aspect of the Goddess is more mature and is represented by the full moon. This facet of the Goddess contains the energy of healing, fertility, productivity, and insight.

5. *Rain sticks* are made in many tropical cultures from bamboo and certain types of beans which when tilted create a very real rain-like sound. This is believed to help bring the rains when combined with appropriate rituals.

6. Many magical people research different countries and cultures to find a Patron God and/or Goddess to call on consistently in their rites. This does not mean that they can not implore other aspects if the occasion arises that a different God/dess is more appropriate; however, for most common functions, only those chosen are used.

7. A *pomander* in the Middle Ages was a little cache of herbs, often roses, cinnamon, ginger, myrrh, and ambergris, believed to ward off the plague. These herbs were carried in a decorative container and also helped combat the odors of a people who were superstitious about bathing.

FINAL NOTES

Writing this book has been a wonderful experience for me. Through each section, I found myself re-examining my own way of looking at magic and the world we live in. As a result, many of the things I used to take for granted are now much more important and alive, including my own self-worth. In sharing these pages with you, I can only hope that some of this transformational energy is given with each word.

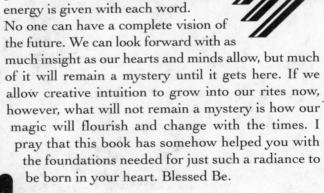

No one can have a complete vision of the future. We can look forward with as much insight as our hearts and minds allow, but much of it will remain a mystery until it gets here. If we allow creative intuition to grow into our rites now, however, what will not remain a mystery is how our magic will flourish and change with the times. I pray that this book has somehow helped you with the foundations needed for just such a radiance to be born in your heart. Blessed Be.

Bibliography

Andrews, Ted. *Magical Name.* Llewellyn Publications, Minnesota 1991.

Beyerl, P. *Master Book of Herbalism.* Phoenix, Washington 1984.

Black, George. *Folk Medicine.* Burt Franklin Company, New York 1883.

Bravo, Brett. *Crystal Healing Secrets.* Warner Books, New York 1988.

Buckland, Raymond. *Practical Color Magic.* Llewellyn Publications, Minnesota 1985.

Campbell, Joseph. *Power of Myth.* Doubleday, New York 1988.

Chase, A. W. *Doctor Chase's Last and Complete Work.* F. B. Dickerson Company, Minnesota 1908.

Clarkson, R. E. *Herbs and Savory Seeds.* Dover Publishing, New York 1972.

Clarkson, Rosetta. *Golden Age of Herbs and Herbalists.* Dover Publishing, New York 1940.

Cristiani, R. S. *Perfumery and Kindred Arts.* Baird and Company, Pennsylvania 1877.

Crowley, Brian and Esther. *Words of Power.* Llewellyn Publications, Minnesota 1991.

Culpeper's Herbal. D. Potterton, editor. Sterling Publishing, New York 1983.

DeGivry, Grillot. *Witchcraft, Magic and Alchemy.* Ballantyne and Company Limited, Spottiswood, England 1931.

Doorn, Joyce V. *Making Your Own Liquors.* Prism Press, New York 1977.

Dyer, T. F. *Folklore of Plants.* D. Appleton and Company, New York 1889.

Farrar, Janet and Stewart. *Spells and How They Work.* Phoenix, Washington 1990.

Fox, Dr. William. *Family Botanical Guide,* 18th Edition. Sheffield, 1907.

Freethy, Ron. *Book of Plant Uses, Names and Folklores.* Tanager Books, New York 1985.

Gordon, Lesley. *Green Magic.* Viking Press, New York 1977.

Griggs, B. *History of Herbal Medicine.* Viking Press, New York 1981.

Haggard, Dr. Howard N. *Mystery, Magic and Medicine.* Doubleday Company, New York 1933.

Hall, Manly P. *The Secret Teachings of All Ages.* Philosophical Research Society, California 1977.

Hawthorne, Nan. *Loving the Goddess Within.* Delphi Press, Illinois 1991.

Hutchinson, Ruth. *Every Day's a Holiday.* Harper and Brothers, New York 1961.

Ickis, Marguerite. *Book of Festival Holidays.* Dodd, Mead and Company, New York 1964.

Ingpen, Robert. *Encyclopedia of Mysterious Places.* Viking Studio Books, New York 1990.

Keirsey, David. *Please Understand Me.* Prometheus Books, California 1978.

Kieckhefer, R. *Magic in the Middle Ages.* Cambridge University Press, Massachusetts 1989.

Kunz, G. F. *Curious Lore of Precious Stones.* Dover, New York 1913.

LeStrainge, R. *History of Herbal Plants.* Arco Publishing, New York 1977.

Mercatante, A. S. *Zoo of the Gods.* Harper and Row, New York 1974.

Mystic Places. Time-Life Books, Virginia 1987.

Northcote, Lady Rosaline. *Book of Herb Lore.* Dover Publishing, 1912.

Palaiseul, Jean. *Grandmother's Secrets.* Putnam's Sons, New York.

Rhode, Eleanour S. *Old English Herbals.* Dover, 1922.

Riotte, Louise. *Sleeping with a Sunflower.* Garden Way Publishing, Vermont 1987.

Rodale's Illustrated Encyclopedia of Herbs, W. H. Hyton, editor. Rodale Press, Pennsylvania 1987.

Rose, Jeanne. *Kitchen Cosmetics.* Aris Books, California 1978.

Sams, J., and D. Carson. *Medicine Cards.* Bear and Company, New Mexico 1988.

Schapira, David. *Book of Coffee and Tea.* St. Martin Press, New York 1906.

Schaun, George. *American Holidays and Special Days.* Maryland Historical Press, Maryland 1986.

Singer, C. *From Magic to Science.* Dover Publishing, New York 1928.

Starhawk. *The Spiral Dance.* Harper and Row, California 1989.

Summer Rain, Mary. *Earthway.* Pocket Books, New York 1990.

Walking for Health, Julian Barr, editor. Consumer Guide, Illinois 1988.

Wallis Budge, E. A. *Amulets and Superstitions.* Dover, New York 1930.

Watson, Naomi. *Energize with Isometrics.* Butterfly Press, Texas 1977.

Wootton, A. *Animal Folklore, Myth and Legend.* Blandford Press, New York 1986.

Zink, David. *Ancient Stones Speak.* E. P. Dutton Company, New York 1979.

Index

STAY IN TOUCH

On the following pages you will find some of the books now available on related subjects. Your book dealer stocks most of these and will stock new titles in the Llewellyn series as they become available. We urge your patronage.

To obtain our full catalog, to keep informed about new titles as they are released and to benefit from informative articles and helpful news, you are invited to write for our bimonthly news magazine/catalog, *Llewellyn's New Worlds of Mind and Spirit*. A sample copy is free, and it will continue coming to you at no cost as long as you are an active mail customer. Or you may subscribe for just $10.00 in the U.S.A. and Canada ($20.00 overseas, first class mail). Many bookstores also have *New Worlds* available to their customers. Ask for it.

Llewellyn's New Worlds of Mind and Spirit
P.O. Box 64383-785, St. Paul, MN 55164-0383, U.S.A.
❖   ❖   ❖

TO ORDER BOOKS AND TAPES

If your book dealer does not have the books described, you may order them directly from the publisher by sending full price in U.S. funds, plus $3.00 for postage and handling for orders under $10.00; $4.00 for orders over $10.00. There are no postage and handling charges for orders over $50.00. Postage and handling rates are subject to change. We ship UPS whenever possible. Delivery guaranteed. Provide your street address as UPS does not deliver to P.O. Boxes. UPS to Canada requires a $50.00 minimum order. Allow 4-6 weeks for delivery. Orders outside the U.S.A. and Canada: Airmail—add retail price of book; add $5.00 for each non-book item (tapes, etc.); add $1.00 per item for surface mail.

FOR GROUP STUDY AND PURCHASE

Because there is a great deal of interest in group discussion and study of the subject matter of this book, we offer a special quantity price to group leaders or agents. Our Special Quantity Price for a minimum order of five copies of *The Urban Pagan* is $39.00 cash-with-order. This price includes postage and handling within the United States. Minnesota residents must add 6.5% sales tax. For additional quantities, please order in multiples of five. For Canadian and foreign orders, add postage and handling charges as above. Credit card (VISA, MasterCard, American Express) orders are accepted. Charge card orders only ($15.00 minimum order) may be phoned in free within the U.S.A. or Canada by dialing 1-800-THE-MOON. For customer service, call 1-612-291-1970. Mail orders to:

LLEWELLYN PUBLICATIONS
P.O. Box 64383-785, St. Paul, MN 55164-0383, U.S.A.

A VICTORIAN GRIMOIRE
Romance • Enchantment • Magic
by Patricia Telesco

Like a special opportunity to rummage through your grandmother's attic, *A Victorian Grimoire* offers you a personal invitation to discover a storehouse of magical treasures. Enhance every aspect of your daily life as you begin to reclaim the romance, simplicity and "know-how" of the Victorian era—that exceptional period of American history when people's lives and times were shaped by their love of the land, of home and family, and by their simple acceptance of magic as part of everyday life.

More and more, people are searching for ways to create peace and beauty in this increasingly chaotic world. This special handbook—Grimoire—shows you how to recreate that peace and beauty with simple, down-to-earth "Victorian Enchantments" that turn every mundane act into an act of magic . . . from doing the dishes . . . to making beauty-care products . . . to creating games for children. This book is a handy reference when you need a specific spell, ritual, recipe or tincture for any purpose. What's more, *A Victorian Grimoire* is a captivating study of the turn of the century and a comprehensive repository of common-sense knowledge. Learn how to relieve a backache, dry and store herbs, help children get over fears of the dark, treat pets with first aid, and much, much more.

0-87542-784-7, 368 pgs., 7 x 10, illus., softcover $14.95

CUNNINGHAM'S ENCYCLOPEDIA OF MAGICAL HERBS
by Scott Cunningham

This is the most comprehensive source of herbal data for magical uses ever printed! Almost every one of the over 400 herbs are illustrated, making this a great source for herb identification. For each herb you will also find: magical properties, planetary rulerships, genders, associated deities, folk and Latin names and much more. To make this book even easier to use, it contains a folk name cross reference, and all of the herbs are fully indexed. There is also a large annotated bibliography, and a list of mail order suppliers so you can find the books and herbs you need. Like all of Cunningham's books, this one does not require you to use complicated rituals or expensive magical paraphernalia. Instead, it shares with you the intrinsic powers of the herbs. Thus, you will be able to discover which herbs, by their very nature, can be used for luck, love, success, money, divination, astral projection, safety, psychic self-defense and much more. Besides being interesting and educational it is also fun, and fully illustrated with unusual woodcuts from old herbals. This book has rapidly become the classic in its field. It enhances books such as *777* and is a must for all Wiccans.

0-87542-122-9, 336 pgs., 6 x 9, illus., softcover $12.95

THE MAGICAL NAME
A Practical Technique for Inner Power
by Ted Andrews

Our name makes a direct link to our soul. It is an "energy" signature that can reveal the soul's potentials, abilities and karma. It is our unique talisman of power. Many upon the spiritual path look for a magical name that will trigger a specific play of energies in his or her life. *The Magical Name* explores a variety of techniques for tapping into the esoteric significance of the birth name and for assuming a new, more magical name.

This book also demonstrates how we can use the ancient names from mythology to stimulate specific energies in our life and open ourselves to new opportunities. It demonstrates how to use the names of plants, trees and flowers to attune to the archetypal forces of nature. It provides techniques for awakening and empowering the human energy field through working with one's name.

The Magical Name fills a gap in Western magic, which has been deficient in exploring the magic of mantras, sounds and names. It has been said that to hear the angels sing, you must first hear the song within your own heart. It is this song that is echoed within your name!

0-87542-014-1, 360 pgs., 6 x 9, illus., softcover $12.95

PRACTICAL COLOR MAGICK
by Raymond Buckland, Ph.D.

Color magick is powerful—and safe. Here is a sourcebook for the psychic influence of color on our physical lives. Contains complete rituals and meditations for practical applications of color magick for health, success and love. Find full instructions on how to meditate more effectively and use color to stimulate the chakras and unfold psychic abilities. Learn to use color in divination and in the making of talismans, sigils and magick squares.

This book will teach all the powers of light and more. You'll learn new forms of expression of your innermost self, new ways of relating to others with the secret languages of light and color. Put true color back into your life with the rich spectrum of ideas and practical magical formulas from *Practical Color Magick!*

0-87542-047-8, 160 pgs., illus., softcover $6.95

All prices subject to change without notice.